THE SHARED TABLE

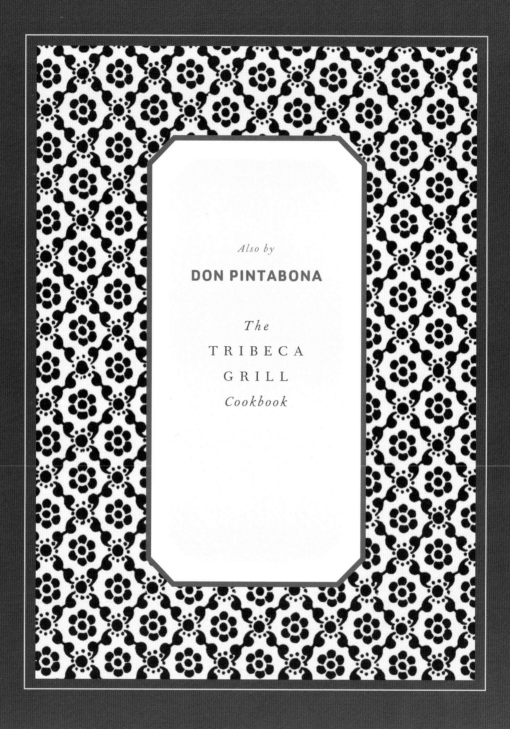

Also by

DON PINTABONA

The
TRIBECA
GRILL
Cookbook

THE
SHARED
TABLE

*Cooking with Spirit for
Family and Friends*

Don Pintabona

with *Judith Choate*

PHOTOGRAPHS BY STEVE POOL

RANDOM HOUSE
New York

All rights reserved under International and
Pan-American Copyright Conventions. Published in the
United States by Random House, an imprint of The Random
House Publishing Group, a division of Random House, Inc.,
New York, and simultaneously in Canada by Random
House of Canada Limited, Toronto.

Random House and colophon are registered
trademarks of Random House, Inc.

Library of Congress Cataloging-in-Publication Data
Pintabona, Don.
The shared table : cooking with spirit for family and friends /
Don Pintabona with Judith Choate.
p.   cm.
Includes index.
ISBN 0-375-50922-4
1. Cookery, Italian. I. Choate, Judith. II. Title.

TX723.P493   2004   641.5945—dc22   2003066724

Printed in China on acid-free paper
Random House website address: www.atrandom.com

2 4 6 8 9 7 5 3 1

FIRST EDITION

Book design by Barbara M. Bachman

Dear
Alex, Daniela and Nicolas

Love,
Daddy

 · ACKNOWLEDGMENTS

A BOOK LIKE THIS REACHES BACK MANY YEARS, SO IT IS NEARLY IMPOSSIBLE TO THANK EVERYONE WHO helped inspire me to write it. I am forever grateful to all those—friends, family, and even complete strangers—who have opened their hearts and homes to me over the years.

My gratitude especially goes to:

Jimmy Canora, a longtime trusted friend who has worn many, many hats in my life, a chef's toque being only one of them. On this project, not only did he help develop and test recipes, but he kept us laughing—sometimes at ourselves.

Judith Choate and Steve Pool, a couple I've grown to love and respect—Judie for her gift with the pen and Steve for his passion behind the lens.

Mickey Choate, for cutting the deal and sharing a meal.

Mary Bahr and Laura Ford, for their patience and more patience and even more patience.

Barbara Bachman, for putting it all together so beautifully.

Aris Mixon, for his gentle manner and keen eye.

My wife, Christine, for her endless support.

Those who so generously shared their recipes with me so that I could, in turn, share them on these pages: Joy Boggio, Maureen Fiorentino Buck, Miriam Cohen, Vincenzina DiPaola, Rose Klein, Anna Tasca Lanza, Miss Millie, Ricardo De Montoya, Anna Nurse, Carman Pintabona, Nancy Pintabona, and my beloved uncle, the late Vincenzo Pintabona.

Rosalie Arlotta, Chris Smith, Gerry Hayden of Amuse Restaurant, and Michael Steward and Horton Foote, Jr., of Tavern on Jane, for assisting with recipe testing and photo locations.

And, of course, my mentors, Georges, Daniel, Kiyomi, and Charlie.

PREFACE

his is more than a cookbook. It is a notebook of aromatic memories infused with my recollections of moments around a table overflowing with the spirit of giving; it is *abbondanza,* the generosity of life that so identifies my Italian heritage. My earliest days in the kitchen with my parents and my father's mother, my beloved nana, are where the memories begin. I close my eyes and can immediately be transported back to that warm room filled with the smells and tastes of Sicily. It was here that I began to understand that food without family and friends to share it is mere sustenance; shared, it nourishes the body and nurtures the mind and soul. It was, I now believe, the community of the table that made me want to be a chef.

Throughout my culinary career, whether in front of the restaurant range or traveling to a remote destination in search of new ideas and tastes, I have been struck, over and over again, with what hospitality really means. *Webster's* might define it as "the friendly and generous reception and entertainment of guests or strangers," while *Roget's* might say it

equals "neighborliness," but to me, it clearly evokes the complete comfort given to guests (there are no strangers) as they enjoy the food and drink that has been especially prepared for them, in good humor and with courtesy and thoughtfulness. To me, genuine hospitality should leave your guests reluctant to go and anxious to return once they do.

Over the years, I have often found myself in isolated areas of the world welcomed with hospitality by people to whom I was not only a complete stranger but a complete unknown. The warmth and companionship shown at the table ensured that I was a welcome guest with an open invitation to return (even when it was clear to me that the diet of my hosts was a meager one). At the opposite end of the spectrum, I have attended lavish events hosted by chefs and restaurants all across the globe in support of their local charities. Hospitality reigns supreme as hosts generously donate food and wine in support of community endeavors.

In the urgent aftermath of the tragic events of September 2001, I once again saw the extent to which food plays a role in bringing people together in harmony and friendship. Friends and colleagues joined me in turning the foodstuffs filling the refrigerators, freezers, and shelves at the shuttered Tribeca Grill (then my home base), located just a few blocks from the site, into quick meals for the rescue workers. It didn't take us long to realize that the workers needed more than the simple sandwiches and cold salads that we were transporting down to them. Warm meals along with a quiet space and fresh clothing were equally required to give the relief workers the

sustenance they needed to continue their very difficult work. Uniting with other chefs, food service companies, and a cruise line made such a venture possible. It brought the combination of community and table that was needed. Once again, I learned that one without the other makes a meal incomplete.

All of my experiences in the restaurant business have led me to believe that the shared table is the heart of community. The intimacy produced is at least as potent as language. Drawing around the fire, the passing of food and drink—nourishing our strength and bolstering our sometimes flagging spirits—these rituals of joining family, immediate and extended, have held throughout humankind. These customs have been passed to me by family, friends, and acquaintances with love, strength, and the bonds forged over sharing at the table.

CONTENTS

LIST OF RECIPES

BREADS AND PASTRY

THE SHARED TABLE

PART ONE

Growing Up

I don't think that you can grow up in an Italian family without knowing that the table is more than just the food set upon it. First of all, almost no meal is prepared without the expectation that an unannounced guest will appear around mealtime, so there is always more than enough food to share. In fact, there really are no guests at an Italian table—anyone sitting there immediately becomes family. Meals are never taken in silence; the food is there to nourish the talk, and the talk is often boisterous and expressive. To Italians, food is life!

My parents, Nancy and Carman, are first-generation Americans; my mom's family came from Naples and my dad's from Sicily. I grew up in Oceanside, a suburban community on Long Island, a short commute from New York City. My dad was employed by the Grand Union supermarket chain (for which he worked for fifty-two years), and my mom kept house and a watchful eye on five kids: my two brothers, Michael and Robert; my sisters, Rosanne and Carole; and me. She was lovingly assisted by my father's mother, Rosina (Nana), who lived with us.

My mom's mother had passed away when she was a little girl, and my dad's father had also passed away at a young age, so Nana was particularly treasured in our house. She was a surrogate mother to my mom and taught her everything that she knew about keeping a strong Italian home, so, although my mother's heritage was Neapolitan, Mom learned to cook in Nana's Sicilian style. Nana was a gentle, loving influence on all of us kids, telling us stories of her childhood of poverty in Italy as she helped prepare our bountiful meals. It has been said that two women should never share a kitchen, but in our house, the sounds of my mom and Nana working together in the kitchen were always happy ones. Looking back, I now realize how dependent they were upon each other and how they each seemed to have a sixth sense about what the other was going to do. The love that they felt for each other was more than evident in the meals that they served. They were a great team in the kitchen!

Every family event was celebrated from our kitchen. Communions, confirmations, weddings, birthdays, christenings, anniversaries—you name it, and Nana, Mom, and my aunts were cooking for it. For days in advance of the celebration, Mom and Nana worked hand in hand, planning, shopping, preparing, and cooking. They were often in the kitchen until the wee hours of the morning as they made the last-

minute preparations. All of the women had assigned kitchen jobs and the excitement that flowed from the cooks was as irrepressible as the aromas that filled the house were enticing.

The overriding memory of my childhood is of a houseful of people gathering to eat and celebrate. All of my parents' siblings lived within a couple of miles of our home, and my mom's father had a large house complete with garden and grapevines that was also only a short hop away. I'm sure that some of our meals must have been with the immediate family alone, but it is almost impossible to remember them. The stronger memories are of aunts bustling in the kitchen with Mom and Nana, uncles playing cards and talking sausage and wine with Dad, and tons of cousins playing stickball, touch football, and other games while sneaking whatever bits and pieces of antipasto they could find.

When I think back, it wasn't only family but also friends who filled the house. With five kids in the family, there were lots of neighborhood and school friends who were always welcomed with a bite from the antipasto ingredients, a hero sandwich, or a plate of pasta. Our neighborhood friends knew that on Sunday mornings, when our kitchen began to fill with the aroma of frying meatballs, their names would be in the pan. I guess that Mom and Nana must have always prepared an extra batch for "the boys," because the platter was always full at dinnertime and I know that every kid had a meatball or two when they were being made.

All the while that meals were being prepared and eaten, there would be talk: tales from the old country; news of relatives still in Italy; gossip about family joys and problems; updates on the recent arrival of a near-relative from Sicily; the rapid exchange of recipes for traditional dishes and new American tastes; and, from the men, word from the workplace along with reports on the volume of wine left from the last bottling and plans for the next year's vintage. Bits of gossip "not fit for the kids" were whispered (always in Italian), but other than those quiet moments, we were included in everything.

Reminiscing about those days has made me realize how much impact my childhood had on my choice of a career in the kitchen. Hard work didn't come from the kitchen, only big, nourishing meals served with so much love, you could feel it. It was the warmth and caring that I took with me as I grew up: my mom and Nana working closely as they cooked, humming and chatting; my dad appreciative of his job, sharing his enthusiasm with us. Never once did we see how much hard work their celebration of the table meant. I am forever grateful to them for making this joy a part of my life.

Is It Sauce or Is It Gravy?

One of the great debates in an Italian American household is "Is it sauce or is it gravy?" To my Neapolitan relatives, any sauce for pasta was called "gravy" or "*ragù*," and all of the Sicilian relatives called any sauce "sauce." Arguments over this would often become quite heated. In our kitchen, peace was kept by calling my mom's Sunday sauce or any hearty meat sauce "gravy" and any sauce made by Nana and Dad "sauce."

Hearty meat-based sauces are the stars of the southern Italian home kitchen. These sauces are always part of any holiday or celebratory meal. The recipes are often handed down by the newly acquired mother-in-law to a young bride so that the continuity of the family table will continue. Great pride is still taken in the back-of-the-stove, slow-cooked sauces that are the heart of great Italian peasant cooking.

Each family has its own recipe. In the old days, the amount of meat was often dictated by the level of wealth: Little money meant little meat; a solid bank account, and two or three types of meat made it into the pot. Some recipes call for whole tomatoes, some for paste and water. Some require poultry; others have no need of a chicken. Strong red table wine is a must for some, a no-no for others. Each recipe is the soul of a family.

To be fair-handed, I offer three sauce recipes, each reflecting the touch of a Pintabona family cook: Nana's basic sauce, Dad's expansion on it, and my mom's famous Sunday gravy. These, I think, are the gold standards of great Italian sauces. (The two pasta dishes that close this chapter are the soul of the Italian table.) Feel free to improvise. The following recipes lend themselves to the inspirations of your family's particular DNA.

Nana's Fresh Marinara Sauce

Time spent in the kitchen with Nana is one of the fondest memories of my childhood. I believe that it is from her joy of cooking that I first understood the possibilities of the community of the table.

This is her version of the most basic of all Italian tomato sauces. She always had a pot ready for what was to her a quick and simple meal—marinara over perciatelli, veal cutlets or grilled sausage, and a tossed salad with spicy greens and a zesty red-wine-vinegar dressing. Sometimes Nana would add some red pepper flakes or fresh peppers to the sauce to add a little spice, but as often as not, it was just this straightforward recipe. Since the flavor of the sauce is so dependent upon the sweet ripeness of the tomatoes, seasoning is very personal. Sometimes you need a

Makes 3 quarts

. . . .

healthy dose of sugar and sometimes the tomatoes themselves are almost too sweet. Salt is also important to bring out the intense flavor of the tomatoes and to balance the sweet and the tart, so use your palate to determine the amount required. In the summertime, when ripe, luscious tomatoes fill the marketplace, I still make this sauce in big batches and either freeze or can it for many winter meals. When great fresh tomatoes are not available, I use canned San Marzano tomatoes with equally tasty results.

$^1/_2$ cup olive oil

1 large white onion, peeled and finely chopped

3 cloves garlic, peeled and thinly sliced

5 pounds very ripe Italian plum tomatoes, peeled, cored, and lightly
     crushed (or four 28-ounce cans San Marzano whole peeled
     tomatoes, with juice, lightly crushed)

Coarse salt and freshly ground pepper

About 1 teaspoon sugar, or to taste (optional)

$^1/_2$ cup chopped fresh basil

$^1/_4$ cup chopped fresh flat-leaf parsley

1.   Heat the oil in a large saucepan over medium heat. Add the onion and sauté for about
3 minutes, or just until the onion begins to soften. Stir in the garlic and sauté for 2 minutes
more, or just until the garlic begins to color. Immediately add the tomatoes and stir to
incorporate the oil into the tomatoes. Season with salt and pepper to taste and bring to
a bare simmer. Lower the heat and simmer, stirring frequently with a wooden spoon, for
25 minutes. Midway through the cooking process, taste and, if necessary, add just enough
sugar to balance the acidity of the tomatoes.

2.   Stir in the basil and parsley and cook for 5 minutes more. Taste and, if necessary,
adjust the seasoning with salt, pepper, and sugar. Serve over pasta, as a dipping sauce
for fried shellfish or calamari, or as a sauce for grilled poultry.

Dad's Blue Crab Sauce

Shellfish is plentiful in Sicily and there are all kinds of pasta sauces prepared using it. This is one of my dad's specialties using the blue crabs (and sometimes clams) that flourish in the waters off Long Island. Blue crabs are found in the Atlantic all up and down the eastern seaboard but can easily be replaced with any fresh local shellfish. The one problem with blue crab is that although it has lots of flavor, it doesn't have much meat. But because the meat is so sweet and delicious, we choose to suck whatever meat we can from the shells—messy but fun! If this is too much work, cook the sauce a bit longer to infuse it with the crabs' flavor and then simply discard the crabs before saucing the pasta.

When Dad returned home with a bushelful of crabs, we knew that we were in for a treat. Dad is a great cook, but with Mom and Nana in the kitchen, he didn't often get his chance at the stove. This was the one time that he took over. He served his sauce, three crabs per person, with linguine and so do I, but I bet it would be great with polenta, also. When I was a boy, the sauce would go in a big bowl in the center of the table and everyone would help themselves. Self-serve communal dining still works in my house!

Serves 6

. . . .

18 live blue crabs, cleaned

$^1/_4$ cup olive oil

3 cloves garlic, peeled and slivered

1 cup dry white wine

3 quarts Nana's Fresh Marinara Sauce (page 8)

Red pepper flakes

Coarse salt and freshly ground pepper

$^1/_4$ cup chopped fresh flat-leaf parsley

2 pounds linguine, cooked

1.   Place the crabs in the kitchen sink and shock them by running very hot water over them for a few minutes. Drain and set aside.

2.   Heat the oil in a large saucepan over medium heat. Add the garlic and sauté for about 4 minutes, or just until the garlic begins to turn golden brown. Immediately add the wine and bring to a boil. Add the crabs and, using tongs, toss in the pan for about 7 minutes, or until the wine has almost evaporated. Stir in the marinara sauce and bring to a boil. Immediately lower the heat and simmer, stirring frequently with a wooden spoon, for 8 minutes if you want to eat the crabmeat or 30 minutes if you want a strongly flavored sauce but do not wish to eat the crabmeat. Season with red pepper flakes, salt, and pepper to taste. Add the parsley and serve over the hot linguine.

Mom's Sunday Gravy with Braciole and Meatballs

Serves 6 to 8

. . . .

"Gravy," the rich, meaty *ragù* that always seems to be simmering on the back of the stove waiting to sauce pasta, eggplant, or whatever the cook puts together to feed the hungry crowd, is also my mom's treasured family recipe. It is not possible to make a small batch, as no Italian cook worth his or her salt would contemplate making just enough to feed six people. There must always be enough for anyone who might stop by and to still have some left over for spontaneous meals during the week. (This recipe makes enough gravy to cook all of the meat specified and to cover about 4 pounds of pasta.) Therefore, you will need a very large (12- to 15-quart) pot for this recipe. However, if you don't have a huge pot, divide the recipe in half and use two saucepans to make the complete recipe, as you might as well make as much as you can, since the sauce freezes well.

This is the gravy that was the center of my childhood Sunday dinner table, and my mom still makes it every Sunday, whether all of the kids come home or not. I would bet that it still appears on most Italian-American tables every Sunday, also. My wife, Christine, is usually in charge of our Sunday dinner and she makes a mean gravy in a pot big enough to serve our friends, who know what they'll find on the stove should they just happen to stop by.

Six 28-ounce cans whole peeled Italian plum tomatoes, with juice

$^1/_2$ cup vegetable oil

Mom's Meatballs for Gravy (recipe follows)

Beef Braciole for Gravy (recipe follows)

3 pounds pork spareribs, trimmed of excess fat and cut into pieces

1 pound sweet Italian sausage

1 pound hot Italian sausage

1 large onion, peeled and finely diced

4 cloves garlic, peeled and minced

One 7-ounce can tomato paste

Coarse salt and freshly ground pepper

About 1 teaspoon sugar, or to taste (optional)

12 fresh basil leaves, well washed and torn into pieces

$^1/_4$ cup minced fresh flat-leaf parsley

1. Place the tomatoes in the bowl of a food processor fitted with the metal blade and process until smooth. This will have to be done in batches. Transfer the pureed tomatoes to a large bowl and set aside.

2. Heat about $^1/_4$ cup of the vegetable oil in a large, heavy-bottomed pot over medium heat. Add the meatballs, a few at a time, and sear, turning frequently, for about 6 minutes, or until nicely browned on all sides. Using a slotted spoon, transfer the browned meatballs to a plate and continue searing until all of the meatballs are browned, adding additional oil as needed. Set the meatballs aside.

3. Using the same pot and adding vegetable oil as needed, place the braciole in the pot and sear, turning frequently, for about 6 minutes, or until nicely browned on all sides. Using a slotted spoon, transfer the browned braciole to a plate and set aside.

4. Using the same pot and adding vegetable oil as needed, brown the spareribs and sausages as above. Using a slotted spoon, transfer the browned spareribs and sausages to a plate and continue searing until all of the spareribs and sausages are browned, adding additional oil as needed. Set the spareribs and sausages aside.

5.   Add the onion and sauté for about 4 minutes, or until the onion is golden and most of the browned bits have been scraped from the bottom of the pot. Add the garlic and sauté for about 1 minute, or just until softened. Immediately add the reserved pureed tomatoes and stir to combine. Add the tomato paste and then add enough water to the paste can to fill it three-quarters full. Using the end of a wooden spoon, stir the water to lift all of the paste from the can. Empty the liquid into the pot. Season with salt and pepper to taste and bring to a simmer. Taste and, if necessary, adjust the seasoning with the sugar.

6.   Add the reserved meatballs, braciole, spareribs, and sausages and again bring to a simmer. Lower the heat and cook at a bare simmer, stirring occasionally with a wooden spoon to keep the meat from sticking to the bottom of the pot, for 2 hours. (When stirring, move the spoon slowly and carefully so that the meat does not break up.)

7.   Twenty minutes before the gravy is ready, add the basil and parsley and stir to combine. Simmer, stirring occasionally, for 20 minutes. Taste and, if necessary, adjust the seasoning with salt, pepper, and sugar.

8.   Remove from the heat and, using a slotted spoon, lift the meats from the gravy and place on a serving platter. Slice each braciole crosswise into 5 pieces. Spoon some of the gravy over the top of the meats and use the remaining gravy to sauce cooked pasta.

MOM'S MEATBALLS FOR GRAVY

Makes about 24

. . . .

2 pounds lean ground beef (or 1 pound lean ground beef
    and 1 pound lean ground pork)

4 large eggs

2 cloves garlic, peeled and minced

1 cup Italian bread crumbs

$^3/_4$ cup cool water

$^1/_4$ cup freshly grated Parmesan cheese

$^1/_4$ cup chopped fresh flat-leaf parsley

1 teaspoon coarse salt

$^1/_2$ teaspoon freshly ground pepper

$^1/_2$ cup vegetable oil

1. Using your hands, combine the meat, eggs, garlic, bread crumbs, water, cheese, parsley, salt, and pepper in a large mixing bowl to just blend. Do not overmix, or the meatballs will be tough. (If the mixture feels dry to the touch, add more water, 1 tablespoonful at a time, to make a moist mixture. My mom says, "If you press your finger into the mixture and it makes an easy indentation, the meatballs will be perfect.") Roll the mixture into 2-inch round balls. (If using meatballs in the Sunday gravy on page 12, proceed to the specific instructions in the recipe.)

2. Heat about 2 tablespoons of the oil in a large cast-iron (or other heavy-bottomed) skillet over medium heat until very hot but not smoking. Add the meatballs, without crowding the pan, and sear, turning frequently, for about 6 minutes, or until nicely browned all over. (If not adding to tomato sauce, lower the heat and continue cooking, turning frequently, for about 8 minutes, or until the meatballs are thoroughly cooked.) Using a slotted spoon, transfer the meatballs to a double layer of paper towels to drain. Continue searing and draining until all of the meatballs are made.

3. Transfer the drained meatballs to your "gravy" and cook as directed in the master recipe.

BEEF BRACIOLE FOR GRAVY

. . . .

1 pound beef or braciole, trimmed of fat and sinew (see Note)

2 cloves garlic, peeled and minced

$^1/_2$ cup freshly grated Parmesan cheese

$^1/_2$ cup chopped fresh flat-leaf parsley

2 tablespoons fresh bread crumbs

Coarse salt and freshly ground pepper

2 tablespoons olive oil

4 thin slices prosciutto (optional)

$^1/_2$ cup shredded mozzarella cheese (optional)

1. Place the beef on a cutting board, and if any fat is still apparent, trim it off. Place a piece of plastic wrap over the beef and, using a mallet or a heavy skillet, pound the meat to a $^1/_8$-inch thickness. Cut the beef into 4 pieces of equal size (which should be about 5 inches wide by 4 inches long). Set aside.

2. Combine the garlic with the Parmesan cheese, parsley, and bread crumbs in a small mixing bowl. Season with salt and pepper to taste and drizzle with the olive oil.

3. Lay the 4 pieces of beef out on a clean, dry work surface. Season each piece lightly with salt and pepper. If using the prosciutto, cover each piece of beef with a slice. Using about 3 tablespoons of the Parmesan cheese mixture and working from the edge closest to you, make a line across each piece of beef. If using the mozzarella, sprinkle about 2 tablespoons over the filling.

4. Using your fingertips, roll up each piece, cigar-fashion, to make a neat package. If necessary, use your fingertips to keep the filling inside of the meat roll. Using kitchen twine, tie each roll in the center and then at both ends.

5. When ready to brown, season each piece with salt and pepper to taste and cook as directed in the master recipe.

NOTE: *Many supermarkets, particularly those in Italian neighborhoods, sell "beef for braciole," which is thinly sliced beef top round. Thinly sliced flank steak can also be used. Whichever type of beef you purchase, it must still be trimmed of all fat and pounded to a ⅛-inch thickness.*

Homemade Cavatelli with Sausage, Onions, and Peas

This is a very hearty home-style dish that can easily be doubled or tripled to feed a crowd. Although the original versions used fresh peas, as I now do, growing up we used canned peas, which make a sauce that is much different in taste. To make homemade cavatelli, you will need a cavatelli machine, an inexpensive device that turns out perfect little curly-edged shells. However, you can also make this using dried cavatelli or any other commercially produced rough-edged pasta that can stand up to the chunky sauce.

Serves 6

. . . .

1/4 cup olive oil

1 pound sweet or hot Italian sausage or Dad's Homemade
     Sausage (page 50), removed from the casing

4 cups Nana's Fresh Marinara Sauce (page 8) or other
     marinara sauce

1 cup diced onions

1 1/2 cups fresh English peas, blanched

Coarse salt and freshly ground pepper

2 tablespoons unsalted butter, softened

1 pound cooked Homemade Cavatelli (recipe follows) or dried cavatelli,
     cooked according to package directions

1/4 cup chopped fresh flat–leaf parsley

1/2 cup freshly grated Pecorino Romano cheese

1. Heat 2 tablespoons of the oil in a large, heavy-bottomed sauté pan over medium heat. Add the sausage and sear, turning frequently, for about 5 minutes, or until the sausage is beginning to color. Lower the heat, cover, and cook, turning frequently, for about 12 minutes, or until the sausage is firm and no longer pink inside. Remove the sausage from the pan and set aside.

2. Place the marinara sauce in a large saucepan over very low heat just to heat through.

3. Return the sauté pan to medium heat. Add the remaining 2 tablespoons oil and the onions and sauté for about 4 minutes, or just until the onions begin to take on some color. Add the peas, season with salt and pepper to taste, and cook, stirring frequently, for about 3 minutes, or just until the peas are heated through. Stir in the butter and remove from the heat. Leave the mixture in the pan.

4. Using a sharp knife, cut each sausage on the bias into 6 or 7 pieces. Add the sausage to the pea mixture and return the pan to medium heat. Cook, stirring frequently, for about 3 minutes, or just until warm. Transfer the mixture to a serving platter (or bowl) and add the cooked cavatelli and just enough of the sauce to lightly coat the pasta. Gently toss to combine. Sprinkle with the parsley and serve with the cheese and the remaining sauce on the side.

Makes 2 pounds

3 cups all-purpose flour

1¼ cups semolina flour (see Note)

1 teaspoon coarse salt

1 pound ricotta cheese

2 large eggs

1. Combine the all-purpose flour, semolina flour, and salt and sift into the large bowl of a heavy-duty electric mixer fitted with a dough hook. Add the ricotta and eggs and mix on medium speed for about 5 minutes, or until the dough pulls together into a ball.

2. Remove the dough from the bowl and form into a disk shape. Wrap in plastic and refrigerate for at least 30 minutes or up to 3 days.

3. When ready to cook (or freeze), using a pasta machine capable of forming cavatelli, form the dough into cavatelli shapes.

4. Bring a large pot of lightly salted cold water to a boil. Add the fresh cavatelli and return to a boil. Boil for about 3 minutes, or just until the pasta rises to the top. Drain well into a colander and proceed as directed in the master recipe.

5. If using in other than the master recipe, drain as above and place in a serving bowl and toss with the desired sauce or with 2 tablespoons softened unsalted butter or olive oil and season with coarse salt, freshly ground pepper, and freshly grated Parmesan cheese to taste. Garnish with chopped fresh flat-leaf parsley or basil and serve immediately.

6. If freezing, line a baking pan with parchment paper and lay the fresh cavatelli out in a single layer. Place the pan in the freezer for at least 1 hour or until the cavatelli are very firm. Transfer the frozen cavatelli to resealable plastic bags, label with the date made, and return to the freezer for up to 3 months. Cook, frozen, as above, increasing the cooking time by about 3 minutes.

NOTE: *Semolina flour (coarsely ground durum wheat flour) is available at Italian markets, specialty food stores, and some supermarkets.*

Working with Carman

All of my dad's kids worked with him at the Grand Union supermarket where he was the manager. Although he is a pretty easygoing guy, he was very strict with us in the store. In fact, he was harder on us than on the regular employees, but he felt that he was giving us an introduction into the business world and that it was important for us to be shown a good work ethic. He showed a lot of confidence in us, giving us responsible jobs that he expected us to fulfill without complaint. Consequently, we all worked hard in trying to meet his expectations.

My dad was extremely popular in the neighborhood and, it was said, knew more people than the local politicos. To us, this translated to "Stay out of trouble, or I'll tell your dad!" Also, since the store was across the street from the Catholic school that we all attended, the nuns could, and often did, shout our transgressions over to Dad before we knew that we had been caught.

I loved to work with the butcher. I was fascinated by all the types of meat and the skill with which the butcher handled each piece. I practiced my Rocky jabs on the sides of beef and then learned how to break the sides down into recognizable parts. It was here, I think, that I developed an interest in charcuterie and in making all sorts of pâtés, terrines, and sausages.

During one of my earliest attempts at hospitality, I learned a very valuable lesson. Besides working in my dad's store when it was open, my friends and I were hired to clean his store (and others) during off-hours. We were to sweep, mop, and, in general, clean up the store for the next day's customers. Having often seen my dad put together meals in the store, one night I decided to feed the crew. I pulled a hibachi, charcoal, and matches from the shelves and got a pretty good fire going to grill up some porterhouse steaks. Unfortunately, I'd forgotten about the fire alarms, which went off almost immediately. In a panic, I put out the fire and quickly threw the whole deal into the dumpster at the back of the store just as the firemen came crashing in looking for the fire. To my relief, of course, there was none. However, in a couple of moments, I heard a fireman yell, "Out back, out back, the fire's out back!" You guessed it—I had ignited the dumpster. I played stupid and got away with it, but, to this day, I have great respect for apparently quiet embers.

Looking back, I see that by allowing us to work with him, my dad taught us the value of honesty, friendship, and trust. He took great pride in the quality of produce and meat featured in the store. The shelves were immaculate and well stocked, as he tried to meet all of the demands of a diversified customer base. He worked hard at a job that he enjoyed. He treated all of his customers and employees as valued friends. I like to think that I carry Carman's ethics with me.

Shrink-Wrap-Machine-Seared Rib Eye Sandwiches with French's Onions

My dad has plenty of tales to tell about his job and more than a few of them involve my youthful hijinks in the store. This recipe evolved when he was looking for a way to feed a bunch of hungry teenage helpers—including his own son. He used some steaks that, although certainly okay to sell and actually better-tasting with age, had begun to discolor around the edges and would be pushed aside by the picky shopper. He sent us up and down the aisles to find condiments and garnishes for what would come to be known as Carman's Specials.

Since the store didn't have a grill at the ready, Dad cooked the steaks on the very hot shrink-wrap machine; then he sliced and stacked the rare meat on day-old French bread that he'd toasted on the hot "grill." Crisp Durkee (now French's) onions were piled on and a spread of his own design was slathered on the warm

Serves 6

. . . .

bread. Sliced tomatoes and romaine from the produce section and mushrooms and peppers straight off of the shelves finished the topping. We had to buy our own drinks! No beer allowed!

I've tried to duplicate Carman's Specials, so I've given the brand names my dad used. There are quite a few ingredients, but since most of them come ready-made, these sandwiches are a cinch to put together. Unfortunately, I can't really recommend the shrink-wrap machine for cooking, so I suggest an outdoor grill, a hibachi (for a Japanese-like *teppanyaki*), or a stove-top grill pan to produce a steak almost as satisfying! Any way you make them, these sandwiches are certain to please a crowd.

$^1/_4$ cup Maille Dijon mustard

1 tablespoon Hellmann's mayonnaise

1 tablespoon Gold's horseradish

1 tablespoon chopped fresh chives

1 teaspoon ReaLemon lemon juice

Three 6-ounce rib eye steaks, trimmed of all fat

McCormick garlic powder

Coarse salt and freshly ground pepper

2 loaves Italian bread, cut in half lengthwise

3 large ripe beefsteak tomatoes, well washed, cored, and sliced crosswise

1 head romaine lettuce, well washed, dried, and chopped

1 can French's French-fried onions

1 small jar Mancini roasted red peppers

1 small can B&B sliced mushrooms

1. Combine the mustard, mayonnaise, horseradish, chives, and lemon juice in a small mixing bowl (Dad "borrowed" a plastic container from the shelves).

2. Preheat a grill.

3. Season the steaks with garlic powder, salt, and pepper to taste. Place on the hot grill and sear, turning once, for about 4 minutes, or until a nice brown crust has formed. Continue to grill, turning once, for about 4 minutes more for rare. Remove from the grill and let rest for a couple of minutes.

4. Place the bread on the grill and toast for about 2 minutes, or until lightly browned.

5. Slice the steaks across the grain into long, thin strips.

6. Slather the sauce on each side of the toasted bread. Layer the tomato slices on one-half of each loaf. Cover the tomatoes with the chopped romaine. Layer the steak strips on top of the romaine on the two halves. Top with the onions, red peppers, and mushrooms. Cover each half with a remaining half loaf and press down to force the ingredients together. Cut each loaf into thirds and, to mimic our experience, reach into the fridge for something cool to drink.

Labor Day in Lynbrook

My mom grew up in Lynbrook, a few towns over from Oceanside, where we lived. She had nine brothers and sisters and it was a family tradition to gather on Labor Day at Papa DeCarlo's, their father's home in Lynbrook. It was a big, rambling house with a cultivated yard complete with a garden and grapevines and an icehouse in the back. It was as rural as Long Island could be and all of the relatives looked forward to a day in "the country." There were horses for carriage rides and wagon pulls; stickball; kick the can; and bocce tournaments. My uncles took wine crates and put wheels on them so the kids could have boxcar races.

As everyone knew about and longed to attend the DeCarlo Labor Day celebration, friends and neighbors often became honorary DeCarlos for the day. By midday, there could be as many as 100 people gathered in the yard, and the kitchen would be overflowing with cooks and helpers. This was without even counting the older generation, who often preferred the quiet of the living room.

Because of the cool shade that they offered, the trellised grapevines were the most popular spot. The men sat in the coolness playing cards and toasting their good fortune with Grandpa's homemade red wine. Big barrels, filled with chunks of ice chopped in the icehouse, held sodas for the kids and littleneck and cherrystone clams for all. The women kept the glasses and barrels filled while they picked vegetables and herbs from the garden for the meal.

Long tables, set in the center of the yard and covered with colorful cloths, were adorned with the standard Sunday Italian supper: antipasto, pasta, meats, vegetables, and salads, with lots of crusty breads to absorb the rich sauces and juices. Desserts were often from an Italian bakery and always in abundance, but the cannoli, cookies, and cheesecake also shared the table with a big bowl of fresh fruit and an assortment of hard and soft Italian cheeses. The party lasted well into the night and renewed everyone's strong feeling of belonging to a wonderfully warm extended family.

My own Labor Day weekend is now focused on putting together the fall wine-making party. For as long as I can remember, the men in my family have made wine. Wanting to continue the DeCarlo family tradition of bottling our own "estate wines," six years ago, I began making wine with two boyhood friends, Kevin Marcari and Danny Casella, who share the same family traditions as I do. (In fact, Kevin's father grew up across the street from my mom, and Danny's dad and my dad have been friends since they were seven years old.) Using eighty percent Merlot and twenty percent Cabernet, we are now turning out a wine we can be proud of.

When we began our project, we were told that it would take about four years to feel confident with the process required to produce a decent red wine. After six years,

our last two vintages have been terrific. One of the secrets to our success has been allowing the wine time to mature in bulk before bottling. This maturing came to us quite by accident when we had to postpone bottling to help friends complete a major construction project. We had kept the wine in bulk storage for one year and had time to bottle just fifteen of our thirty gallons. When we tasted the two wines—one bottled after one year in bulk and the other after two—the difference was extraordinary.

The first equipment that we used belonged to a friend's grandfather and dated from the 1800s. Using it set our imaginations to work, dreaming about all of the men who had made wine through the generations, wondering what parts of Italy they had emigrated from and how many bottles they had created, and so forth. However, the $800 we eventually spent for new stainless-steel equipment was worth every penny. No more bare feet in the vats! Home winemaking is still an activity best done (and much more fun) with a group. We never fail to conclude the harvest with a celebratory feast to extend the delight.

Stuffed Baby Eggplant

In my mom's family, everyone loved eggplant, especially big fat purple ones, except for my mom, who preferred midsummer's little tiny baby ones picked before they became plump and seedy. These were perfect to fill with a savory meat stuffing. She still makes this much-requested dish for family gatherings.

Now that there are so many different types of eggplant available in Asian markets, green markets, and specialty food stores, this is a recipe that can be made year-round. My mom serves this dish hot or at room temperature and I can testify that it is an all-day-long great snack.

You can use only one type of ground meat in the stuffing, but the end result will be more delicious if Mom's mixture of beef, veal, and pork is used.

6 baby eggplants, well washed, dried, and trimmed

2 tablespoons olive oil

$^3/_4$ cup finely chopped onions

2 teaspoons minced garlic

Coarse salt and freshly ground pepper

$^1/_3$ pound lean ground beef

$^1/_3$ pound lean ground veal

$^1/_3$ pound lean ground pork

1 large egg, beaten

$^1/_2$ cup cooked white rice

$^1/_4$ cup Italian Seasoned Bread Crumbs (recipe follows)

2 tablespoons chopped fresh flat-leaf parsley

2 tablespoons chopped fresh basil

$^1/_4$ cup freshly grated Parmesan cheese

About 5 cups Nana's Fresh Marinara Sauce (page 8)

   or other marinara sauce

1. Cut each eggplant in half lengthwise and, using a melon baller or teaspoon, scoop out and discard the center seedy portion; then scoop out and reserve the remaining pulp, leaving a shell about $\frac{1}{8}$ inch thick. Coarsely chop the eggplant pulp and set aside.

2. Heat the oil in a large sauté pan over medium heat. Add the onions and 1 teaspoon of the garlic and sauté for about 2 minutes, or just until slightly soft. Add the eggplant pulp and continue to sauté for about 5 minutes, or until the vegetables are very soft and have begun to take on a little color. Season with salt and pepper to taste, remove from the heat, and set aside to cool.

3. Preheat the oven to 375°F.

4. Place the ground beef, veal, and pork in a mixing bowl. Stir in the egg, then add the rice along with 2 tablespoons of the bread crumbs, the parsley, the basil, and the remaining 1 teaspoon garlic. When blended, add $1\frac{1}{2}$ cups of the cooled eggplant mixture, 2 tablespoons of the Parmesan cheese, and salt and pepper to taste. Stir to combine. The mixture should be quite moist. (If desired, make a small patty and fry over medium heat for about 4 minutes, or until cooked through, to taste for the correct seasoning.) Place equal portions of the ground-meat mixture in each eggplant half, mounding slightly as you stuff.

5. Cover the bottom of a baking pan large enough to hold all of the eggplant halves in a snug single layer with about 1 inch of the marinara sauce. Place the stuffed eggplant halves in the pan, fitting them tightly together. Cover the entire pan with aluminum foil and place in the preheated oven. Bake for 25 minutes. Uncover and bake for 15 minutes more, or until the tops are beginning to brown. Remove the pan from the oven and preheat the broiler.

6. Sprinkle the tops of the eggplant halves with equal portions of the remaining 2 tablespoons cheese and 2 tablespoons bread crumbs and place the pan under the broiler for about 1 minute, or until the tops are bubbling and golden brown. Remove from the heat and serve the eggplant hot or at room temperature.

Makes 7 cups

6 cups fresh Italian bread crumbs, lightly toasted (see step 1, page 40)

1 cup freshly grated Locatelli Romano cheese

$^1/_2$ cup chopped fresh flat-leaf parsley

1 teaspoon dried basil

1 teaspoon dried oregano

1 teaspoon coarse salt, or to taste

Combine the bread crumbs, cheese, parsley, basil, oregano, and salt in a mixing bowl. When well blended, transfer to a clean container with a lid. Store, tightly covered, in a cool, dry place for up to 1 week.

Sautéed Fava Beans

This is my mom's very own recipe. I have never seen fava bean pods used by any other cook. This is one of those dishes that happened at the moment—when a friend's garden had produced a big batch of beans and Mom decided to try using the whole bean. Unfortunately, this recipe is best when the favas are young, tender, and very, very fresh. One indication of this is small, firm pods that are not bursting with fat beans. If the pods are large and tough, discard them and use the beans only.

If, perchance, you have a load of young, tender beans, another great way to enjoy them is raw (peel off the tough outer skin) with shavings of Parmesan cheese and a bottle (or two) of great Italian wine.

Serves 6

. . . .

2 pounds fresh young fava beans in their pods

$1/_4$ cup extra–virgin olive oil

1 tablespoon minced garlic

1 teaspoon red pepper flakes, or to taste

Coarse salt and freshly ground pepper

1.   Wash the fava beans under cold running water. Using a sharp knife, snip the top and bottom from each pod, then cut down the seam lengthwise (on both sides) to open them. Release the beans from the pods and set aside. Cut the pods into 2-inch pieces. Separately reserve the beans and the pods.

2.   Bring a large pot of lightly salted cold water to a boil over high heat. Add the reserved fava beans and return to a boil. Boil for 2 minutes and then add the reserved pods. Return to a boil and cook for 3 minutes more, or just until the beans are tender and the skins are beginning to slip off and the pod pieces have wilted. Remove from the heat and drain well. Cool under cold running water and pat dry.

3. Slip the skins from the beans and set the beans and pods aside. (The beans and pods can be prepared up to this point a few hours before final cooking.)

4. Heat the oil in a large sauté pan over medium heat. Add the garlic and red pepper flakes and sauté for 1 minute. Add the reserved fava beans and pods and sauté for about 3 minutes, or just until heated through. Season with salt and pepper to taste and serve hot.

Summer Tomato Salad

Raw or cooked, tomatoes are the essence of southern Italian cooking. In the summer, tomato salads and raw tomato sauces are at the center of the table. Unfortunately, to be really good, many of these dishes can be made only in the summertime and early fall. Labor Day is perfect timing because the vines are usually falling over with ripe tomatoes ready for the picking. This is a very simple salad that can be enhanced by the addition of olives, capers, fresh herbs, spicy greens, cooked tuna or shrimp, or the classic buffalo mozzarella. There is no acid added to the tomatoes, as I think that their own natural acidity does the trick when hit with the spicy green olive oil.

Serves 6

. . . .

6 large ripe tomatoes, peeled, cored, and cut into chunks

1 large red onion, peeled and cut into slivers

2 cloves garlic, chopped

$^1/_4$ cup extra-virgin olive oil, or to taste

Pinch of dried oregano, or to taste

Coarse salt and freshly ground pepper

8 fresh basil leaves, well washed, dried, and torn into pieces

1. Combine the tomatoes, onion, and garlic in a salad bowl. Add the oil and season with the oregano and salt and pepper to taste. Set aside to marinate for at least 30 minutes before serving.
2. When ready to serve, add the basil and toss to combine. Serve at room temperature.

Roast Chicken with Potatoes and Mushy Peas

Serves 6

This is a simple, transportable Sicilian dish that we often took along when we visited friends and relatives. It puts its stamp on family picnics, as it can be eaten with your fingers straight from the baking dish, either hot or at room temperature. It is a recipe that can easily be doubled or tripled, which makes it perfect for large gatherings. Dark-meat chicken was always used because it took to the longer cooking period required for the vegetables without drying out. You could, of course, use breast meat, but be sure to shorten the cooking time or it will either dry out or become stringy.

6 chicken legs, well washed and dried

6 chicken thighs, well washed and dried

6 chicken wings, well washed and dried

1 medium onion, peeled and diced

2 cloves garlic, peeled and minced

1 teaspoon dried oregano

4 Idaho potatoes, peeled and each cut lengthwise into 6 equal pieces

One 16–ounce package frozen peas, partially thawed

Coarse salt and freshly ground pepper

One 14–ounce can whole peeled Italian plum tomatoes, with juice

$^1/_4$ cup olive oil

5 tablespoons butter

$^1/_4$ cup chopped fresh flat–leaf parsley

1. Preheat the oven to 350°F.

2. Place the chicken pieces in a large nonstick baking pan. Add the onion, garlic, oregano, potatoes, peas, and salt and pepper to taste, tossing well to combine. Squeeze the juice from the tomatoes over the chicken mixture and then add the tomatoes and parsley to the pan and toss to combine. Dot each piece of chicken with butter and drizzle with the olive oil.

3. Cover the pan with aluminum foil and place in the preheated oven. Bake for 30 minutes, then uncover and bake for 30 to 40 minutes more, or until the potatoes are cooked and the chicken is nicely browned. At this point, the peas should be overcooked and will almost create a sauce as their starches meld with the pan juices. Remove from the oven and serve piping hot, straight from the pan, with warm Italian bread to soak up the juices.

A Sicilian Christmas at Home

I would venture to say that every Italian home has a traditional Christmas Eve dinner. It is often the same meal shared by their immigrant ancestors those many years ago. This meatless menu has enormous religious significance, as it is thought to reflect the seven sacraments or seven gifts of the Holy Spirit and always features seven fish courses. Tradition in some Italian households raises the number of fish courses to thirteen. Whatever the menu, the Christmas Eve meal is, without question, the one tradition that almost all Italians keep.

In Oceanside, we always began our Christmas Eve dinner at seven P.M. Of course, we didn't merely have the seven fish courses. First came a huge, meatless antipasto complete with a variety of cheeses, roasted vegetables, and green and black olives. Then Mom and Nana would serve a large platter of the most basic of all pastas, *spaghetti àglio e òlio,* spaghetti with garlic and olive oil, which we all loved. It was so hard not to eat too much pasta, but we knew that there were many more dishes to come and that we had to use caution and save room. This simple but delicious pasta would be followed by the seven fish courses. After such a meal, Mom wisely served a light dessert of fruit and cookies. Eventually, it was time to head off for midnight mass.

After mass, the celebration continued at our house. Nana, Mom, and my aunts went back to the kitchen to do the last-minute preparations for Christmas dinner. Dad took care of the after-mass meal, which never varied—Dad's Homemade Sausage (page 50), roasted and sliced; crusty bread; a big tossed salad; and some red wine. The kids got some before-bed cookies and milk while the men played cards and the women cooked. In the hour or so before Mom shooed us off to bed, we kids would snoop around the house, trying to sneak a peek at the packages under the tree and to search out any gifts that hadn't yet been wrapped.

Once the kids were in bed, the women finished wrapping the gifts and making sure that the tree was perfectly dressed for the excitement of Christmas morning. By this time, it was probably about three or four A.M., and (I now know) the adults would

finally collapse, bone-tired, into bed, only to be awakened at six A.M. by a tangle of
hyperactive kids, wild to open their gifts. And, God love them, Mom and Nana would
be back in the kitchen making frittatas, toasting up Italian bread, and making good,
strong coffee to get them through another day filled with celebration at the table
with loved ones.

Stuffed Calamari with Raisins and Pignoli

Sicilians prefer fresh squid, but today squid is most readily available from the supermarket, frozen. The freezing process does help tenderize the meat, which, when improperly cooked, can be very tough. Squid must be cooked either very briefly or for an extended period of time; anything in between, and you will have

Serves 6

. . . .

plenty of exercise for your jaw! I think that this is a great change from the ubiquitous, flavorless fried calamari that you now find on so many menus.

12 large squid, cleaned, heads and tentacles reserved

6 tablespoons olive oil, plus more as needed

2 tablespoons minced garlic

4 anchovy fillets, finely chopped

$^1/_3$ cup raisins

$^1/_3$ cup pine nuts

Juice and freshly grated zest of 1 lemon

$^1/_4$ cup chopped fresh flat-leaf parsley

$^1/_4$ cup chopped fresh basil

Coarse salt and freshly ground pepper

1 cup fresh bread crumbs, toasted (see step 1, page 40)

$^1/_4$ cup freshly grated Parmesan cheese

$^1/_2$ teaspoon dried oregano, or to taste

1 tablespoon unsalted butter, softened

$^1/_2$ cup chopped onions

1 cup canned crushed Italian plum tomatoes

$^1/_4$ cup water

Red pepper flakes

Lemon wedges

1. Using a sharp knife, chop the squid heads and tentacles. Set aside. Rinse the bodies under cold running water and pat dry. Remove and discard any fine backbone still clinging to the bodies.

2. Heat 3 tablespoons of the oil in a large sauté pan over medium heat. Add 1 tablespoon of the garlic, then the anchovies and the reserved chopped squid. Lower the heat and sauté for 3 minutes, or until the garlic begins to color. Immediately add the raisins, pine nuts, and lemon juice and zest along with 2 tablespoons each of the parsley and basil. Season with salt and pepper to taste and toss to mix. Remove from the heat.

3. Combine the bread crumbs with the squid mixture, mixing well. Add the cheese and oregano. The mixture should be slightly moist; if it seems too dry, add a bit of olive oil.

4. Generously stuff each squid body with the bread crumb mixture. Close the opening by securing it with a toothpick. Continue stuffing until all of the squid have been filled. Set aside.

5. Heat the remaining 3 tablespoons of oil and the butter in a large, heavy-bottomed saucepan over medium heat. Add the onions along with the remaining 1 tablespoon garlic and sauté for about 3 minutes, or just until the onions are softened. Add the stuffed calamari and cook, turning frequently, for about 3 minutes, or just until lightly browned on all sides. Add the tomatoes and $1/4$ cup water and season with salt and pepper to taste. Cover, bring to a simmer, and simmer for 10 minutes. Uncover and simmer for 10 minutes more. Add red pepper flakes to taste along with the remaining 2 tablespoons each of parsley and basil. Serve hot with lemon wedges on the side.

Baked Clams

My dad takes great pride in his baked clams. Nobody can help him make them! They are always on the menu on Christmas Eve and often served as part of an antipasto at Sunday dinner and anytime when the clamming is good. I always ask him to make them for me when I have friends over for a football Sunday. I have

Serves 6

. . . .

to say that although I give you his recipe here, you'll probably have to borrow my dad to get them to taste as good as his do!

6 tablespoons olive oil

³/₄ cup fresh Italian bread crumbs

2 dozen cherrystone or littleneck clams, well scrubbed

¹/₄ cup freshly grated Parmesan cheese

2 tablespoons chopped fresh flat–leaf parsley

1 clove garlic, peeled and minced

1 teaspoon dried oregano (optional)

Juice of 1 lemon (optional)

About ¹/₄ cup water

Freshly ground pepper

1. Heat 2 tablespoons of the oil in a large sauté pan over medium heat. Add the bread crumbs and sauté for about 2 minutes, or just until they are taking on some color. Remove from the heat and set aside to cool.

2. Preheat the oven to 350°F.

3. Working with one at a time, carefully shuck the clams over a small bowl to catch any juices. Discard the top shell and reserve the juice. Loosen the clam meat from the bottom

shell by running a small knife under it. Lay each clam in its shell on a clean baking sheet small enough to fit under the broiler. (See Note.)

4.   Combine the reserved bread crumbs, cheese, parsley, garlic, and oregano (if desired) in a small mixing bowl. Add the reserved clam juice, the lemon juice (if desired), and 2 tablespoons of the remaining oil and toss to combine.

5.   Spoon about 1 teaspoonful of the bread crumb mixture on top of each clam, pressing down lightly so that the breading covers the entire shell. Pour the water into the pan and drizzle some of the remaining 2 tablespoons oil over the top of each clam. Finish with freshly ground pepper over all.

6.   Place the pan in the preheated oven and bake the clams for about 8 minutes, or until the tops are lightly golden and the edges are bubbling. Remove from the oven and preheat the broiler. Place under the broiler at least 5 inches from the heat source and broil for about 30 seconds, or until the tops are slightly crisp. Serve hot with some Italian bread to dip in the liquid from the baking pan.

NOTE: *For cherrystone clams, first chop the clams and place them back in the shell before adding the topping.*

Baccalà Salad

It is said that cod is the fish that has nourished common folk the world over. In Sicilian cooking, this is certainly true, as every household has a recipe for either a salad or a stew featuring dried salted cod, and for many families, the dish will be at the center of the Christmas Eve dinner. Salt cod must be soaked for at least twenty-four hours, with the water changed frequently, before it can be cooked, and, unfortunately, it emits a very unpleasant smell as it soaks. (When I was a boy, the soaking was done outside to keep the smell out of the house.) Many cooks think that once the cod begins cooking, the smell becomes almost fresh, but to me, the smell remains strong and unpleasant. But after you acquire the taste for baccalà, you will be willing to suffer the smell.

Serves 6

. . . .

1 pound salt cod

2 pounds red-skinned potatoes, well washed and cut crosswise
      into $^1/_4$-inch-thick slices

$^1/_2$ cup extra-virgin olive oil

2 cloves garlic, peeled and minced

1 small red onion, peeled and diced

Red pepper flakes

2 ribs celery, well washed, trimmed, and diced

4 tablespoons fresh lemon juice

1 tablespoon freshly grated lemon zest

$^1/_2$ cup diced roasted red bell peppers

$^1/_2$ cup sliced pitted ripe olives

$^1/_4$ cup chopped fresh flat-leaf parsley, plus more for garnish (optional)

3 tablespoons chopped, drained, vinegar-packed capers

6 tablespoons red wine vinegar

Coarse salt and freshly ground pepper

1. Place the salt cod in a deep bowl with cold water to cover. Soak for 24 hours, changing the water and rinsing the cod under cold running water every couple of hours.

2. Bring a large pot of water to a boil over high heat. Add the soaked cod and return the water to a boil. Lower the heat and simmer for 5 to 8 minutes, just until the fish is tender. Remove from the heat and drain well. Set aside to cool.

3. Bring a pot of lightly salted cold water to a boil over high heat. Add the potatoes and bring to a simmer. Lower the heat and simmer for about 6 minutes, or just until tender. Remove from the heat and drain well. Refresh under cold running water, drain, and pat dry. Set aside to cool.

4. Heat the oil in a small sauté pan over medium heat. Add the garlic, onion, and red pepper flakes to taste and sauté for about 3 minutes, or just until the onion has wilted. Remove from the heat.

5. When the fish has cooled, using your fingers, pull it apart into small pieces, discarding any bones and skin. When the fish is in smaller pieces, carefully check for and discard any small pinbones. Place the fish in a large mixing bowl along with the potatoes, celery, lemon juice and zest, roasted peppers, olives, parsley, and capers. Stir in the garlic-onion mixture and vinegar and toss to combine. Cover and refrigerate for at least 2 hours or up to 24 hours to allow the flavors to blend.

6. Uncover and taste. Adjust the seasoning, if necessary, with salt, pepper, and additional red pepper flakes. If desired, garnish the top with additional chopped parsley before serving.

Scampi

Scampi is technically the Italian word for the bodies of small, lobsterlike shellfish, but it has, in America, come to mean a dish made with large shrimp, garlic, olive oil, fresh lemon, and, often, white wine. The shrimp (or prawns) can be sautéed, baked, or broiled and still be called "scampi" on the menu. This is my mom's classic Christmas Eve rendition and the one that I still follow to a tee

Serves 6

. . . .

whenever I want to make a relaxed, informal meal for friends—a big platter of scampi, a great salad, crusty peasant bread, and a few bottles of chilled Verdicchio.

$^1/_2$ **cup olive oil**

8 tablespoons (1 stick) unsalted butter

2 tablespoons minced garlic

2 pounds extra-large shrimp, peeled and deveined

Coarse salt and freshly ground pepper

2 tablespoons fresh lemon juice

$^1/_4$ **cup minced fresh flat-leaf parsley**

$^1/_2$ **cup Italian Seasoned Bread Crumbs (page 30)**

Lemon wedges (optional)

1. Preheat the broiler.

2. Heat $^1/_4$ cup of the oil and 4 tablespoons of the butter in a large sauté pan over medium heat. Add 1 tablespoon of the garlic and stir to blend. Add half the shrimp and sauté for about 4 minutes, or just until the shrimp are opaque. Using a slotted spoon, transfer the shrimp from the sauté pan to a baking pan.

3. Return the sauté pan to medium heat and repeat the cooking process with the remainder of the shrimp, using the remaining $\frac{1}{4}$ cup oil, 4 tablespoons butter, and 1 tablespoon garlic.

4. When all of the shrimp have been transferred to the baking pan, season with salt and pepper to taste and sprinkle with the lemon juice and parsley. Cover the top with the bread crumbs. Place under the preheated broiler and broil for about 2 minutes, or just until the bread crumbs are lightly browned. Remove from the broiler and serve hot with lemon wedges, if desired, and crusty bread to sop up the rich juices.

Crisp Sautéed Eel

This is a dish that holds much more appeal for adults than for kids. When I was younger, my mom could never convince me that the eel wasn't still alive, and I was always certain that I saw it squirm on the plate. Slowly I grew to really love its subtle flavor.

Serves 6

2 cups all-purpose flour

1 teaspoon onion powder

1 teaspoon garlic powder

1 teaspoon paprika

$^1/_2$ teaspoon dried oregano

Pinch of cayenne pepper

Coarse salt and freshly ground pepper

2 pounds eel, skinned and cleaned, cut into 2-inch-long pieces

About 1 cup blended oil (half olive oil and half vegetable oil)

1 tablespoon fresh lemon juice

1. Combine the flour, onion and garlic powders, paprika, oregano, cayenne, and salt and pepper to taste in a large mixing bowl or resealable plastic bag. Add the eel and toss to coat well.

2. Heat enough oil to cover the bottom of a large sauté pan over medium heat. Add the eel, without crowding the pan, and fry, turning frequently, for about 4 minutes, or until golden brown and crisp. Using a slotted spoon, transfer the cooked eel to a double layer of paper towels to drain. Continue heating oil and frying until all of the eel has been fried.

3. Place the eel on a serving platter and drizzle the lemon juice over the top. Serve hot with warm spicy marinara sauce as a dip, if desired.

Steamed Mussels with Wine and Garlic

Steamed mussels are right up there with scampi as one of my favorite crowd-pleasing meals. They are inexpensive, easy to prepare, and even easier to eat. Sometimes we spoon them over pasta and sometimes we use great peasant bread to absorb the pan juices. It is particularly important to add fresh parsley at the last moment, as its fresh pungency really accents the sweet, slightly acidic broth. On Christmas Eve, my mom will often add some clams, and when I can get them, I contribute some scallops still in their shells.

Serves 6

. . . .

¹/₄ cup extra-virgin olive oil

2 tablespoons minced garlic

2 cups dry white wine

4 dozen mussels, well scrubbed and beards removed

2 tablespoons butter

Juice of 2 lemons, or to taste

¹/₂ cup chopped fresh flat-leaf parsley

Coarse salt and freshly cracked pepper

1. Heat the oil in a large saucepan over medium-high heat. Add the garlic and sauté for about 3 minutes, or just until the garlic is soft. Add the wine and bring to a boil. Cook for 3 minutes. Add the mussels and cook, stirring and shaking the saucepan occasionally, for about 5 minutes, or until the shells open. Using a slotted spoon, lift the mussels from the cooking liquid and place them in a shallow bowl.

2. Bring the cooking liquid to a simmer. Add the butter and bring to a boil. Stir in the lemon juice and then the parsley. Season with salt and pepper to taste. Pour the liquid over the mussels and serve with plenty of crusty bread to sop up the juices.

Lobster Fra Diavolo

All kinds of shellfish were part of the Sicilian diet, and many dishes using lobster and crab were simple, everyday fare, particularly in households all around the coast of the island. Unfortunately, between polluted waters and overfishing, recreational fisherman, whether on Long Island or in Sicily, don't find many lobsters on a day's outing, so lobster dishes are saved for holidays and special occasions.

When I was a kid, we used to get our lobsters at Jordan's Lobster Farm, which

Serves 6

offered a very fresh catch at a reasonable price. Although it is now a bit pricey, lobster makes a great communal dining dish, as it is so much fun to have everyone put on a bib and slurp away, extracting every bit of meat from the shells. You can't be squeamish when you work with lobsters—they must be alive and kicking when you start!

6 live 1½- to 2-pound lobsters

1 cup extra-virgin olive oil

3 cloves garlic, peeled and minced

1 onion, peeled and chopped

1 cup dry Marsala wine

½ cup grappa

1 cup clam juice

Three 28-ounce cans whole peeled San Marzano tomatoes,
     with juice, crushed

Coarse salt and freshly ground pepper

¼ cup chopped fresh flat-leaf parsley, plus more for serving

¼ cup chopped fresh basil

½ teaspoon dried oregano

1 teaspoon red pepper flakes

1 pound freshly cooked spaghetti or linguine

1. Working with one lobster at a time, hold the lobster in a large kitchen towel and, twisting, pull the head from the body, then twist off the claws. Place the heads, bodies, claws, and tails each in separate piles.

2. Using a cleaver or a heavy knife, split each head in half lengthwise. Scrape out and discard the gravel sac. Set the head aside. Using the back of the cleaver, make a crack in each claw, leaving the meat and shell intact. Set aside. Using kitchen scissors, cut down the back of each tail to make a neat incision, leaving the meat and shell intact. Set aside. Rinse the cut-up heads and bodies under cold running water. Pat dry and set aside. (As you will only need 3 lobster bodies, you can either discard the remaining 3 or place them in resealable plastic bags and freeze for stock.)

3. Heat the oil in a large pot over medium heat. Add the reserved lobster tails, claws, heads, and 3 bodies and sear, turning frequently, for about 4 minutes, or until bright red. Using tongs, remove and set aside the tails and claws and skim off any white scum that may have formed. Add the garlic and onion to the pot and sauté for about 2 minutes, or until the vegetables are fragrant. Raise the heat and add the wine and grappa. Using a long match, carefully ignite the alcohol. Lift the pot from the heat and allow the alcohol flame to die out. Return the pot to the heat and bring to a boil. Add the clam juice and again bring to a boil. Lower the heat to a vigorous simmer and simmer for about 12 minutes, or until the liquid has reduced by half. Add the tomatoes along with salt and pepper to taste and again bring to a simmer. Lower the heat and cook, at a bare simmer, for 30 minutes, or until the sauce is nicely infused with flavor from the lobster heads and bodies. Remove from the heat and strain the sauce through a fine sieve into a food mill, discarding the solids. Process the sauce through the food mill into a clean saucepan.

4. Place the sauce over medium heat, add the reserved lobster claws, and bring to a simmer. Simmer for 10 minutes.

5. While the sauce is simmering, cut the reserved lobster tails into 2-inch pieces. Add the pieces, along with the parsley, basil, oregano, and red pepper flakes, to the sauce and again bring to a simmer. Simmer for 8 minutes. Remove from the heat and, if necessary, adjust the seasoning with salt and pepper to taste.

6. Place the hot spaghetti in the center of a large serving platter. Using a slotted spoon, transfer the cut-up lobster tails and the claws to the edges of the platter and ladle the sauce over the pasta. Sprinkle with chopped parsley and serve hot.

Dad's Homemade Sausage

For all of my life, my dad has made sausage. He was taught to make it by his godfather and surrogate father, Frank Lenzo. Dad does all of the cutting by hand and still uses the sausage-making equipment that was passed on to him by Uncle Frank. To try it at home, you'll need a manual or electric sausage stuffer (or a stuffing attachment for a heavy-duty electric mixer) with a small funnel, a meat grinder, a heavy-duty electric mixer with a paddle, and natural casing, which is available from specialty butchers and butcher supply houses and through mail order.

Makes 10 pounds

Medium (1 1/4 -inch round) natural casing (see Notes)

10 pounds lean pork butt, cut into 1–inch cubes

4 tablespoons coarse salt, or to taste

1 tablespoon freshly ground pepper

1/2 cup fennel seeds

1/2 cup chopped fresh flat–leaf parsley (optional)

1 tablespoon minced garlic (optional)

1. Soak the casing in cold water to cover for 5 minutes, then hold the casing under the tap and run cold water through it to rinse thoroughly, checking constantly for any holes or weak spots, which will burst when the casing is stuffed. Set the casing aside.

2. Place the large bowl of a heavy-duty electric mixer in the freezer or refrigerator to chill thoroughly.

3. Using the 3/8-inch disk on a meat grinder, grind the pork into the chilled mixing bowl, or cut by hand into small, 3/8-inch dice. Add the salt, pepper, fennel seeds, and, if desired,

the parsley and garlic. Mix just long enough to blend the ingredients without warming the fat. Cover with plastic wrap. Refrigerate for at least 1 hour or up to 4 hours.

4. Place the funnel on either an electric or a manual sausage stuffer and slide one end of the casing over the opening. Pack the chilled meat mixture into the stuffer, taking care that there are no air pockets. Fill the casing with a slow, steady force, continuing to avoid forming any air pockets. If the casing is filled too fast, heat will also build up and the fat will begin to melt. When the casing is completely filled, any visible air pockets that have formed can gently be pricked with a toothpick. The sausage may be left in a long coil or twisted off into individual sausages. If the latter is done, make sure that there is enough casing to twist each sausage closed.

5. The sausage will keep, tightly wrapped in plastic and refrigerated, for a couple of days. For longer storage, wrap in freezer paper, label with the date made, and freeze for up to 6 months.

6. When ready to cook, grill, turning frequently, over medium-high heat for 12 minutes, or until crisp and juicy, *or* bake, turning occasionally, in a preheated 350°F oven for 15 minutes, or until nicely browned and juicy, *or* cut into pieces and fry, turning frequently, for about 15 minutes, or until nicely browned and juicy, *or* sear lightly and place in a sauce or casserole to finish cooking.

NOTES: *Sausage-making ingredients and equipment are available from The Sausage Maker (see Sources, page 335).*

Natural casings (usually made from hog) come in a variety of sizes and are sold by the hank, bundle, cap, or ounce. They are available either dry salt packed, slush or preflushed packed, or pretubed. The largest amount, a hank, will usually be sufficient for about 150 pounds of sausage. One pound of meat will usually require about 2 feet of casing. One ounce of medium (1¼-inch round) casing, the size used to make Italian sausage, will stuff about 8 feet of sausage. Natural casing keeps for years, packed in salt and refrigerated. Fibrous casing, which is extremely strong and unbreakable, is generally used when making dry sausage, which has to be tightly packed. The interior of fibrous casing is coated with a protein substance that will allow it to shrink and bind the sausage as it dries.

To make hot sausage, simply add cayenne pepper or red pepper flakes, usually no more than a tablespoonful (or to taste), when the fennel seeds are added. Anise-flavored liqueur, such as Sambuca, can also be added to hot sausage to round out the spiciness.

Meeting My Family in Sicily

Until very recently, American travelers to Italy "discovered" Rome, Venice, Florence, and, if they were in the fashion industries, Milan, while the rest of the boot went unexplored. For me, these well-known cities held less interest—it was the unsung communities of Sicily, the region left by my emigrating family, which lured me back home. From my first visit to this ancient part of the world, I've always felt as though I truly belonged there. Fortunately, I have been able to return repeatedly and feel my comfort level grow.

Because of my swarthy complexion and black hair, I am frequently asked about my heritage. When I reply "Sicilian," my response is always greeted with, at best, a questioning look and more often, "You don't look Italian; you sure you're not Lebanese?" "Indian?" and so on. I could be a bit of all of those, as, through the centuries, Sicily has been aggressively visited and occupied by a great many invaders. Arab, Saracen, and Greek are but a few of the influences on the cuisine, customs, and even the genealogy of this rugged land.

My grandparents left the mountain town of St. Angelo di Brolo, located between Messina and Palermo, in 1927, when my grandmother was pregnant with my father. The town is now dotted with houses that are, for the most part, abandoned, their inhabitants either having left in the great American migration of the twenties and thirties or having moved from the harshness of the land to an expected easier life in the cities of their own country. From time to time, these homesteads are converted into summer cottages for the more affluent and the warmer months once again welcome bustling activity.

I first discovered St. Angelo in 1983 during my six-month-long hitchhiking tour of Europe. I had met my great-uncle Vincenzo, who still lived in the village, some years before, when he had visited my family in New York. He had urged me to visit anytime and this seemed the perfect anytime. When I arrived in Italy, I telephoned Zìo Vincenzo to let him know that I would be visiting the next day. When my cousin answered the ring with the customary abrupt Italian "*Pronto!*" which I thought meant "Hurry up," in a nervous burst of American Italian I managed to say my name and hoped that I said that I would be arriving the next day.

When I arrived at Zìo Vincenzo's door, looking a bit scruffy, it was clear that, although everyone welcomed me with open arms, they were surprised to see me. There was no food in evidence—a sure sign that no one was expected. The arrival of a guest inspires the whole town to come out in force and fill the tables to overflowing with food and wine. However, once the word got out that a Pintabona had returned from America, the party began. Perfect strangers pulled me to their chests, eager to meet a descendant of my beloved grandfather, who was never able to return home after his departure to America. Hugs and kisses enveloped me wherever I went. People stopped by just to take a peek at me. Everyone made me feel as though I were part of one huge, exuberant family.

The most moving (and frequently amusing) moments were those I spent with Zìo Vincenzo. Determined to hear me properly pronounce the family name, he spent a full day coaching me on how to hit all the right inflections in the nine letters that need to be hit to get the full measure of "Piinntaabooona." His expressions as he taught the infidel ran the gamut, with much hand-wringing and shrugging of shoulders accompanying his exasperation. When I finally got it out—sounding just like a native—he rewarded me with a bear hug and many kisses.

My relatives were so eager to share their history with me, and I was so eager to learn it, that we were able to communicate despite the language barrier. By day, aunts and uncles, cousins and second cousins led me around the towns, pointing out monuments and clan landmarks. Each building where a family milestone had occurred was highlighted with enthusiasm. I could almost picture the weddings, births, funerals, and other events remembered and retold in detail for me.

However, it was around a table groaning with food, laughter, and simultaneous conversations that I learned the connections and journey of my family. Through stories and remembrances, punctuated by passed serving dishes and midsentence taste thrills from the forkfuls of food stuffed, often by someone else, into my ever-eager mouth, I learned all of my lessons in Sicilian hospitality.

After the first few dinners, I couldn't really detect a connection between the meals of my Italian American family and those of my Sicilian one, so I began to politely inquire about "real" food. I was surprised and saddened to learn that many Sicilians consider their cooking to be mere "peasant" food and therefore unfit for visitors and honored guests. I finally got my courage up and asked a cousin (French-speaking and my full-time translator) to explain that I really wanted to experience the most treasured of our family recipes just as they had been served for generations. It was my great honor to be part of my St. Angelo family and I did not want to be treated as a guest. From then on, I feasted on every possible take on Sicilian "peasant" dishes.

When it came time to leave, I carried with me many warm memories of family and the community of food. And tucked in my knapsack was a treasured notebook of family recipes written so that, whenever I felt a longing for the tables of St. Angelo, I could go

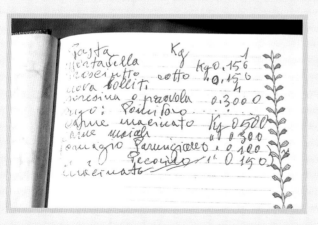

to the stove and transport myself back "home." But I also deeply felt that the recipes would always be incomplete without the warmth of a shared table.

Wedding Soup

here is no way to make a wedding soup for just a couple of people! It's a great nostalgic dish fit for a big, hungry crowd. I first tasted this soup at the home of relatives who still lived much as they had in Italy in, of all places, West Virginia. Coming from New York, it reminded me of the matzo ball soup served in the Jewish delis that I had grown to love. It is basically

Serves a crowd

. . . .

the same thing—a simple but rich broth filled with nourishing meats, a starch, and vegetables. Although it is very filling, you'll still want a couple of loaves of crusty bread to dunk in the rich broth.

1 bunch fresh flat-leaf parsley, well washed and dried

2 tablespoons olive oil

4 ribs celery, well washed, trimmed, and chopped

3 large carrots, peeled, trimmed, and chopped

2 cloves garlic, peeled and chopped

1 large onion, peeled and chopped

One 4- to 5-pound roasting chicken, well washed and dried

1 tablespoon black peppercorns

Coarse salt

Mom's Meatballs for Gravy (page 15), formed into thumbnail-sized balls

2 cups blanched, chopped escarole

3 large eggs, beaten

$^1/_2$ cup freshly grated Pecorino Romano cheese, plus more for serving
   (optional)

1$^1/_2$ cups cooked pastina or other tiny dried pasta

Freshly ground pepper

1. Pick and chop the leaves from the parsley, separately reserving the stems.

2. Heat the oil in a large pot over medium heat. Add the celery, carrots, garlic, and onion and sauté for about 5 minutes, or just until the vegetables have begun to sweat their liquid but have not taken on any color. Add the chicken, peppercorns, and reserved parsley stems. Add enough cold water to cover the chicken by 3 inches (about 6 quarts). Raise the heat and bring to a boil. Immediately lower the heat, season with salt to taste, and simmer for about 2 hours, or until the chicken meat is falling off the bones.

3. Remove the pot from the heat and strain the liquid through a fine sieve into a clean saucepan.

4. Pick the chicken meat from the strainer, discarding the vegetables, skin, and bones. Shred the chicken meat and set aside.

5. Return the strained broth to medium heat and bring to a simmer. Add the meatballs and return to a simmer. Simmer for 10 minutes or until the meatballs begin to float to the top. Add the escarole and simmer for 10 minutes more.

6. While the soup is simmering, combine the eggs and the cheese. Set aside.

7. Bring the soup to a boil and add the pastina. Whisking constantly, add the egg mixture in a slow, steady stream. Whisk vigorously until the egg is set (it should resemble Chinese egg-drop soup). Stir in the reserved chicken. Taste and, if necessary, adjust the seasoning with salt and pepper. Stir in the reserved chopped parsley leaves and serve hot, sprinkled with extra cheese, if desired.

Zìo Vincenzo's Pasta al Forno

Serves 8 to 12

Here it is—the best lasagna that you'll ever eat. It does not have the expected ricotta cheese that Italian Americans generally use. The kind with ricotta was what I knew before I feasted on Vincenzo's authentic St. Angelo version. This is what I now make—we don't miss the ricotta and I can guarantee that you won't either. It also doesn't have any salt added, as the meats and cheeses are salty enough to adequately season the dish. Be sure that you use really good imported Italian cheeses, as their intense flavor really makes all the difference in the world. Coupled with the smoky prosciutto and mozzarella, the flavors add a whole new dimension to this homespun preparation.

2 tablespoons olive oil

1 pound lean ground beef

1 pound lean ground pork

Freshly ground pepper

Two 16-ounce boxes lasagna noodles

8 cups Nana's Fresh Marinara Sauce (page 8) or other marinara sauce

8 ounces mortadella cheese, thinly sliced

2 pounds smoked mozzarella cheese, cubed

8 ounces Parmigiano-Reggiano cheese, freshly grated

8 ounces Pecorino Romano cheese, freshly grated

8 ounces prosciutto, thinly sliced

1 cup chopped fresh flat-leaf parsley

1 cup chopped fresh basil

4 large eggs, hard-boiled and chopped

1. Heat the oil in a large sauté pan over medium heat. Add the ground beef and ground pork and sauté for about 5 minutes, or just until the meat has begun to color. Season to taste with some freshly ground pepper and set aside to cool.

2. Preheat the oven to 375°F.

3. Bring a large pot of lightly salted cold water to a boil over high heat. Add the lasagna noodles and cook according to package directions. Drain well.

4. Place a thin layer of marinara sauce on the bottom of a lasagna pan. Cover with one-quarter of the lasagna noodles. (This will probably be about 8 noodles.) Sprinkle about one-quarter of the cooked ground meats over the noodles, then cover with all of the mortadella slices. Layer with one-quarter of the cubed mozzarella and then sprinkle with one-quarter of the grated cheeses. Ladle some more marinara sauce over all and then cover with another layer of lasagna noodles. Top with one-half of the prosciutto slices, followed by another layer of mozzarella and grated Parmigiano-Reggiano and Pecorino Romano, and a light layer (one-third) of the chopped parsley and basil. Add another layer

of the ground meats and cover with more marinara sauce. Top with one-half of the hard-boiled eggs. Place another layer of lasagna noodles in the pan and repeat the previous layering, ending with a layer of lasagna noodles. Cover this last layer of lasagna noodles with a final layer of the ground meats, then the grated cheeses followed by mozzarella. Cover with a final layer of marinara sauce. Sprinkle the remaining parsley and basil over the top and grind some pepper over all. Cover the entire pan with aluminum foil, making sure that the foil does not touch the top of the lasagna, or the cheese will stick to it and pull off when you remove the foil. Place in the preheated oven and bake for about 40 minutes, or until the cheeses are melted and the flavors have melded together.

5.   Remove the pan from the oven and place on a wire rack to rest for 30 minutes before cutting the lasagna into 3 × 5-inch serving pieces. (This resting time is necessary so that the cooking liquid that formed during baking will have time to be absorbed by the noodles.) Serve hot.

Swordfish Braciole

This is a classic Sicilian dish that my great-aunt Carmela made for me. The stuffing can be used for beef or veal, but in Sicily, stuffed meat rolls were usually prepared only in the kitchens of the wealthy landowners, with the more readily available fish used for stuffing in the poorer households. The bit of meat offered by the prosciutto gave just a taste of luxury

to the dish. This stuffing combines many of the basic flavors of Sicilian cooking that, when combined, serve to identify the cuisine.

$^{1}/_{4}$ cup dried currants

2 tablespoons brandy

About $^{1}/_{4}$ cup olive oil

3 cloves garlic, peeled and minced

1 onion, peeled and minced

$^{1}/_{4}$ cup finely chopped prosciutto

1 cup Italian Seasoned Bread Crumbs (page 30)

$^{1}/_{4}$ cup chopped fresh flat-leaf parsley

2 tablespoons chopped fresh mint

2 tablespoons pine nuts, toasted

Coarse salt and freshly ground pepper

Twelve 3-ounce, $6 \times 4 \times ^{1}/_{4}$-inch pieces swordfish

Juice of 1 lemon

Lemon wedges (optional)

1. Place the currants in a small bowl. Add the brandy and enough hot water to cover the currants by $^{1}/_{2}$ inch. Set aside.

2. Heat 2 tablespoons of the oil in a large sauté pan over medium heat. Add the garlic and onion and sauté for about 5 minutes, or until golden but not brown. Remove from the heat and scrape into a mixing bowl. Stir in the prosciutto and set aside.

3. Drain the currants, discarding the soaking liquid. Add the currants, bread crumbs, parsley, mint, and pine nuts to the prosciutto mixture. Season with salt and pepper to taste and stir to combine.

4. Preheat the oven to 350°F.

5. Lightly oil a baking pan large enough to hold the rolled-up swordfish in a single layer. Set aside.

6. Place the swordfish pieces on a clean, dry work surface. Place a piece of plastic wrap over each piece of swordfish and, using a metal meat pounder or cleaver, pound the fish until very thin. Place an equal portion of the stuffing in the center of each piece of fish. Working with one piece at a time, roll the swordfish up, cigar-fashion, to make a tight, neat roll. Secure each roll with a couple of toothpicks. Place the fish rolls in a single layer in the prepared baking pan. Using a pastry brush, lightly coat the rolls with the remaining 2 tablespoons oil. Cover the entire pan with aluminum foil and place in the preheated oven. Bake for 20 minutes, or until the filling is hot and the fish is cooked through. Remove the fish from the oven.

7. Preheat the broiler. Place the fish under the broiler and broil, watching carefully to prevent burning, for about 4 minutes, or until the tops are golden brown but not dry. Remove from the heat and drizzle with the lemon juice. Serve hot, with lemon wedges on the side, if desired.

Sea Bass Messina

Serves 6
. . . .

Many of my relatives still reside in and around Messina, an important port on the east side of the island from which you can almost touch the Calabrian coast. This is, therefore, a Pintabona family classic. You can use almost any type of firm fish, either in fillets or steaks, to prepare this dish. We often make it when we expect a crowd, as it is easy to put together and the sauce keeps the fish from drying out if it has to sit out on the dinner table.

$^1/_2$ **cup olive oil**

2 cloves garlic, peeled and minced

1 large onion, peeled and diced

1 rib celery, well washed, trimmed, and diced

1 cup dry white wine

1 cup canned diced Italian plum tomatoes

1 cup clam juice

$^1/_2$ **cup julienned pitted green olives**

$^1/_4$ **cup salt-packed capers, well rinsed and dried**

$^1/_4$ **cup raisins**

3 tablespoons pine nuts, toasted

Coarse salt and freshly ground pepper

1 cup all-purpose flour

Six 6-ounce pieces boneless, skinless sea bass (or other firm white fish)

$^1/_4$ **cup chopped fresh basil**

1. Heat ¼ cup of the oil in a large, shallow, nonstick, ovenproof casserole-type pan over medium heat. Add the garlic, onion, and celery and sauté for about 3 minutes, or just until the vegetables have softened. Raise the heat and add the wine. Bring to a boil, then lower the heat and simmer for about 5 minutes, or until the wine has reduced by half. Add the tomatoes and again bring to a simmer. Simmer, stirring occasionally, for 10 minutes. Add the clam juice, olives, capers, raisins, and pine nuts and again return to a simmer. Season with salt and pepper to taste and cook at a bare simmer for 10 minutes.

2. Preheat the oven to 375°F.

3. While the sauce is cooking, prepare the fish. Place the flour with salt and pepper to taste in a shallow bowl. Cut each piece of fish into 3 equal portions. Dip the fish into the seasoned flour, coating both sides evenly. Shake off any excess flour.

4. Heat the remaining ¼ cup oil in a large sauté pan over medium heat. When very hot but not smoking, add the fish and sear for about 3 minutes, or until the bottom is golden brown. Using a slotted spoon, transfer the fish to the sauce, browned side up. Place in the preheated oven and bake for 10 minutes, or until the fish is firm and cooked through. Remove from the oven, sprinkle the top with the basil, and serve hot, directly from the pan.

Rabbit Cacciatore

raises and stews such as this tomato-based dish were popular in Italian peasant cooking because a little meat could be stretched to flavor a sauce that could then be extended with pasta, rice, or bread. Rabbit dishes could also be found at the heart of almost any peasant cooking, since rabbit was (and still is) fairly easily caught and offers good, lean protein at no cost, except to the nerves of the hunter. Cacciatore-style was also used to cook poultry; however, in poorer families,

Serves 6

. . . .

chickens were not easily given up to the stewpan, as the eggs that they provided were even more important to the table. Most specialty butchers now carry rabbit as well as wild hare, so recipes once almost impossible to duplicate unless you had a hunter in the family are now simple to prepare.

6 white peppercorns

2 cloves garlic, peeled and chopped

1 teaspoon chopped fresh rosemary

1 teaspoon freshly grated lemon zest

$^1/_2$ teaspoon coarse salt, plus more to taste

$^1/_4$ cup plus 3 tablespoons olive oil

One 3-pound rabbit, cleaned, well washed, and cut into pieces

$^1/_4$ cup all-purpose flour

12 ounces button mushrooms, stemmed and cleaned

2 ribs celery, well washed, trimmed, and diced

1 onion, peeled and diced

1 large carrot, peeled, trimmed, and diced

3 cups dry red wine

One 28-ounce can crushed peeled Italian plum tomatoes

2 cups chicken broth

1 bay leaf

Freshly ground pepper

Red pepper flakes

$^1/_4$ cup chopped fresh flat-leaf parsley

1. Place the peppercorns, garlic, rosemary, lemon zest, and salt in a mortar. Pour in the 3 tablespoons oil and, using the pestle, grind the mixture into a coarse paste.

2. Rub the seasoning into the rabbit pieces. Place the seasoned rabbit in a shallow dish, cover, and marinate for 30 minutes.

3. Lightly dust the rabbit with the flour, shaking off any excess.

4. Heat the $^1/_4$ cup oil in a large, heavy-bottomed casserole-type pan over medium-high heat. Add the rabbit and sear, turning frequently, for about 7 minutes, or until nicely browned. Add the mushrooms, celery, onion, and carrot and sauté for about 5 minutes, or until the vegetables have just begun to soften. Add the red wine and bring to a boil. Lower the heat and simmer for about 6 minutes, or until the liquid has reduced by half. Raise the heat and add the tomatoes, broth, and bay leaf. Bring to a boil, season with salt, pepper, and red pepper flakes to taste, and lower the heat to a simmer. Cover and cook at a bare simmer for about $1^1/_2$ hours, or until the meat is very tender and the sauce has thickened. Remove and discard the bay leaf. Stir in the parsley and remove from the heat. Serve hot with pasta, gnocchi, rice, polenta, or mashed potatoes.

Learning to Cook

I didn't expect to be a cook. After graduating from high school, I went to college—the University of South Florida—to become an accountant. Like so many other students, I financed my education by working in restaurants. My first job was over a stifling-hot fryer making hush puppies by the thousands at a busy Tampa seafood restaurant called the Sea Wolf.

As I worked my way through a couple of years of college, my studies began to suffer. When sitting in the classroom, I would think about what I might get to cook at the restaurant, and soon recipes were replacing my accounting books. With three years under my belt, it finally dawned on me that I belonged in cooking school.

More than anything in the world, I loved to travel, so one of the main reasons that a culinary career appealed to me was that it seemed to be a portable profession. Once I got the basics down, all I would need were my knives and a change of clothes and I could cook anyplace in the world. I knew that I could work my way up in restaurant kitchens, but I felt that culinary school would be the quicker route to a good, solid foundation that could take me anywhere.

My goal was to complete culinary school and then head straight for France, where I could immerse myself in the classics and learn the language. Next would come Italy, cooking and learning the language of my heritage, and then I would be off to a land I had always dreamed of, Japan. I had it all figured out.

Until I actually enrolled in the Culinary Institute of America, in Hyde Park, New York, I hadn't taken into consideration the costs. I had hoped to work in a restaurant kitchen while at school, but, unfortunately, the pay was so low that I couldn't afford the experience. I was fortunate in that I had driven a cab all over New York City and Long

Island during summers and vacations and knew that if I worked a good schedule, I could make enough money to see me through.

I lived off campus in Poughkeepsie in a tiny apartment above the Nite Cap Pub, whose neon sign blinked off and on all night across my bedroom and whose patrons did their best to keep a racket going until closing time. I was a group leader in class, so I didn't have a lot of time for myself. As soon as classes were over on Friday evenings, I would head for my cab, a two-hour trip to the city. I picked up the cab at midnight and gave $50 to the dispatcher and $50 to the mechanic to ensure that I would be given the best fares and that the odometer would be disconnected so that no one could trace my hours. I would sign back in at noon on Sunday, when I usually had $800 cash in my pocket and a ticket back to Hyde Park.

Although I had taken up cab driving for financial reasons only, I used the opportunity to scout out ethnic neighborhoods and adventures in eating while making a little money. An additional benefit was that I got to meet a lot of people I would never have known under other circumstances. When passengers saw me reading a cookbook as I sat parked in my cab or heard that I was in culinary school, I got stories, recipes, cooking hints, maps to culinary adventures in local ethnic restaurants and markets, and generally good conversation. I really did love meeting new people and talking about food. It was such a universal subject that almost everyone felt comfortable sharing their own dining experiences, whether with home cooking or in restaurants featuring the cuisines of their homelands. Once again, I saw what a powerful connection food was to the community.

I did well at the Culinary Institute and passed with honors and enough money to plan a six-month-long backpacking trip through Europe. I had my passport, a Eurailpass, and an open-ended itinerary—I would go wherever the kitchens carried me.

Miss Millie's Fried Chicken

Of all of the passengers I met in my cab, Miss Millie was my favorite. She was an elderly African American woman who asked that I take her to church every Sunday morning and then pick her up and take her home after the service and the big Sunday meal served in the church hall. On the ride back, Miss Millie would hand me a brown paper bag with some of her fried chicken. It was so delicious—truly finger-lickin' good. I finally got her to share the recipe with me, and it is one that I have

Serves 6

. . . .

treasured through the years. I can't even guess at the number of times I have used it for restaurant events, barbecues, kids' parties, and summer picnics. I always think of Miss Millie's gentleness and generosity. And her chicken is always a hit.

2 cups buttermilk

2 teaspoons paprika

2 teaspoons cayenne pepper

2 teaspoons garlic powder

2 teaspoons onion powder

2 teaspoons dried parsley

1 teaspoon chili powder

1 teaspoon ground coriander

1 teaspoon ground fennel

1 teaspoon dried thyme

1 teaspoon dried oregano

$1/2$ teaspoon ground cumin

Coarse salt and freshly ground pepper

One 3-pound frying chicken, cut into serving pieces,
well washed and dried

2 cups all-purpose flour

About 6 cups solid vegetable shortening (see Note)

1. Combine the buttermilk with 1 teaspoon each of the paprika, cayenne, garlic powder, onion powder, and parsley and 1/2 teaspoon each of the chili powder, coriander, fennel, thyme, oregano, and cumin, along with salt and pepper to taste, in a nonreactive container with a lid, large enough to hold all of the chicken. Add the chicken and toss to combine. Cover and refrigerate for at least 2 hours and up to 8 hours.

2. Combine the flour and the remaining 1 teaspoon each paprika, cayenne, garlic powder, onion powder, and parsley and 1/2 teaspoon each chili powder, coriander, fennel, thyme, oregano, and cumin along with salt and pepper to taste in a large resealable plastic (or brown paper) bag.

3. Line a couple of baking pans with wire racks. Set aside.

4. Remove the chicken from the buttermilk marinade, shaking off the excess liquid and reserving the marinade. Place the chicken in the seasoned flour, a few pieces at a time, and shake to coat evenly. When all of the chicken is coated, quickly dip each piece into the reserved buttermilk marinade. Then toss the chicken again, a few pieces at a time, in the seasoned flour. Place the coated chicken on the wire racks and set aside for 30 minutes to dry slightly.

5. Place the shortening in a large cast-iron skillet over

high heat, allowing it to melt. You want about 1½ inches of fat in the pan. When the fat reaches 350°F on an instant-read thermometer, add the chicken, skin side down. Keeping the fat at a constant 350°F, cover and fry for about 5 minutes, or until the chicken is nicely browned on the bottom. Turn the chicken, cover, and fry for 5 minutes more, or until crisp and golden brown. Lower the heat so that the fat temperature stays at about 300°F, turn the chicken, and fry, uncovered, turning from time to time so that all of the chicken cooks evenly, for 10 minutes more, or until all of the pieces are crisp, golden brown, and cooked through. Remove from the skillet and place on the wire racks to drain. Season with additional salt and pepper, if desired. Serve warm or at room temperature.

NOTE: *I have found that Crisco shortening is the best possible fat to use. It is difficult to estimate the amount of fat needed, as you want to have 1½ inch of hot fat in the pan at all times. If it should get too hot and the particles of flour in the bottom begin to burn, drain the fat from the pan through a fine sieve. Rub the skillet clean with paper towels, return the hot fat to the pan, and continue frying the chicken. If the oil gets too hot and the flour begins to burn, the chicken will take on an unpleasant burned flavor.*

New York: Charlie Palmer

❋ •*Learning Charcuterie*

Although my six months of backpacking travel had taken me to many countries and through many cuisines just as I had hoped, my money was running out and I had to get back to work. I knew that if I was going to build a career in the kitchen, I would have to experience working with the best chefs in America, many of whom were located in New York. So back I went.

Upon arrival, I poked around the city, asking questions, learning about the current "best" restaurants and "hot" chefs, and trying to discover the chef from whom I could learn the most. More often than not, the name Charlie Palmer came up. Charlie was the chef at the River Café on the water's edge in Brooklyn and his reviews had made him the talk of the town. I went to see Charlie, who, to my amazement, was almost as young as I. We hit it off immediately and I had a job.

One of Charlie's areas of expertise was charcuterie. It had become his specialty under his mentor, Chef Leon Dhanens, at our shared alma mater, the Culinary Institute of America. Ever since my days at Grand Union helping the butchers, curing, salting, and making sausages had fascinated me. I expressed this interest to Charlie and he set me to work experimenting with new techniques and perfecting old ones as we made traditional French cured meats and put our own stamp on some new variations.

I particularly loved the long process of making charcuterie, the French term for cooked or cured meats made mainly from pork as well as the name of the store where such meats are sold. The term itself is a combination of the words *chair* ("meat") and *cuite* ("cooked"), and the art has been practiced in France for eons. Galantines, *crépinettes,* headcheeses, rillettes, pâtés, and sausages all take time to put together and, for many of them, time to cure. I always had (and still have) a feeling of great accomplishment when I created perfect charcuterie. In addition, once made, many items of charcuterie keep well for months and make great spur-of-the-moment snacks or hors d'oeuvres.

The recipes that I have chosen to represent this period are relatively simple to make, and they could be part of a large platter of charcuterie that might include commercially prepared items along with some of the traditional garnishes of pickled vegetables, particularly tiny onions, cornichons, different mustards, and fruit chutneys. Of course, baskets of breads and crackers would add even more heft to the feast. There is nothing that more represents the community of the table than this welcoming mixture of peasant food and haute cuisine to be shared with friends and family.

Working with Charlie at the River Café was not only a great learning experience but lots of fun. We were all young, enthusiastic, and full of curiosity and energy. Many of America's greatest chefs came out of those early years at the café. It was a real community of cooks, learning and sharing. We have remained friends throughout our careers, sending out a helping hand when needed, working together at charitable events across the country and all over the world.

Country Pâté

This is a very basic, classic French *pâté de campagne* from which you can build variations using different meats. You will want to keep the fat, as it is the amount of fattiness that gives it a nice, moist texture rather than the more dense, meaty country loaf. I like the strong liver flavor of this pâté, but if you prefer a milder flavor,

Makes one 12-inch terrine

replace the duck livers with chicken livers. If you want to keep the pâté for a long period of time, keep it in the terrine and cover the top with melted duck fat.

2 pounds very lean pork butt

8 ounces pork fatback

1 tablespoon unsalted butter

2 shallots, peeled and minced

1 small onion, peeled and minced

1 clove garlic, peeled and minced

3 sprigs fresh thyme

2 bay leaves

1 tablespoon *sel rose* (see Note)

1 cup applejack brandy

About 1 pound (20 strips) thinly sliced lean bacon

1 pound duck livers

1 large egg, at room temperature

1 cup heavy cream

$^1/_4$ cup all-purpose flour

$^1/_4$ cup Madeira wine

1 tablespoon coarse salt, or to taste

$^1/_2$ teaspoon freshly ground white pepper

$^1/_4$ teaspoon five-spice powder

1 cup finely diced lean cooked ham

1 cup chopped unsalted pistachios

¹/₄ cup chopped fresh flat-leaf parsley

1. Cut the pork butt and fatback into a fine dice. Place in a cold-proof bowl in the freezer for about 30 minutes, or until just starting to freeze.

2. While the meat is chilling, melt the butter in a sauté pan over medium-low heat. Add the shallots, onion, and garlic and sauté for about 4 minutes, or just until the vegetables have begun to sweat their liquid but have not taken on any color. Remove from the heat and allow to cool.

3. Remove the chilled pork meat and fat from the freezer. Add the cooled shallot mixture, thyme, and bay leaves.

4. Add the *sel rose* to the brandy and stir to dissolve. When dissolved, add the mixture to the pork. Cover with plastic wrap and refrigerate for 2 days.

5. Line a 12 × 4¹/₂ × 4-inch terrine with plastic wrap, leaving about 2 inches hanging over all of the sides. With the strips of bacon, cover the bottom and the sides of the terrine completely with at least 2 inches hanging over all of the sides. Set aside.

6. Place the meat mixture in a fine sieve and drain off and discard all of the liquid.

7. Remove the thyme sprigs and bay leaves from the meat mixture and then run the chilled meat mixture through the large disk of a meat grinder. Return the ground meat to the freezer to chill for 30 minutes, then run the chilled meat mixture through the medium disk of a meat grinder into a clean bowl.

8. Preheat the oven to 325°F.

9. Using a spatula, push the livers through a fine sieve into the meat mixture.

10. In a separate bowl, whisk together the egg and cream. When well blended, whisk in the flour. Pour the egg mixture into the meat mixture, a little bit at a time, using your hands to incorporate. Add the Madeira, salt to taste, white pepper, and five-spice powder and stir to combine. Fold in the ham, pistachios, and parsley.

11. Fill the terrine to the top with the meat mixture, pressing down to make a neat surface. Bang the terrine on the countertop to help any air bubbles escape. Pull the bacon up and over the meat mixture to completely cover it. Fold the excess plastic wrap tightly up and over to cover.

12. Place the terrine in a baking pan large enough to hold it leaving about 2 inches all around. Fill the pan with boiling water to come halfway up the sides of the terrine. Place in the preheated oven and bake for about 90 minutes, or until an instant-read thermometer inserted into the center reads 150°F. (The terrine will continue to cook to reach 160°F.) Remove from the oven and transfer the terrine to another baking pan. Fill the baking pan with ice to come halfway up the sides of the terrine, so that the pâté will cool quickly.

13. When the pâté is cool, cover the top with plastic wrap and then place a heavy object (such as a large juice can or a small cast-iron pan) on top of the pâté to weigh it down. Refrigerate for 24 hours.

14. Remove the weight and keep the pâté refrigerated, in the mold, until ready to serve.

15. When ready to serve, cut crosswise into ¼-inch-thick slices and serve, if desired, with cornichons, grainy mustard, Cranapple-Ginger Chutney (page 79) or other chutney, and toast points or crackers.

NOTE: Sel rose *("pink salt")* is a nitrate preservative available at specialty food stores.

Cranapple–Ginger Chutney

This sweet-spice mixture is the perfect garnish for pâtés, dry sausage, cured meats, or simple grilled chicken or pork. Mix it with a little mayo and mustard, and you have a very tasty condiment for sandwiches. All in all, it's a great addition to the pantry! It makes quite a large amount, but it does keep for quite a long time and it makes a great gift from the kitchen. You can also preserve the chutney in a hot-water canner according to manufacturer's directions and it will then keep unrefrigerated.

Makes 4 quarts

. . . .

Two 3-inch cinnamon sticks

2 star anise

1 cardamom pod

1 tablespoon vegetable oil

4 jalapeño chili peppers, well washed, stems removed, seeded, and finely diced

2 large red onions, peeled and finely diced

$^1/_4$ cup finely chopped fresh ginger

5 pounds Granny Smith apples, peeled, cored, and diced

3 cups sugar, plus more to taste

1 tablespoon unsalted butter

1 cup dry white wine

2 pounds fresh cranberries, well washed and dried

$1^1/_2$ pounds golden raisins

1 pound dark raisins

$^1/_2$ pound dried apricots, finely diced

$^1/_4$ cup freshly grated orange zest

1 cup apple cider vinegar

4 cups water

Coarse salt and freshly ground white pepper

1. Tie the cinnamon sticks, star anise, and cardamom pod in a cheesecloth bag. Set aside. Heat the oil in a large saucepan over medium heat. Add the jalapeños, onions, and ginger and sauté for about 3 minutes, or just until fragrant. Add the apples, $1\frac{1}{2}$ cups of the sugar, and the butter. Raise the heat and sauté for about 10 minutes, or until the apples begin to caramelize. Add the wine and cook, stirring occasionally, for about 5 minutes, or until the pan is almost dry.

2. Stir in the cranberries, golden raisins, dark raisins, apricots, and orange zest. Then add the remaining $1\frac{1}{2}$ cups sugar, the reserved spices tied in the cheesecloth bag, and the vinegar. Stir to combine and then add the water. Bring to a boil, then lower the heat and simmer, stirring often, for about 40 minutes, or until very thick. Remove from the heat. Taste and season with additional sugar, if needed, and salt and white pepper to taste.

3. Immediately pack into sterilized containers with lids. Cover and refrigerate until ready to use or for up to 3 months.

France: Georges Blanc

※ *I Can Do It!—Becoming a Pastry Chef*

While working with Charlie Palmer, I expressed an interest in going to France. Charlie had a connection to Georges Blanc, who was, at that time, at the height of his fame. A couple of telephone calls later, I was on my way to Vonnas, France, and a job at Restaurant Georges Blanc.

The restaurant had been family owned and operated for over 100 years. It was in a country château situated in an absolutely idyllic setting. The family were all still involved, but it was the fabled chef who was in control. Georges Blanc was young, charismatic, and challenging. Unlike older French chefs, he was very open and approachable, and I was eager to learn from him. And I even got paid! (I may have been one of the last *stagiaires* to be paid to work in a three-star kitchen—nowadays, cooks often have to pay for the privilege of this experience.)

There were cooks from all over the world on the line, but I was the only American. Because of my longstanding interest in Japan, I made an immediate connection with a Japanese cook, Makoto Ono. Makoto had lived in France for seven years. Although he was very well known in Japan as a respected teacher at the Tsuji Cooking School, he was content to move from three-star restaurant to three-star restaurant to continue to hone his skills and learn new techniques. He was not alone, as all of the cooks were serious about learning and worked extremely hard under not-always-the-greatest conditions. There was terrific camaraderie as we all moved through every station in the kitchen.

The pastry chef was a guy named Michel Paulot, who came from a small town near Cannes. He had his own pastry shop and was quite famous throughout the south of France. He had come to Vonnas to add some luster to his career but didn't really need the job. Since he had also spent some time in California and spoke great English, we became fast friends. On our days off, we would drive the five hours to the Côte d'Azur to check out the business in his shop and to eat in the off-the-beaten-track family-owned restaurants that only he knew.

Because Michel was so successful in his own right, he often butted heads with Georges Blanc. Sometimes their disagreements would become quite heated and Michel would turn and leave. One night, Michel had had enough and left for good. He didn't tell anyone—except me—that he was not coming back. He not only told me that he was leaving, but left me copies of all of his dessert recipes, with the admonition, "Don't share these with anyone; they are only for you. Guard them well, but use them when you can."

Since Michel had left more than once, everyone expected him to be back in the morning. As the day progressed and no Michel appeared, whispers grew to nervous talk. The restaurant had a very ambitious pastry program, and dinner guests expected to be wowed at the end of the meal. There were a couple of signature desserts on the menu that were part of the family heritage, but most of the desserts belonged to Michel. There was a staff of six in the pastry kitchen, but none of them knew how to prepare all of the components of Michel's desserts.

Monsieur Blanc was furious when he realized that Michel was gone for good. "Can any of you do these desserts for me?" Chef Blanc asked. There was silence for a few moments, and then someone said, "No, only Michel had the recipes." "The *opéra*, the *opéra* [a classic chocolate cake that every pastry chef does a spin on]—someone must know how Michel made it." Very quietly, I said, "I think I can make it."

The only problem was that I had hidden the recipes behind the staff commode, so, to make the cakes, I had to keep running to the john to sneak a peek at the handwritten recipe. After a while, everyone began asking me if I was sick. "No, no, it's just so hot in here that I have been drinking a lot" was my cover. To everyone's amazement, my *opéras* looked and tasted just like Michel's. This gave the chef a lot of confidence in my abilities and he kept asking me to duplicate Michel's desserts. I continued to be successful, but I had to listen to a lot of kidding about my weak bladder. Although tempted when the ribbing got out of control, I never gave up my secret stash.

Served on a *chariot* that was wheeled through the dining room, the desserts at Georges Blanc were, for the most part, pretty classic. The desserts that follow are representative of those classics, adapted for an American kitchen. They are all relatively easy to prepare and all together would make a great dessert cart for a large party. Of course, each one stands alone beautifully and, like all good food, will taste even better when shared with friends.

Poached Prunes in Red Wine and Armagnac

This is one of the most classic French desserts. You will find it everywhere from bistros to brasseries to salons of fine dining. Fresh fruit as well as dried fruit can be used. In France, seasonal poached fruits are always on the menu—berries in the spring, luscious peaches and apricots in the height of summer, and pears in the fall. The basic poaching liquid can be used with any seasonal fruit, with a change of the liqueurs to pair with the type of fruit used (see Note). Since fruit preserved in this manner keeps so well, it is a great dessert to have on hand at all times. It can be served warm or chilled with a dollop of crème fraîche and a sprig of mint as the perfect ending to almost any meal.

Serves 6

. . . .

1 large orange

1 lemon

3 cups hearty, dry red wine (alcohol content at least 14%)

3 cups sugar

1 vanilla bean

One 3-inch cinnamon stick

1 cup freshly brewed very strong English breakfast tea

2 pounds dried plums (prunes)

³/₄ cup Armagnac

1. Carefully remove the peel from the orange and lemon, taking care not to leave much pith attached to the peel. Set aside the peels, then juice the orange and lemon. Set aside the juice.

2. Place the wine in a heavy-bottomed saucepan over medium-high heat. Bring to a boil. Using a long wooden match, ignite the wine and, shaking the pan slightly, boil for about 1 minute, or until the flame dies out. Add the sugar along with the reserved citrus peels and juice. Stir to combine.

3. Cut the vanilla bean in half lengthwise and add it to the pan along with the cinnamon stick. Bring to a boil and boil for about 10 minutes, or until syrupy. Add the tea and again bring to a boil. Add the dried plums to the boiling syrup. Again, bring the mixture to a boil and boil for 5 to 8 minutes. Remove from the heat and allow to cool.

4. When cool, stir in the Armagnac. Cover and let marinate in a cool, dark spot for at least 24 hours before serving. For longer storage, transfer to a nonreactive container, cover, and refrigerate for up to 1 week.

NOTE: *Following this same procedure but changing the alcohol, you can prepare all types of fruit in this manner. In addition, when using fresh fruit rather than dried, you obviously do not have to rehydrate the fruit. This is the perfect recipe to showcase perfectly ripe fruit in season. If the fruit is pale, use white wine in place of the red and a matching fruit liqueur in place of the Armagnac. A slightly sweet Sauternes is a perfect match for ripe white peaches, and pears meet their match with a fine Poire William. There is also room to play with the spices—star anise, cardamom, nutmeg, even a bit of chili pepper can make magic.*

Tarte au Chocolat

Although not an *opéra*, this is a Georges Blanc classic. It is a dense, rich cake that, unlike American layer cakes, is quite thin. The quality of chocolate that you use will determine the quality of the cake. Georges Blanc used Swiss chocolate, but there are now so many wonderful American chocolates available (such as Guittard and Scharffen Berger) that great quality is easy to come by. Since this is so dense and a little bit goes a long way, it will keep, covered and refrigerated, for a few days.

Makes one 10-inch cake

. . . .

4 ounces bittersweet chocolate

8 tablespoons (1 stick) unsalted butter

$^1/_2$ cup plus 2$^1/_2$ tablespoons superfine sugar

$^1/_4$ cup cake flour

3 large eggs, at room temperature

Chocolate Ganache (recipe follows)

$^1/_4$ cup cocoa powder

1. Preheat the oven to 375°F.

2. Lightly butter a 10-inch springform cake pan. Cut a piece of parchment paper into a 10-inch circle and fit it into the bottom of the pan. Lightly butter the parchment paper and set the pan aside.

3. Combine the bittersweet chocolate and butter in the top half of a double boiler over boiling water. Heat, stirring constantly, for about 4 minutes, or until the chocolate and butter have melted and blended. Set aside.

4. Combine the sugar and flour in the bowl of an electric mixer fitted with the whisk attachment. Add the eggs one at a time, beating on low speed to combine. Whisking constantly, add a bit of the hot chocolate mixture to temper the egg mixture. When blended, with the mixer still running, add the remaining chocolate mixture. Beat on low for about 8 minutes, or until the batter is very thick and smooth. Pour the batter into the prepared cake pan, smoothing the top with a spatula. (The batter should be no more than 1 inch high in the pan or the cake will not hold together.)

5. Place the cake in the preheated oven and bake for 30 minutes, or until a tester or toothpick inserted into the center comes out clean. Remove from the oven and let stand for 5 minutes. Open and remove the springform. Invert the cake onto a wire rack and allow to cool.

6. When cool, place the cake on a cake plate and, using a metal spatula, lightly coat the entire cake with the ganache. Allow the cake to rest for about 15 minutes, or just long enough for the ganache to harden slightly.

7. Using a sharp knife, score a crisscross pattern into the top of the cake. Place the cocoa in a fine sieve and lightly tap the side to sprinkle cocoa on top of the cake. Cut into small slices and serve at room temperature with a dollop of whipped cream, crème fraîche, or fine vanilla ice cream.

CHOCOLATE GANACHE

3 ounces semisweet chocolate

1 teaspoon unsalted butter

6 tablespoons heavy cream

1. Combine the chocolate and butter in the top half of a double boiler over boiling water. Heat, stirring constantly, for about 3 minutes, or until the chocolate and butter have melted and blended. Remove from the heat.

2. While the chocolate is melting, bring the cream to a simmer in a small saucepan over medium heat. Immediately remove from the heat and whisk the hot cream into the chocolate, whisking until the mixture is smooth and glossy.

3. Set aside to cool slightly before icing the cake.

Tarte aux Pommes Caramélisées

This tart was a fabled Blanc family recipe. Madame Blanc took great pride in its perfection and she would have a fit if the finished tart did not meet her expectations. It had to have just the right amount of crispness and be emblazoned with just a touch of caramelized sugar. Sometimes we would have to remove the tart from the oven and give it a number of

Makes one 10-inch tart

. . . .

extra brushings with the butter-sugar mixture to achieve her goal. I have to say, though, this is about as perfect an apple tart as you'll ever eat!

> 7 tablespoons unsalted butter, melted
>
> Pâte Brisée (recipe follows)
>
> 9 tablespoons superfine sugar, plus more for sprinkling
>
> 3 Golden Delicious apples

1. Preheat the oven to 450°F.
2. Using about 1 tablespoon of the melted butter, lightly coat a baking sheet large enough to hold the pastry circle. Set aside.
3. Roll the Pâte Brisée out on a lightly floured board to make 1 large, very thin (about $1/16$-inch-thick) circle (or 2 small circles). Use a small, sharp knife to trim the edges, making a neat edge all around. Prick the pastry with the tines of a dinner fork. Using a pastry brush, lightly coat the pastry with 1 tablespoon of the melted butter and then sprinkle with about 2 tablespoons of the sugar. Set aside.
4. Combine the remaining 6 tablespoons butter and 7 tablespoons sugar in a small mixing bowl. Set aside.

5. Peel the apples and cut them in half lengthwise, then core and seed each half. Using a mandoline or Japanese vegetable slicer, cut each half into paper-thin slices. Arrange the slices, slightly overlapping, in a neat circle around the edge of the pastry. Using a pastry brush, lightly coat the apples with the butter-sugar mixture. Continue making overlapping circles, working in toward the center and brushing each layer of apples with the butter-sugar mixture before making a new layer, until the entire top is covered with apples. Sprinkle the entire top with a light coating of sugar.

6. Place the tart in the preheated oven and bake for 10 minutes. Remove from the oven and again sprinkle the top with sugar. Return to the oven and bake for about 10 minutes more, or until the top is nicely caramelized and golden brown. Remove from the oven and let stand for 5 minutes. Cut into wedges and serve warm with whipped cream or vanilla ice cream, if desired.

. . . .

1 to 1¼ cups all-purpose flour

2 tablespoons superfine sugar

Pinch of salt

8 tablespoons (1 stick) cold unsalted butter, cut into small pieces

1 large egg yolk

About 2 tablespoons ice water

1. Sift the flour, sugar, and salt together into the bowl of a food processor fitted with the metal blade. With the motor running, add the butter and process, using quick on-and-off turns, for about 1½ minutes, or until the mixture has turned to fine crumbs.

2. Transfer the flour mixture to a mixing bowl. Whisk the egg yolk with 1 tablespoon of the ice water, then add the liquid to the flour mixture, pulling together with a fork just until a soft dough forms, adding additional ice water as needed.

3. Transfer the dough to a lightly floured work surface and, using a few turns, quickly knead it into a ball and then flatten into a small disk. Wrap in plastic and refrigerate for 2 hours before rolling out into the desired shape.

Madeleines

At the restaurant, we served both cold and warm petits fours (small cakes) at the end of every meal. Madeleines—moist, slightly crisp, and buttery—were always the most popular of the miniature display. To make these little French cakes, you will need three madeleine pans, known as *plaques à coques,* which turn out the classic elongated shell-shaped cakes. Madeleines do not hold well and are best served, after a brief rest, right after they are pulled from the oven. Their fragrant, enticing aroma usually makes even this brief wait seem interminable.

About 3 tablespoons clarified unsalted butter

About $^1/_4$ cup Wondra flour

$^3/_4$ cup plus 2 tablespoons cake flour

$^1/_3$ teaspoon baking powder

Pinch of salt

6 tablespoons unsalted butter, softened

$^1/_2$ cup superfine sugar

$^1/_2$ vanilla bean, split lengthwise

1 tablespoon honey

1 tablespoon heavy cream

2 large eggs, separated, at room temperature

1. Preheat the oven to 350°F.

2. Using the clarified butter and a pastry brush, lightly coat each madeleine mold. Sprinkle with the Wondra flour and then turn the pans upside down and knock off any excess flour. The molds should be only lightly coated. Set aside.

3. Sift the cake flour, baking powder, and salt together. Set aside.

4. Place 3 tablespoons of the softened butter in a small pan over medium-low heat. Cook, stirring frequently, for about 1 minute, or just until the butter begins to turn golden brown and is very aromatic. Immediately remove from the heat and stir to cool down quickly.

5. Combine the remaining 3 tablespoons butter with the sugar in the bowl of an electric mixer and beat for about 2 minutes, or until combined. Scrape the seeds from the vanilla bean into the sugar mixture, reserving the bean to flavor sugar or sauces (see page 213). Add the cooled brown butter, honey, and cream and beat to incorporate. Add the egg yolks, one at a time, and beat to blend, frequently scraping down the sides of the bowl. With the mixer on low speed, slowly add the sifted dry ingredients, beating just to incorporate.

6. Using an electric mixer, beat the egg whites until stiff peaks form. Gently fold the egg whites into the batter. Heat the prepared pans in the oven until hot.

7. Spoon an equal amount of batter into each prepared mold without pressing the batter down. Place in the preheated oven and bake for about 12 minutes, or until the edges of each madeleine are golden and a toothpick inserted into the center comes out clean.

8. Remove from the oven and let rest for 1 minute. Carefully remove the cakes from their molds and place, rounded side up, on wire racks to cool slightly. Serve warm.

Îles Flottantes

Îles flottantes are known in English as floating islands. They can be made any of three ways—as one large meringue floating in a sea of custard sauce, as individual meringues floating in their own little lakes of custard (known as *oeufs à la neige,* or snow eggs), or as an entirely different classic French dessert of a liqueur-soaked sponge cake or brioche cut into layers and filled with (usually) berry jam and nuts, covered with whipped cream, and set in a pool of light custard.

Serves 6

. . . .

At Georges Blanc, we did individual meringues served in a classic crème anglaise with a few berries scattered around the edge. This is a dessert that is not done much anymore but one that, to me, signifies the ending of a classic French meal.

2 cups milk

11 tablespoons superfine sugar

2 strips orange zest

$^1/_2$ vanilla bean, split lengthwise

5 large eggs, separated, at room temperature

About 1 tablespoon unsalted butter, softened

2 tablespoons pure vanilla extract

$1^1/_2$ cups fresh raspberries, blueberries, or strawberries,
     well washed and dried

1. Combine the milk with 3 tablespoons of the sugar, the orange zest, and the vanilla bean in a medium nonstick saucepan over medium-low heat. Bring just to a simmer. Immediately remove from the heat and allow to cool for 1 hour.

2. Combine the egg yolks and 3 tablespoons of the remaining sugar in a mixing bowl, whisking until well blended.

3. Return the infused milk to low heat. When warm, whisk about $\frac{1}{2}$ cup into the egg mixture until tempered. Whisking constantly, beat the egg mixture into the warm milk. Cook, stirring constantly with a wooden spoon, over low heat for about 7 minutes, or until the custard coats the back of a metal spoon. Do not allow the custard to boil.

4. As soon as the custard has thickened, immediately pour it through a fine sieve into a clean bowl, discarding the orange zest and scraping the vanilla seeds into the smooth custard. Cover lightly with plastic wrap and place in the refrigerator to cool.

5. Preheat the oven to 225°F.

6. Lightly butter and then, using about 1 tablespoon of the remaining sugar, coat the insides of six 2-inch round ceramic ramekins. Set aside.

7. While the custard is cooling, place the egg whites in the bowl of an electric mixer and beat until soft peaks form. Slowly add the remaining 4 tablespoons sugar and the vanilla extract and beat until stiff peaks form, but without drying the meringue.

8. Spoon an equal portion of the meringue into the prepared ramekins, filling to the top. Place the ramekins in a baking pan with cold water to halfway up the sides of the ramekins. Place in the preheated oven and bake for about 20 minutes, or just until the meringue has set.

9. Remove the meringues from the oven and from the water bath. Immediately place in the refrigerator to cool rapidly. (The meringues may be made up to 12 hours in advance of use.)

10. When ready to serve, ladle an equal portion of the chilled custard into each of 6 shallow soup bowls. Loosen the meringues by gently tapping the bottom of each ramekin and quickly turning the ramekin over so that a meringue falls into the center of each of the bowls. Scatter some berries around the edge and serve immediately.

Candied Grapefruit Peel

andied fruit peel is a wonderful treat to keep on hand. I've noticed that many restaurants now place a small bowl of candied peel on the table when coffee is served. It offers just a hint of sweetness nicely balanced by the sharpness of the peel. You can candy any citrus peel, but orange and grapefruit are the most commonly used.

Makes about 56
. . . .

4 large pink grapefruits, well washed

About 3 cups sugar

1. Cut the top and bottom from each grapefruit, making even cuts so that the grapefruit will sit straight. Using a sharp knife and cutting downward, remove the peel in neat, even strips following the shape of the fruit. Reserve the pulp for another purpose.

2. Cut the grapefruit peel into thin strips about $2\frac{1}{2}$ inches long by $\frac{1}{4}$ inch thick. You should get about 14 strips from each grapefruit.

3. Place the strips in cold water in a medium saucepan over high heat. Bring to a rapid boil and boil for 1 minute. Drain well and repeat the boiling process, always using fresh cold water, 3 more times.

4. After the final boil, pat the peel dry. Using a kitchen scale, weigh the boiled peel, then combine the weighed peel with an equal weight of sugar in a heavy-bottomed saucepan. (It should be about 1 pound of peel to about 1 pound [2 cups] of sugar). Add enough water (about $\frac{1}{4}$ cup) to just cover the bottom of the saucepan. This will help the sugar melt quickly. Place over medium heat and bring to a boil. Lower the heat and cook at a bare simmer for about 40 minutes, or until the peel is transparent. Remove from the heat and drain well.

5. Place the peel in single layers on wire racks to drain and dry for at least 3 hours or up to 8 hours.

6. Place the remaining 1 cup sugar in a resealable plastic bag. Add the dried peel, seal the bag, and toss until each piece is well coated with sugar. Remove the sugared peel from the bag and serve. (Alternately, place the sugared peel in a tightly covered container in a cool, dry spot for up to 1 month).

Back in New York: Daniel Boulud

My time in France ended with an invitation to realize my dream of cooking in Japan. My friend Makoto Ono was returning home. Of course, we had to share a farewell dinner and, after a few drinks too many, I told him that he must find me a job once he got to Japan. Three days later, I got a call. "I got job; when you coming?" Once again, I didn't have any money, so I had to return to New York for a short stint before I could take off to the Land of the Rising Sun.

I immediately went back to New York and sought out the best job I could find—one that would pay me enough and teach me a lot. Le Bernardin was just opening and I thought that it would be a great place to start, but when I told the chef that I wanted to work for only six months, he had no interest and booted me out the door.

I did a little more research and was told that the up-and-coming French chef was a guy named Daniel Boulud at the Hôtel Plaza Athénée. Since I also learned that he had been a sous-chef at Georges Blanc, I thought I might just have a good chance at a job with him. I met Daniel and told him of my six-month plan. He was enthusiastic about my sense of adventure and put me right to work.

Although I worked with Daniel for only six months, an amount of time I wouldn't normally even list on a résumé, it was a great learning experience for me. One thing I learned was that sometimes a mentor does not have to be in your life for very long to effect a change in your way of thinking. I absorbed more in those six months than at any other time of my life, particularly about the running of a great restaurant. Daniel's work ethic, respect for both his cooks and his restaurant guests, sociability in the dining room, demand for pristine ingredients, creativity, and sense of experimentation together made a profound impression on me. I found that it is sometimes more than recipes or cooking techniques that create a culinary learning experience.

At the Plaza Athénée, Daniel featured a special roast every day. The whole roast was shown tableside, carved, and served with complementary accompaniments that were rolled through the dining room on a silver serving cart. This was an old-fashioned way of service in French restaurants that had recently begun to make a comeback in New York. The restaurant guests loved it and so did I. The recipes that I have chosen to highlight my few months with Daniel are, like the whole roast in the restaurant, geared to the middle of the table: great classic recipes that serve a crowd well, formally or informally.

Daniel Boulud was instrumental in bridging the gap between the new crop of American chefs and their French counterparts. Up until this time, French chefs had tended to look down on American-trained cooks. Daniel changed all of that. He helped make the New York culinary scene an international one comprised of equals. He has remained a good friend to me and to all other American chefs of my generation, joining in, when needed, for charity and fun. I continue to learn from him—his integrity, passion, and professionalism are an inspiration. He truly is an expert in the community of food.

Fruit-Stuffed Loin of Pork

Pork with dried fruit is a classic French combination. Although I don't think that we served anything exactly like this when I worked with Daniel Boulud, this is a perfect roast for communal dining. It is rich, slightly sweet, and beautiful on the plate—I can't imagine anyone not

Serves 6

. . . .

liking it. Best served warm, it can also stand up to room temperature on an elegant buffet.

4 tablespoons (¹/₂ stick) unsalted butter, softened

2 large shallots, peeled and finely minced

¹/₂ cup finely diced apples

¹/₄ cup brandy

¹/₂ cup finely diced dried apricots

¹/₂ cup finely diced dried plums (prunes)

¹/₄ cup slivered almonds, toasted

Juice of 1 lemon

Coarse salt and freshly ground pepper

One 3¹/₂-pound pork loin, boned with chine and rib bones reserved

1 teaspoon paprika

1 teaspoon garlic powder

1 tablespoon canola oil

3 cloves garlic, peeled

1 carrot, peeled, trimmed, and diced

1 large onion, peeled and diced

1 bay leaf

1 tablespoon plus 1 teaspoon chopped fresh thyme

1 tablespoon plus 1 teaspoon chopped fresh rosemary

2 cups chicken broth

$^1/_2$ cup dry white wine

$^1/_4$ cup sugar

$^1/_4$ cup apple cider vinegar

1. Heat 2 tablespoons of the butter in a large sauté pan over medium heat. Add the shallots and sauté for 3 minutes. Add the apples and sauté for 3 minutes more, or until the apples have softened. Add the brandy and, off the flame, ignite it with a long wooden match. Immediately add the apricots, dried plums, and almonds, stirring until the brandy flame dies out, and return the pan to the heat. Stir in the lemon juice and season with salt

and pepper to taste. Remove from the heat and allow to cool to room temperature.

2. Preheat the oven to 400°F.

3. Trim and set aside any excess fat and connective tissue from the pork. Butterfly the pork by cutting lengthwise, almost through the loin, leaving about 1 inch of connecting meat. Open both sides to make an almost flat rectangle of meat. Season with salt and pepper to taste.

4. Arrange the cooled fruit mixture in a neat row about 2 inches from one of the long sides of the meat. Fold the 2-inch piece of meat up and over the stuffing and then continue tightly rolling the meat into a firm cylinder. Using kitchen twine, tie the pork closed in about 5 or 6 places. Season the pork with the paprika, garlic powder, and additional salt and pepper to taste.

5.   Combine 1 tablespoon of the butter with the oil in a Dutch oven over medium heat. Add the stuffed loin along with the reserved trimmings, chine, and rib bones. Sear, turning occasionally, for about 8 minutes, or until the meat is beginning to brown on all sides. Add the garlic, carrot, onion, and bay leaf and sear for 5 minutes more, or until the meat is nicely browned and the vegetables have taken on some color. Sprinkle the 1 tablespoon thyme and the 1 tablespoon rosemary on top of the meat and vegetables. Add the broth and wine and bring to a boil. Transfer to the preheated oven and immediately lower the heat to 375°F. Roast, turning and basting the meat every 15 minutes, for about 1 hour, or until an instant-read thermometer inserted into the thickest part reads 145°F.

6.   Remove the meat from the pan and place on a platter. Lightly tent with aluminum foil to keep warm.

7.   Place the Dutch oven on the stove top over medium-high heat and bring the roasting liquid and vegetables to a boil. Lower the heat and simmer for about 12 minutes, or until the liquid has been reduced to about $1/2$ cup. Remove from the heat and strain through a fine sieve into a small bowl, discarding the solids. Set aside.

8.   Combine the sugar and vinegar in a small, heavy-bottomed saucepan over medium-high heat and bring to a boil. Lower the heat and simmer for about 3 minutes, or just until the liquid has begun to caramelize. Remove from the heat and swirl in the reserved reduced pan juices. Add the remaining 1 tablespoon butter along with the 1 teaspoon thyme and the 1 teaspoon rosemary. Taste and, if necessary, adjust the seasoning with salt and pepper.

9.   Using a sharp knife, cut the pork crosswise into slices about $1/2$ inch thick. Drizzle sauce over the top and serve the remaining sauce on the side.

Cassoulet of Spring Beans

From Daniel Boulud, I learned to take advantage of the bounty of each season. Part of his insistence on this came, I'm sure, from the frugality of the French kitchen—use the best available to you and use it all—and part from his desire to capture the essence of each of the ingredients with which he was working. This cassoulet is my tribute to Daniel, so if you can't find all of the beans I call for, go ahead and make the recipe with

the best of what is available to you. And don't worry if you can't find dried lavender; although it adds a lovely scent, the beans are delicious without it. Again, this is perfect for the center of the table, as it is as good at room temperature as it is warm.

¹/₄ cup hazelnut oil

2 large shallots, peeled and thinly sliced

12 ounces haricots verts, well washed, trimmed, and blanched

12 ounces yellow wax beans, well washed, trimmed, and blanched

Coarse salt and freshly ground pepper

2 tablespoons unsalted butter, softened

1 cup cooked fresh cranberry beans

1 cup steamed fresh fava beans

1 teaspoon dried lavender

¹/₄ cup chopped hazelnuts, toasted (optional)

Place a large sauté pan over medium heat. When hot, add the oil and then the shallots. Sauté for about 3 minutes, or just until the shallots have begun to sweat their liquid but have not taken on any color. Add the haricots verts and the wax beans, season with salt and pepper to taste, and sauté for about 3 minutes, or until the beans begin to take on

some color. Add the butter and then the cranberry beans, tossing to warm through.
Add the fava beans and, lastly, the lavender. Sauté for about 2 minutes, or just until
heated through. Taste and, if necessary, adjust the seasoning with salt and pepper.
Remove from the heat and transfer to a serving bowl. Sprinkle the top with the chopped
hazelnuts, if desired, and serve.

Root Vegetable Gratin

Everybody loves a traditional French potato gratin, so I have taken two not-always-so-popular vegetables and given my spin on that classic dish. The herby flavor of the celery root is mellowed by the sweet turnips, which, in turn, give a sugary earthiness to the finished casserole. Gratins are perfect "company's coming"

Serves 6

dishes, as they can be made ahead and reheated before serving. They can also be cut into serving pieces and plated for buffet service.

2 tablespoons unsalted butter, softened

2 large eggs

1 large leek (white part only), well washed, dried, and finely diced

2 cups heavy cream

1 tablespoon roasted garlic, minced

1 cup freshly grated Parmesan cheese

2 large celeriac (celery root), peeled and cut crosswise into
$1/8$–inch–thick rounds

1 large rutabaga, peeled and cut crosswise into $1/8$–inch–thick rounds

1 large sweet potato, peeled and cut crosswise into $1/8$–inch–thick rounds

1 tablespoon minced fresh parsley, thyme, or tarragon

$1/2$ teaspoon freshly grated nutmeg, or to taste

Coarse salt and freshly ground white pepper

Six to eight $1/8$–inch–thick slices Gruyère cheese

3 tablespoons fresh bread crumbs

1. Preheat the oven to 375°F.

2. Using 1 tablespoon of the butter, generously grease an $11 \times 7 \times 2$-inch baking pan. Set aside.

3. Place the eggs in a mixing bowl and whisk to loosen. Set aside.

4. Heat the remaining 1 tablespoon butter in a medium saucepan over medium-low heat. Add the leek and sauté for about 4 minutes, or just until the leek has begun to sweat its liquid but has not taken on any color. Add the cream and garlic and raise the heat to medium. Bring to a boil, watching carefully so that the cream does not boil over. As soon as the cream comes to a boil, lower the heat and whisk in $^1/_2$ cup of the Parmesan cheese. When well incorporated, remove from the heat.

5. Pouring very slowly, whisk about $^1/_4$ cup of the hot cream mixture into the reserved eggs to temper them. When tempered, whisk the egg mixture into the remaining hot cream mixture. Set aside.

6. Place the celeriac, rutabaga, and sweet potato in a large mixing bowl. Season with the minced parsley, nutmeg, and salt and white pepper to taste. Pour in the hot cream mixture and, using a rubber spatula, carefully toss to coat well without breaking up the vegetables. Place an even layer of the vegetables in the prepared baking pan. Sprinkle with some of the remaining $^1/_2$ cup Parmesan cheese, pressing down slightly to even out the layer. Continue making layers of seasoned vegetables and Parmesan cheese, reserving 2 tablespoons of the Parmesan.

7. Layer the Gruyère slices over the top of the casserole, then sprinkle the bread crumbs over the cheese. Finally, sprinkle the reserved 2 tablespoons Parmesan over all. Place in the preheated oven and bake for 45 minutes, or until the point of a small, sharp knife can easily be inserted into the center and the top is golden brown and bubbling.

8. Remove from the oven and let rest for 15 minutes before cutting into squares. (If you cut the gratin too quickly, it tends to break apart.)

Japan: Kiyomi Nishitani

❋ • Cooking French in a Far-Off Land

After an inspiring six months working with Daniel Boulud, I had enough money to head to Japan, where I was assured of a job at, of all places, a French restaurant called Gentille Alouette (after the children's song). I had absolutely no idea of what to expect, but that didn't dissuade me one bit. As far as I was concerned, the community of the kitchen was always a welcoming one, whether you spoke the local lingo or not.

Gentille Alouette was owned by a marvelous Japanese chef named Kiyomi Nishitani who reveled in all things French. The staff was just four—the chef and three cooks—

each of whom was expected to do everything needed to keep the restaurant running. This meant sweeping and mopping as well as shopping and cooking. Nishitani-san spoke no English and I spoke no Japanese, so French was our common language. He had a great sense of humor and loved to tell guests that he had a Frenchman working in the kitchen and then tell me not to worry—nobody would know the difference because we all looked alike.

The staff spent a great deal of time together. We really became a family. We had our own baseball team that played against other kitchens; we were all avid baseball fans and would go to professional games when we could manage it; we fished, we drank, we ate together—in short, we were comrades. The only thing that I couldn't do for the first five months was touch the fish. As a foreigner, they just didn't trust me to have the respect necessary to properly appreciate the beauty of their seafood.

And what beautiful seafood it was. I had never experienced anything like the Tsukiji market in Tokyo. The respect shown the "catch of the day" was almost religious in nature. The shrimp were alive and kicking, packed in sawdust rather than frozen solid in blocks of ice as I had experienced in my first cooking job in Florida. Tuna was a sacred icon! The lessons I learned there made it possible for me to work with seafood in a way I had never contemplated.

We really did cook French food, but the ingredients that we worked with were quintessentially Japanese. It was a challenge to take the experience of Georges Blanc and Daniel Boulud and translate it into the Japanese approach to the kitchen. As I struggled with the language and the traditions of this very alien land, the support of the Japanese cooks made it possible for me to share my knowledge and to absorb theirs. The months at Gentille Alouette are, perhaps, the most memorable of my entire career.

I was at the restaurant for eight months before immigration caught up with me. It was obvious that I wasn't going to get a visa that would allow me to stay in the kitchen, and because I desperately wanted to master the language, I developed a four-pronged strategy to being awarded a visa that would allow me to stay in Japan: I would teach English and try for a teacher's visa; I would study Japanese in hopes of getting a student visa; I'd try for a straight working visa; and if all else failed, I'd opt for a cultural visa by studying karate and ikebana. I found that if I taught English for twenty hours a week, I could make more money than I had working eighty hours a week in the kitchen and could, therefore, sustain my stay. So I began my teaching career on the sly, working in a little culture through karate at the same time.

I stayed in contact with all of my kitchen buddies, who encouraged me to immerse myself in karate. Never one to say no, I found myself the only non-Japanese student in a well-known dojo. Although I was no match for the tough guys who were regulars, once they found that I was a cook, they took me under their wing and made me their "mascot." Food, once again, was the social glue.

The regulars were huge—big, mean guys with multiple black belts who loved to eat. After working out, we would all go for "all you can eat" *yakiniku,* which is simply every cut of beef imaginable marinated in a soy-based sauce and then grilled over red-hot coals. The grilling is usually done at the table by the individual diner—sort of self-serve—and you can believe that the guys kept the grill going. I know that the restaurant must have lost money on our nights out. Those guys could eat!

After some weeks, much prodding, and too much sake, the regulars convinced me to enter a karate *shiai,* an all-Japan tournament. It was to feature the 250 top karate men from around the country. These were guys who had been at it for many, many years, and I had just a few months under my not-so-black belt. As the day neared, I began to panic. I was alone, I didn't have the greatest command of the language, and most important (since I expected to be killed), I had no health insurance. Like an idiot, I applied for national health insurance.

The night of the tournament, I won my first round on a bye when my opponent didn't show. I nervously watched as the first 125 guys lost their matches, leaving the best of the lot to finish. I anxiously waited for my turn, knowing that I had to meet my opponent or lose face. The end came quicker than I'd hoped. With one roundhouse kick to the back of my head, I didn't know where I was, where I'd been, or where I was going. On that cold Thursday night, I got my butt kicked, and on Saturday morning, my bruised body was not-so-gently escorted to the airport and put on a plane for New York. My application for national health insurance had done me in, and I was deported for visa violations two hours less than a year to the day that I had arrived to fulfill my dream.

Yakiniku: The Communal Barbecue

Although traditionally made only with beef, you can make *yakiniku* from anything. The best is made with Kobe beef, but you don't have to pick the pricey cuts to make great skewers. I've used pork tenderloin, lean lamb, dark and white poultry meat, shrimp, salmon, and on and on. This recipe makes just enough for six, but you can make any amount that you like—just up everything so that everyone has at the least two skewers. For feeding a crowd, I like to make up the skewers and the dipping sauces and then let everyone grill for themselves, even the kids. In the summer, we often have a *yakiniku* party in Brooklyn, grilling the skewers in my outdoor pizza oven.

1 pound well-marbled beef sirloin, cut into ³/₄–inch cubes

12 small shiitake mushroom caps, scored

12 scallions (white part only), well washed and cut into 1–inch pieces

Twelve 1–inch diamond-shaped pieces red bell pepper

Twelve 1–inch diamond-shaped pieces green bell pepper

Yakiniku Marinade (recipe follows)

Ponzu Dipping Sauce and/or Miso-Mustard Dipping Sauce (recipes follow)

1. Place twelve 8-inch-long bamboo skewers in cold water to cover and let soak for at least 1 hour.

2. Prepare a very hot charcoal grill.

3. Place an equal portion of the meat and vegetables in an attractive pattern on each skewer. Using a pastry brush, lightly coat each skewer with the marinade.

4. Place the skewers on the hot grill and grill, turning and brushing with the marinade frequently, for about 5 minutes, or until the meat is cooked to the desired degree of doneness and the vegetables have taken on some color.

5. Remove from the grill and serve warm with one or both of the dipping sauces.

. . . .

^{3}/$_4$ cup low-sodium soy sauce

^{1}/$_2$ cup sake

^{1}/$_4$ cup mirin (see Note)

2 tablespoons sugar

1 tablespoon minced fresh lemongrass

1 tablespoon minced fresh ginger

^{1}/$_2$ teaspoon minced garlic

Combine the soy sauce, sake, mirin, sugar, lemongrass, ginger, and garlic in a small mixing bowl. Use to baste the prepared *yakiniku* as it is grilled. The marinade may be made up to a week in advance of use and stored, covered and refrigerated, until ready to use.

NOTE: *Mirin is available at Asian markets, specialty food stores, and some supermarkets.*

PONZU DIPPING SAUCE

. . . .

1 cup low-sodium soy sauce

$^1/_2$ cup fresh lemon juice

$^1/_2$ cup fresh lime juice

$^1/_4$ cup rice wine vinegar (see Note)

$^1/_4$ cup mirin (see Note)

$^1/_4$ cup bonito flakes (see Note)

One 2-inch piece kelp (see Note)

1. Combine the soy sauce, lemon juice, lime juice, rice wine vinegar, mirin, and bonito flakes in a small mixing bowl. Add the kelp, cover, and refrigerate for 24 hours.

2. Remove from the refrigerator and strain through a cheesecloth-lined fine sieve into a clean bowl. Serve immediately or cover and store, refrigerated, for up to 1 month.

NOTE: *Rice wine vinegar, mirin, bonito flakes, and kelp are available at Japanese markets, specialty food stores, and some supermarkets.*

MISO-MUSTARD DIPPING SAUCE

. . . .

2 tablespoons *karashi* (see Note)

1 tablespoon water

2 tablespoons fresh lemon juice, plus more to taste

2 tablespoons sugar

¾ cup white miso (see Note)

1 tablespoon rice wine vinegar (see Note)

1 tablespoon sake

1. Combine the *karashi* and water in a small mixing bowl, stirring to make a paste. Set aside.

2. Combine the lemon juice and sugar, stirring until the sugar has dissolved. Set aside.

3. Combine the white miso, rice wine vinegar, and sake in a small mixing bowl. Whisk in the reserved *karashi* and lemon juice–sugar mixture. If necessary, thin the sauce with up to 1 tablespoon water and adjust the flavor with additional lemon juice. (The dipping sauce can be made ahead and stored, covered and refrigerated, for up to 2 months.)

NOTE: Karashi *(Japanese mustard), white miso, and rice wine vinegar are available at Japanese markets and some specialty food stores.*

✳ • OSECHI RYORI JUBAKO: NEW YEAR'S TIERED BOXES

In Japan, the sharing of good fortune through food is no more evident than during the New Year's holiday—so much so that there is even a special name for Japanese New Year's food: *osechi ryori*. The preparation and eating of New Year's foods is an ancient tradition going back almost 700 years. *Osechi ryori* consists of many, many different dishes, quite a few of them with special meaning, packed into layers in beautiful tiered lacquered boxes called *jubako*.

There are usually four tiers of *jubako*. The first tier (*ichi-no-ju*) is the most significant, as it is tightly packed with colorful traditional dishes that represent wishes for health, a long life, a bountiful harvest, riches, and all good things necessary to make a prosperous life. Frequently, the second tier (*ni-no-ju*) holds vinegared or pickled dishes, the third (*san-no-ju*) is filled with grilled and fried foods, and the fourth (*yo-no-ju*) contains cooked vegetables that are creatively arranged primarily for eye appeal.

Traditionally, *osechi* are prepared prior to New Year's Eve so that the cook (most often the woman of the house) can enjoy the first three days of the New Year also. They are usually dishes that can be eaten at room temperature or chilled and shared with family and friends without extensive last-minute preparation. Many of the dishes are as much a feast for the eyes as for the palate. Each dish, as well as each type of food, has a traditional meaning, and all of them send greetings for spiritual and financial good fortune in the coming year. *Osechi* are also offered to the household god.

When I first discovered this tradition, I was absolutely fascinated with the foods and with learning their individual meanings. I wondered how sweet chestnut paste came to mean treasure or bamboo shoots to mean virtue and fidelity or burdock to mean energy. Eventually, I discovered some of the history and found that the pronunciation of a word or its written character might, in some way, reflect something about the food and, from that, the symbolism translated to meaning.

There are some regional differences in the foods that comprise the *osechi,* but, for the most part, the dishes are traditionally prescribed. I loved watching the *osechi* being prepared and then configured into the *jubako.* It was both a culinary art and an act of generosity that had taken many, many generations to develop.

Although many of the foods are relatively easy to prepare, the fact that there are usually so many necessary to complete a bountiful *jubako* makes the preparation of these traditional boxes extremely time-consuming for the cook. In the days preceding the New Year, at Gentille Alouette, we worked twenty-hour shifts preparing both the traditional *osechi* and some classic French dishes for the chef's unique *osechi ryori jubako.* I remember wondering how Japanese housewives managed to do all of the work alone.

Nowadays, many people purchase at least some of the *osechi* in grocery stores and more than a few order the whole *jubako* just as we would order take-out food. Remembering that sea bream, signifying celebration, is always eaten at times of joy, I have selected just a few recipes that might be added to a simple broiled sea bream (see page 119) in a small *osechi ryori jubako* of your own making.

Sesame-Soy Tofu Squares

Serves 6 to 8

. . . .

One 1-inch piece fresh ginger, peeled and cut crosswise into thin slices

$^3/_4$ cup pineapple juice

$^1/_2$ cup low-sodium soy sauce

$^1/_4$ cup Worcestershire sauce

$^1/_4$ cup packed light brown sugar

2 tablespoons sesame oil (see Note)

$^1/_2$ teaspoon freshly ground pepper

1 pound grilled tofu, cut into 1-inch cubes (see Note)

2 tablespoons sesame seeds

1. Combine the ginger, pineapple juice, soy sauce, Worcestershire sauce, brown sugar, sesame oil, and pepper in a mixing bowl. Add the tofu and toss to coat. Cover with plastic wrap and refrigerate, tossing every hour, for at least 2 hours or up to 4 hours.

2. Preheat the oven to 375° F. Lightly coat a nonstick baking sheet with vegetable spray.

3. Remove the tofu from the marinade and place the cubes in a single layer on the prepared baking sheet. Place in the preheated oven and bake for 15 minutes.

4. Remove from the oven and sprinkle with the sesame seeds. Return to the oven and bake for 5 minutes more, or until the tofu is firm and golden brown.

5. Remove from the oven and serve warm or at room temperature. (The tofu squares can be made ahead and stored, covered and refrigerated, for up to 3 days. Bring to room temperature before serving.)

NOTE: *Sesame oil and grilled tofu are available at Asian markets, specialty food stores, and some supermarkets.*

Sake-Steamed Heads-On Shrimp

. . . .

12 jumbo heads-on shrimp, rinsed and patted dry

Juice of 2 large limes

$^1/_2$ cup sake

2 tablespoons mirin (see Note)

1 teaspoon rice wine vinegar (see Note)

$^1/_8$ teaspoon *shottsuru* or other Asian fish sauce (see Note)

Pinch of coarse salt

1. Leaving the tail intact and the shell on, make a slight cut in each shrimp down the center of the back. Devein if necessary.

2. Place the lime juice, sake, mirin, rice wine vinegar, *shottsuru,* and salt in a sauté pan over high heat. Bring to a boil and add the shrimp. Return to a simmer, lower the heat, and cover. Simmer until the shrimp have turned a deep pink, no more than 3 minutes. Remove from the heat and, with a slotted spoon, transfer the shrimp to a plate. Strain any excess cooking liquid and use it to make aïoli, or discard. Refrigerate the shrimp for about 20 minutes, or just until slightly cooled.

3. Remove the shrimp from the refrigerator. Peel and discard the shells. Serve plain or with any Asian dipping sauce, aïoli, or tartar sauce.

NOTE: *Mirin, rice wine vinegar, and* shottsuru *(Japanese fish sauce) are available at Japanese or other Asian markets and some specialty food stores.*

Miso-Glazed Sea Bream

Serves 6

. . . .

3 sea bream fillets, skin on and pinbones removed (see Notes)

About 1 teaspoon coarse salt, plus more to taste

Juice of 1 large lemon

$^1/_2$ cup plus 2 tablespoons mirin (see Notes)

$^1/_2$ cup low-sodium soy sauce

$^1/_2$ cup sake

$^1/_4$ cup white miso (see Notes)

Freshly ground pepper

6 lemon or lime wedges (optional)

1. Sprinkle each side of the fish fillets with the salt. Place in a single layer in a glass baking dish and set aside for 20 minutes.

2. Combine the lemon juice, $^1/_2$ cup mirin, soy sauce, sake, and white miso. Pour over the fillets and set them aside to marinate for 30 minutes. Set aside the 2 tablespoons mirin in a small bowl.

3. Preheat the broiler.

4. Remove the fillets from the marinade and pat dry. Reserve the marinade.

5. Lightly coat a nonstick baking pan with vegetable spray. Season the fillets with salt and pepper to taste and place them, skin side up, on the prepared baking pan. Using a pastry brush, lightly coat the skin with some of the reserved marinade. Place under the preheated broiler and broil, brushing with additional marinade every 2 minutes, for about 5 minutes, or just until the flesh is barely firm to the touch. About 1 minute before the fish is ready, using a pastry brush, lightly coat the fillets with the reserved mirin and continue to broil just until the skin is nicely glazed. Do not overcook.

6. Remove from the broiler. Cut the fillets in half and serve hot or at room temperature with a wedge of lemon or lime, if desired.

NOTES: *This recipe is sufficient for 6 tasting portions; however, the marinade is enough to season 6 fillets that could then be used as a main course.*

Mirin and white miso are available at Asian markets, specialty food stores, and some supermarkets.

Chicken Roulades with Dashi and Soy

Serves 6

. . . .

1 tablespoon peanut oil

5 shallots, peeled and minced

1 clove garlic, peeled and minced

3 red chili peppers, well washed, stems removed, and, if desired, seeded

$^3/_4$ cup dashi (see Notes)

$^1/_2$ cup rice wine vinegar (see Notes)

3 tablespoons sugar

2 tablespoons low-sodium soy sauce

1 tablespoon dark soy sauce

Coarse salt and freshly ground pepper

8 chicken roaster legs, skin on, boned, with excess fat removed

     (see Notes)

1 cup julienned carrots

1 cup julienned leeks

1 cup julienned daikon radishes (or celery)

About 2 cups Wondra flour

About 6 cups vegetable oil

1.   Heat the peanut oil in a saucepan over medium heat. Add the shallots and garlic and sauté for about 2 minutes, or just until the vegetables begin to wilt. Add the chili peppers, dashi, vinegar, sugar, low-sodium and dark soy sauces, and salt and pepper to taste and bring to a boil. Remove from the heat and allow to cool.

2.   Lay each chicken leg out flat on a clean, dry work surface. Place an equal amount of the carrots, leeks, and daikon radishes in the center of each piece of meat. Roll the chicken up

and around the vegetables. Using kitchen twine, tie each roulade in about 3 places to secure tightly.

3. Place the flour in a resealable plastic bag. Season with salt and pepper to taste. Working with a few at a time, toss the roulades in the seasoned flour. Shake off the excess flour and set aside the roulades.

4. In a large cast-iron skillet or deep fryer, heat the vegetable oil to 365° F on an instant-read thermometer.

5. Add the roulades, a few at a time, and fry for about 3 minutes, or until golden brown and cooked through. Using a slotted spoon, remove the roulades from the oil and place on paper towels to drain. Continue frying until all of the chicken is cooked.

6. Place the hot roulades in a glass baking dish. Pour the cooled marinade over the roulades and toss to coat. Cover with plastic wrap and refrigerate for at least 24 hours or up to 3 days.

7. When ready to serve, cut each roulade crosswise into 3 pieces and serve at room temperature with any Asian dipping sauce, if desired.

NOTES: *Dashi is a broth made from bonito flakes, kelp, and water. It is available in an instant form, either powdered, granulated, or as a concentrate, at Japanese or other Asian markets and some specialty food stores, as is rice wine vinegar.*

The chicken may be replaced with duck or turkey with great results.

Japanese Sweet Potatoes and Chestnuts

Serves 6

5 yams, peeled and halved lengthwise

1 pound fresh chestnuts, cooked and peeled

1 cup pure maple syrup

1/2 cup cinnamon honey

1/4 cup mirin (see Note)

1 tablespoon packed dark brown sugar

1 teaspoon ground cinnamon

Coarse salt and freshly ground pepper

1. Preheat the oven to 450° F.

2. Cut each yam half crosswise into 1-inch-thick slices. Combine the yams and chestnuts in a baking dish.

3. Whisk the syrup, honey, mirin, brown sugar, and cinnamon together in a small mixing bowl. Pour over the yam-chestnut mixture and toss to coat well. Season with salt and pepper to taste.

4. Place in the preheated oven. Immediately lower the heat to 350°F and bake, stirring from time to time to prevent sticking, for 40 minutes, or until the yams are tender and golden brown. Remove from the oven and serve hot or at room temperature. (This dish can be made up to 1 week in advance and stored, covered and refrigerated. Bring to room temperature before serving.)

NOTE: *Mirin is available at Asian markets, specialty food stores, and some supermarkets.*

Pickled Lotus Root

Serves 6

. . . .

2 cups rice wine vinegar (see Note)

1 cup water

¹/₄ cup sugar

10 juniper berries

1 small red beet, peeled, trimmed, and cut into quarters

1 bay leaf

1 large fresh lotus root, peeled and thinly sliced crosswise (see Note)

1. Combine the rice wine vinegar, water, and sugar in a saucepan. Stir in the juniper berries, beet, and bay leaf and place over medium-high heat. Bring to a boil. Lower the heat and cook at a bare simmer for 15 minutes.

2. Add the lotus root and return to a boil. Lower the heat and simmer for 5 minutes.

3. Remove from the heat and place a weight (a small, heatproof plate will work) in the saucepan to hold the lotus root down in the liquid. Cover the saucepan with plastic wrap and allow the lotus root to steam until cool. Remove the quarters of beet, which are used for color only.

4. When cool, serve, or store, covered and refrigerated, for up to 1 week.

NOTE: *Rice wine vinegar and lotus root are available at Asian markets and some specialty food stores.*

Sweet Asian Plums

Serves 6

. . . .

1 cup water

$^1/_2$ cup sugar

Juice of 1 lemon

$^1/_2$ cup sweet, dark rice wine vinegar (see Note)

$^1/_2$ teaspoon chili paste (see Note)

Pinch of coarse salt

1 pound small Asian plums, well washed, dried, cut in half
       lengthwise, and pitted

1. Combine the water and sugar in a saucepan over medium heat and bring to a simmer. Simmer for 3 minutes. Add the lemon juice, vinegar, chili paste, and salt and bring to a boil. Add the plums and lower the heat. Cover and cook at a bare simmer for about 15 minutes, or until the plums are very soft and the liquid is slightly thick. Remove from the heat and allow to cool to room temperature.

2. Serve at room temperature or place in a nonreactive container with a lid, cover, and refrigerate for up to 1 week.

NOTE: *Sweet, dark rice wine vinegar and chili paste are available at Asian markets and some specialty food stores.*

Acquiring New Tastes

I think that in many ways, learning to eat is much more important than learning to cook. For me, it has always been easier to learn how and what and why to eat through travel. I have ventured far and wide to learn why people eat what they eat—the customs, traditions, and ancient beliefs that tell you how a cuisine has come about. It is an adventure to learn how foods have made their way across the globe; what is served with what, and why; what is drunk with what meal, and why; what foods heal; and on and on and on.

I have been to almost every corner of the earth, always a student learning recipes and traditions. I have worked hand in hand with local cooks to learn their "secrets." In France, it was how the classic, many-coursed menu came about and how to successfully pull such a menu together. In Japan, I found that many garnishes are served with a purpose beyond decoration or taste, an example being freshly grated daikon radishes served with tempura to act as a digestive balance to the fat in the tempura. Every cuisine is filled with intoxicating mysteries.

In order to cook like a native, I had to eat like one. After cooking school, I began crisscrossing the globe, and I haven't stopped yet. I once felt that I should do all of my traveling before I married. But after I had a family, I realized that traveling with children offered a different but equally satisfying adventure. Throughout my years of cooking and training, I traveled all over the world—often with other chefs—promoting American foods abroad, cooking at charitable events, and sometimes as a guest chef featured on a cruise ship or in a hotel dining room. The food was always the tie that bound our different cultures and traditions together.

I believe that until you've eaten the cuisine of a country in its native setting, you never truly understand how to translate its ingredients into your own culinary vocabulary. Shizuo Tsuji, in his book *Japanese Cooking: A Simple Act,* used a baseball analogy to describe this very same thought: "If an American, for instance, wants to try a bit of French cuisine, he or she might go out and buy a copy of Child and Beck's *Mastering the Art of French Cooking.* He or she would start out with a very good idea of what the end result should be. To use a baseball simile, he or she would know where the 'strike zone' was. With a Japanese recipe, however, unless you have been to this country and eaten the food, you will probably have little idea of what you are aiming at."

Travel to me is the real deal. You become the pitcher, the catcher, the mitt, and the strike zone. Once people have opened their homes, hearts, and tables to you, you can truly understand the origin of a dish and the culture that has created it. And once you have experienced this type of global warming, your own life is expanded in unimaginable ways. Learning to eat teaches you to taste, which makes you a better cook. And once you learn how to eat, you learn how to share.

Europe

My first trip to Europe came right after I graduated from the Culinary Institute of America. It was an extensive trip done on the cheap. I planned to be gone for six months—three with a Eurailpass and three by thumb. My passage over was booked on a bargain fare offered by Cunard Line: $299 round-trip, Philadelphia to Southampton, England, on the *Queen Elizabeth 2*. Since I had never been on an ocean liner, the "luxury" journey across the water presented as much of an adventure as the trip itself.

My knowledge of ocean cruises was from the movies, so I expected to see the captain's table and elegantly dressed couples dining in splendor and walking the decks, drinking champagne. I had never seen cramped, four-to-a-tiny-room cabins or tables filled with ancient ladies looking for dancing partners and perhaps, as the night wore on, a little more. I walked the decks and was befriended by an eighty-seven-year-old retired ship's captain who patiently explained the ins and outs of ocean travel. It was he who told me that the French-cuffed shirt that I had purchased for my "elegant" attire should have had the cuffs turned back to hold only one set of cuff links per cuff, not the two sets that I had fitted into the rather long cuff on each sleeve.

Rather than dig into my Eurailpass, I began my trip through Europe by hitchhiking from Southampton to London, where I spent a week getting my balance while still in an English-speaking country. I had been warned that hitchhiking was more dangerous in southern Europe, so I began my explorations south using the Eurailpass (see page 53 for my visit to Sicily). I took very long trips so sleep on the train could substitute for hotel rooms that I could ill afford. I was especially taken by the coastal regions of France, Italy, and Greece. The more relaxed lifestyle of these regions held great appeal, as did the weather, diet, and geography. I remained extremely observant of what people were eating and saw how similar the cuisines of the regions were.

My days in Paris were absolutely intoxicating. I walked endlessly. I peered in the windows of every restaurant that I passed. I wandered the markets in a state of wonder. Of course, I couldn't afford meals in the Michelin-starred restaurants, but there were so many extraordinary cheeses, meats, breads, and fruits that I could put together my own four-star meals on the fly. The inherent respect that the French give their meals was no more evident than when I observed a homeless man in the Metro savoring every bite of the white asparagus spears that he elegantly lifted from a can.

My pied-à-terre was a locker in the Amsterdam train station where I kept most of my belongings. I had discovered that I loved Amsterdam—the people were so welcoming and the atmosphere convivial. I slept in youth hostels while I was in "residence," always carrying a change of clothes, a diary, and a few personal items with me. Since Amsterdam was in the center of my various destinations, I could easily thumb my way out for days or weeks at a time.

Hitchhiking throughout northern Europe was a true adventure. I especially enjoyed Germany, Denmark, and Sweden, where I always got a great reception and easy rides. Other than my brush with the law in then-Communist East Germany (that's another book), I was free and easy during my visits to these countries.

I was heading back to Amsterdam one day in the autumn of 1983 when my ride left me off at a roadside rest stop in northern Sweden. The air was getting chilly, so I thought I'd have no trouble hitching a ride, but sixteen hours later, I was still sitting there with a near-frozen bottom and my thumb in the air. But for every storm there is a rainbow, and mine appeared in the form of a busload of beautiful blonde Norwegian girls on a school trip to London.

As the girls, all about eighteen years old, streamed off the bus, I prayed that they spoke English. Not only did they speak English, but they invited me to join them on their adventure. Their teacher-chaperone was a bit skeptical, but when she learned that I was an American chef taking an extended learning trip through Europe, and after I agreed to teach her students conversational English in exchange for a ride, she allowed me to hop on.

At dinnertime, we pulled into a rest stop, where the students prepared our meal over campfires. This was one of the most delicious meals I have ever eaten. The girls made warm potatoes and dill with herring and sour cream. So simple, and yet a perfect combination that would evoke memories of Sweden for the rest of my life. We spent three days together, the girls and their chaperone demonstrating some of their traditional dishes while I taught them colloquial English. The following menu puts me right back on that bus.

Homemade Gravlax with Mustard Sauce

This simple cured salmon is so easy to make and keep on hand for a last-minute smorgasbord. It is more dense and somewhat sweeter than smoked salmon, but its uses are similar. Although salmon is the fish of choice in Sweden, you can cure almost any rich, fatty fish in this fashion. Gravlax is perfect party food

Makes 3 1/2 pounds
. . . .

served with whole wheat crisps or dark brown bread, sweet butter, and iced aquavit or vodka.

One 3 1/2-pound center-cut piece Atlantic or wild king salmon,
      backbone and pinbones removed
1/4 cup coarse salt
1/4 cup sugar
2 tablespoons cracked black peppercorns
1 cup chopped fresh dill
3 tablespoons vodka, preferably Swedish
Mustard Sauce (recipe follows)
Pickled Onions (recipe follows)

1.   Using a sharp knife, cut the salmon piece in half lengthwise. Run your fingertips along the fish, against the grain, to locate any remaining bones. If bones are found, use a tweezer to carefully remove them. Place 1 piece of the salmon, skin side down, in a shallow glass dish large enough to hold it.

2.   Combine the salt, sugar, and cracked peppercorns in a small bowl. Sprinkle half the mixture over the salmon, then evenly spread the chopped dill over all. Drizzle the vodka over the dill-covered salmon. Place the remaining piece of salmon, skin side up, on top of the dill, pressing down to make a neat fit.

3. Cover the entire dish with plastic wrap, then with heavy-duty aluminum foil. Use a cast-iron pan, a heavy platter, or any heavy piece of equipment or utensil that will fit on top of the salmon to weigh it down. (It is very important that enough pressure be put on the salmon to press the top piece down onto the bottom.) Place in the refrigerator and marinate, uncovering the dish, reversing the 2 pieces of salmon, and basting with the liquid that has formed in the dish every 12 hours, for 3 days. It is important to keep the weight in place for the entire period of marination.

4. When the gravlax is ready, remove the salmon from the dish, separate the 2 pieces, and gently scrape off the seasonings and dill.

5. If serving immediately, place the salmon on a cutting board, 1 piece at a time, and, using a slicing knife, cut very thin slices on the bias, taking care that the flesh is free of any skin. Place the slices, slightly overlapping, on a platter, with the mustard sauce and pickled onions on the side. If storing for later use, after scraping off the seasonings and dill, tightly wrap the salmon in plastic. Refrigerate for up to 3 days. Slice just before serving as above.

MUSTARD SAUCE

¼ cup heavy cream

2 tablespoons fresh lemon juice

2 tablespoons Dijon mustard

1 tablespoon freshly grated white onion

1 tablespoon sherry vinegar

2 tablespoons vegetable oil

Coarse salt and freshly ground pepper

1 hard-boiled large egg yolk, chopped

1 tablespoon chopped fresh dill

1. Combine the cream, lemon juice, mustard, onion, and vinegar in a small mixing bowl. Add the oil and, if necessary, a drop or two of water to thin the sauce. Season with salt and pepper to taste.

2. Cover and refrigerate for at least 1 hour or up to 2 days to allow the flavors to blend. Serve chilled, garnished with the chopped egg yolk and dill.

. . . .

1 cup water

$^1/_2$ cup white wine vinegar

$^1/_2$ cup sugar

1 bay leaf

1 teaspoon coarse salt

1 teaspoon black peppercorns

1 teaspoon juniper berries

2 large onions, peeled and thinly sliced crosswise

1. Combine the water, vinegar, sugar, bay leaf, salt, peppercorns, and juniper berries in a saucepan over medium heat. Bring to a boil and boil for 2 minutes.

2. Place the onions in a large, shallow, heatproof bowl. Pour the hot liquid over the onions and cover with plastic wrap. (If the onions are not completely immersed in the liquid, place a plate on top to keep them covered.) Set aside to cool.

3. When cool, transfer to a nonreactive container, cover, and refrigerate for up to 1 week.

Aquavit-Poached Haddock

Haddock is such a mild-flavored fish that it makes a marvelous sponge for the potent caraway-flavored aquavit in the poaching liquid. The poaching liquid gets reduced to make a delicate sauce for the fish. For large-scale entertaining, you could easily poach a whole fish in this manner, then serve the whole fish on a

Serves 6

. . . .

beautifully decorated platter. This is a bit fancier than the roadside meals I had in Sweden, but the flavors are so reminiscent of Swedish cooking that I had to include it.

Juice of 1 lemon, or more to taste

2 cups water

1 cup dry white wine

1 cup aquavit

2 tablespoons canola oil

1 tablespoon juniper berries

1 bay leaf

1 tablespoon white peppercorns

1 teaspoon coarse salt, or more to taste

Six 7-ounce boneless, skinless haddock fillets

6 lemon wedges (optional)

1. Combine the lemon juice, water, wine, aquavit, oil, juniper berries, bay leaf, peppercorns, and salt in a shallow pan or casserole, with a lid, that is large enough to hold the fish in a single layer. Place over medium-high heat and bring to a boil. Lower the heat and simmer for 5 minutes. Submerge the fish in the liquid, making sure that the liquid just barely covers it. (Add a bit more water, if necessary.)

2. Cover, raise the heat, and again bring to a boil. Lower the heat and cook at a bare simmer for about 5 minutes, or until the fish is still undercooked in the center.

3. Using a slotted spoon or a fish spatula, carefully remove the fish from the pan and place on a platter to cool slightly. Then cover with a clean damp kitchen towel and refrigerate for at least 2 hours or until well chilled.

4. Serve chilled, with lemon wedges, if desired, or any chilled sauce or vinaigrette.

New Potatoes and Creamed Herring

More than any other dish that I experienced in Sweden, I remember this one. No, not because it was cooked by a bunch of beautiful young women! Tossing the hot potatoes in the butter softens them a bit and then their buttery

Serves 6

. . . .

warmth loosens the slightly sweet-sour taste of the herring. Dill adds a wonderful grassy, fresh taste to the warm dish.

1 ¹/₂ pounds tiny new potatoes or other small heirloom potatoes,
    well washed

4 tablespoons (¹/₂ stick) unsalted butter, softened

¹/₂ cup finely diced red onions

1 cup prepared pickled herring in sour cream

2 tablespoons chopped fresh dill

Coarse salt and freshly ground pepper

1. Place the potatoes in a saucepan with lightly salted cold water to cover. Place over high heat and bring to a boil. Lower the heat and simmer for about 12 minutes, or just until the potatoes are barely tender when pierced with the point of a small, sharp knife. Remove from the heat and drain well.

2. While the potatoes are still very hot, carefully cut them in half lengthwise.

3. Heat the butter in a large sauté pan over medium heat. Add the onions and sauté for 1 minute. Add the potatoes and toss until nicely coated with the melted butter and the onions. Sauté for about 2 minutes, or until very hot. Gently fold in the herring and cook, tossing gently, for about 1 minute, or just until heated through.

4. Remove from the heat and fold in the dill. Taste and, if necessary, adjust the seasoning with salt and pepper. Serve hot along with Aquavit-Poached Haddock (page 137) or other poached fish.

Southeast Asia

I had been preparing for a trip to Southeast Asia when I was unexpectedly hired to open the Tribeca Grill. The restaurant was still under construction, so I did not have to cancel my long-planned excursion, although, since the restaurant was due to open in eight weeks, it seemed it would not be as long as I had hoped. I promised that I would have no problem returning and that I would call from time to time, checking on construction progress. As usual in almost any new construction, there were many delays, and the scheduled eight weeks ended up being seven months, so my trip lasted even longer than I had originally planned.

During the period that I cooked in Japan (see page 107), I had the opportunity to visit a number of other Asian countries because I had to leave Japan to renew my three-month tourist visa. I tried to go someplace different each time and was able to visit mainland China, Hong Kong, and Korea on these short hops. Food was managed much differently in each of these countries than in Japan. In China, it seemed to me that anything that walked was considered edible, and Korean cuisine seemed more robust and spicy.

The brief visits to all of these countries served only to whet my appetite for more Asian adventures. But this time around, it was the nonindustrialized countries that I really wanted to see—Thailand, in particular. The focal point of my curiosity was the hill tribes of northern Thailand, who, I'd heard, lived much as they had centuries ago. Indonesia, Malaysia, and Singapore were also high priorities. I wanted to experience the cultures of these places, eating in homes and learning in restaurant kitchens.

I had a three-month tourist visa good for travel in Thailand that would allow me to explore to my heart's content. I hooked up with a guide in Chiang Mai. He was a soft-spoken man who loved to play the guitar and who could speak seven languages, including English and all of the local dialects. He assured me that he could lead me anywhere I wanted to go, even to the most remote hill tribes. His rate was a bit too steep for me, so I had to find some fellow adventurers willing to ante up the pot.

It took a couple of days, but I eventually found two Canadians and a New Zealander to join me and we were on our way.

As we traveled up the Mekong River into the hill country, we stopped at every village that came into view. The first village was a sea of activity, with dogs and elephants in profusion. We later learned that these particular villagers did not eat dog, they just raised the dogs to sell to other villages that did. The elephants were a sign of the prosperity that dog farming had brought to the village.

We did most of our traveling on the backs of elephants, climbing into the hills during the day and then setting up camp for the night. Our guide, besides being an excellent escort, turned out to be a fantastic campfire cook. Once he learned that I was a cook, he appointed me his assistant in the preparation of each meal. Under his direction, I was responsible for the nightly *mise en place* (that is, having all the components of the menu in place), while he put it all together in the most proficient manner. He was expert at balancing chili peppers and spices, which he turned into fragrant sauces for our jasmine or sticky rice.

The farther into the hills we got, the more the remote villages seemed to exist outside of time. The last village that we visited was located high on a mountaintop near the Burmese (now Myanmar) border. We had to walk a full day into the village, as the path was so steep, even the elephants couldn't navigate it.

As we entered the village, the tribal leader determined that our presence was nonthreatening, so he gave his approval to our visit (we were the first westerners they had ever seen). This led to our being welcomed like family. The children gathered around us, fascinated by my camera and its zoom lens, thinking it was alive. The older clansmen lay around smoking opium, while a group of younger men ceremoniously killed chickens in our honor that would be prepared by the village women for our meal later in the evening. It was an amazing banquet.

When our guide learned that I wanted to go to Laos (even though I knew it was off-limits to Americans) to visit the famed wild-game markets, he explained that this was very dangerous for me and I shouldn't risk the trip. However, he could easily go and bring us something delicious to eat from the market. The next morning, he was gone by sunup, and before noon he was back, calling, "Lunch, I've got lunch." In his hand was a three-foot-long iguana.

We were all a bit alarmed but willing to give it a try. The guide took me to his grandmother's house, where he taught me how to clean the iguana, a task, I must admit, I have not had to perform since. He then cooked it in a spicy stir-fry that he served over a bowl of aromatic jasmine rice. The meat was quite sweet and rather luxe. I recommend it highly should you chance upon it at your local supermarket.

The flavors and spirit of Thai cuisine became very much a part of me. Lemongrass, mint, sweet basil, coconut milk, cilantro, galangal, fish sauce, and garlic all blended together to make perfect harmony on the plate. The cooking methods were quick, easy, and accessible, much like the Thai people themselves, who believe that life should be *sanuk,* or fun.

Heading toward Malaysia, I made my way through Thailand and ended up in a small bungalow colony on the beach in Koh Samui, a poor man's island paradise. Or I thought it was, perhaps because all of the dishes featured at the local restaurants began with "magic mushroom": You could have a magic mushroom omelet, magic mushroom soup, magic mushroom stir-fry, and so forth. I lingered for some time, eating, sunbathing, eating, sleeping, eating, partying. I did a lot of eating and no cooking!

When I finally left Thailand, hopping on a bus that would take me on a fourteen-hour ride across Malaysia to Singapore, I had just a few clothes and some souvenirs in my backpack. Some of those souvenirs were knives I had purchased for my collection, and at the Malaysian border, rather than hide them, I naïvely unpacked my bag and presented them to the guards. I was taken from the bus and very aggressively interrogated. While the guards were searching me, they were studying my visa, which, I was told, had expired. "That's impossible—it's a three-month visa." "Yes, but you've been here for four." After forking over some cash to avoid a "problem," I was promptly escorted out of the country.

Singapore amazed me: a very cosmopolitan country with a multicultural population, a complete turnaround from Thailand. The food was extraordinary. There was not one style of cooking but many. Although there was some influence from the British, Portuguese, and Dutch cuisines, Chinese, Indian, Malay-Indonesian, and Nonya cuisines had the most important roles to play. The Nonya style of cooking was the most unique, as it resulted from the marriage of early Chinese settlers to local Malay women. The four main styles of cooking were often interdependent, sharing, borrowing, and integrating ingredients and techniques to produce dishes that were singularly Singaporean. It is said that Singapore was the home of the first fusion cuisine. And like the food, the people were warm and inviting.

I was most intrigued by the hawker stalls that featured home-style cooking. Hawker stalls were outdoor, mobile carts that were generally set up in the evening in open spaces that served as other things (such as parking lots or picnic grounds) during the day. They were most often family-run, with the parents cooking and the kids serving. For generations, the stalls had given immigrants a chance to get a start in the community with a small investment and lots of hard work. The meals served were usually one-dish (some stalls featured only one kind of meal) that could be eaten on the run, although some stall owners did set up a couple of tables and a few chairs. Everything was cooked to order, fresh and delicious. Since my first visit, fancy air-conditioned government-initiated food courts in indoor malls offer a cleaner, more orderly alternative, but to me, the hawker stalls are still the best way to experience the varied cuisines of Singapore.

Even though I could have stayed in Singapore indefinitely, sampling dish after dish, Indonesia beckoned. I made my way to Bali, where I spent six unbelievable weeks. If Koh Samui was paradise, Bali was paradise plus one when it came to natural beauty. However, it was overrun with tourists, so I headed out to the Gili Islands, three remote spots north of Lombok, a large island east of Bali. To get to these islands, I had to take a large boat that connected with a smaller boat, then a moped, a horse, and a donkey. Finally, the last leg of the trip was in a small rowboat with an old fisherman who shared his rice wine moonshine as we rowed. Once there, I found no electricity and plenty of peace and quiet along with some spectacular scenery.

I spent my days snorkeling for the most incredible seafood that I have ever eaten. I stayed in a small family-run beach compound of thatched huts, where the family cook prepared my daily catch for me. The native spices added heat and flavor to the rice that we ate at every meal. I watched the women in the kitchen as they cooked extremely elaborate meals but was never permitted to join them—I never knew if it was because of Muslim custom or because they thought that a man in the kitchen was too crazy to contemplate.

As much as I hoped otherwise, I knew that eventually my every-two-week checking-in telephone call would find my services required at the Tribeca Grill. After seven months of being on the move, learning more about ingredients, techniques, and cuisines unknown than I had anticipated, I was called home. I then realized that I was actually excited to be heading back to the kitchen. It was going to be a time of great exploration for me, as many of the dishes that I had tasted and ingredients that I had discovered were imprinted on my palate. It was going to be up to me to fuse them into the menu that I would introduce in New York.

Thai Shrimp Toasts

Everyone has tried the shrimp toasts in their neighborhood Chinese restaurant, but these are the real thing. The secret is to have clean, clear oil when you fry so that the delicate shrimp flavor can shine. I have used this recipe a million times for restaurant events because the toasts can be put together early in the day and fried at the last minute for a terrific hot hors d'oeuvre.

Makes 32

. . . .

8 slices day-old home-style white bread

2 cloves garlic, peeled and chopped

3 tablespoons chopped fresh cilantro

2 large eggs

2 tablespoons milk

1 pound medium shrimp, peeled and deveined

4 ounces lean ground pork

1/4 cup bias-cut scallion slices

2 tablespoons *nam pla* fish sauce (see Note)

1/2 teaspoon freshly ground white pepper

About 4 cups canola oil

1. Preheat the oven to 325°F.

2. Trim the crusts from the bread and cut each slice into quarters. Place the bread on a baking sheet in a single layer in the preheated oven. Bake for about 6 minutes, or until the bread is lightly toasted. Remove from the oven and set aside.

3. Place the garlic and cilantro in a mortar and grind them to a paste with a pestle. Set aside.

4. Combine 1 of the eggs with the milk in a small, shallow bowl. Set aside.

5. Place the shrimp in a food processor fitted with the metal blade and process, using quick on-and-off turns, until finely ground. Transfer the shrimp to a mixing bowl. Add the garlic-cilantro mixture, the remaining 1 egg, the pork, scallion slices, fish sauce, and white pepper, mixing until well blended.

6. Spread an equal portion of the shrimp mixture on the top of each piece of toast, smoothing down around the edges to make a neat fit. Using a pastry brush, lightly coat the shrimp mixture with some of the egg-milk mixture.

7. Heat the oil in a deep fryer over high heat until it reaches 350°F on an instant-read thermometer.

8. Add the shrimp toasts, a few at a time, and fry for about 2 minutes, or until the shrimp-covered side is golden. Using a slotted spatula, turn each toast and fry until the bottom is golden. Carefully remove the toasts from the oil and place on a double layer of paper towels to drain. Continue frying until all of the toasts are done. Serve hot.

NOTE: Nam pla *(Thai fish sauce) is available at Asian markets, specialty food stores, and some supermarkets. It may be replaced with other fish sauces such as Vietnamese* nuoc mam *and Filipino* patis.

Green Pea Fritters

This is typical of the many types of fritters served throughout Asia. Hot and crispy, they make a great snack or a terrific hors d'oeuvre served with a slightly spicy dipping sauce or fruit-based chutney. They are also quite sweet, so they can also be turned into a dessert, served warm with ice cream melting over the top.

Makes about 36

. . . .

One 16-ounce package frozen peas

3 cups vegetable broth

3/4 cup granulated sugar

3/4 cup packed light brown sugar

1 cup freshly grated coconut or unsweetened coconut flakes

Coarse salt

1/2 cup plus 6 tablespoons all-purpose flour

12 ounces rice flour

2 tablespoons baking powder

1 teaspoon ground turmeric

2 cups water

1 large egg

About 6 cups vegetable oil

1. Combine the peas and vegetable broth in a saucepan over high heat. Bring to a boil. Lower the heat and simmer for 12 minutes, or until the peas are beginning to burst open and are very soft. Add the sugars and stir to dissolve. Stir in the coconut and cook, stirring

constantly, for about 5 minutes, or until the mixture is beginning to thicken. Season with salt to taste, remove from the heat, and allow to cool.

2. Combine the 6 tablespoons all-purpose flour with the rice flour, baking powder, turmeric, and a pinch of salt in a small mixing bowl.

3. Combine the water and egg and whisk to blend. Whisk the egg mixture into the flour mixture, whisking to make a loose batter. Refrigerate for at least 1 hour to chill.

4. Place the cooled pea mixture in the bowl of a food processor fitted with the metal blade. Add the $\frac{1}{2}$ cup all-purpose flour and process, using quick on-and-off turns, until the flour is barely incorporated. You should have a thick, lumpy batter.

5. Using a tablespoon, scoop up balls of the batter and place them on a flat plate. You should have about 24 balls. Place in the freezer for about 10 minutes, until firm.

6. Heat the oil in a deep fryer over high heat until it reaches 350°F on an instant-read thermometer.

7. Working with a few at a time, dip the pea balls into the reserved rice flour batter to coat well, allowing the excess to drip off. Immediately place in the hot oil and fry for about 3 minutes, or until golden brown. Using a slotted spoon, transfer the fried fritters to a double layer of paper towels to drain. Serve hot with any sweet or savory Asian dipping sauce, if desired.

Singapore Spicy Curry Noodles

I have seen Singapore *mai fun* on many Chinese restaurant menus and I've ordered it from quite a few of them, but I've never tasted one as good as this one. I brought this recipe back with me and have made it over and over again, changing the vegetables from time to time but never the spicy curry sauce. It is a terrific buffet dish, since it tastes as good at room temperature as it does warm. I often make

Serves 6

. . . .

two versions—this one and one without eggs and with the chicken broth in the sauce replaced with vegetable broth, so that vegetarians have their own interpretation of this authentic dish.

1 pound rice noodles or rice sticks (see Notes, page 151)

4 large eggs

6 teaspoons sesame oil (see Notes, page 151)

Coarse salt

2 tablespoons peanut oil

1 jalapeño chili pepper, well washed, stem removed, seeded, and minced

1 shallot, peeled and minced

1 clove garlic, peeled and minced

$^1/_4$ cup julienned yellow squash

$^1/_4$ cup julienned zucchini

$^1/_2$ cup bean sprouts, blanched

$^1/_4$ cup julienned leek

$^1/_4$ cup julienned carrot

$^1/_4$ cup julienned red bell pepper

Yellow Curry Sauce (recipe follows)

Freshly ground pepper

¹/₄ cup julienned scallion

¹/₄ cup chopped fresh cilantro

1. Place the rice noodles in a bowl with warm water to cover by 2 inches and soak for 15 to 20 minutes. Drain well and set aside.

2. Combine the eggs with 2 teaspoons of the sesame oil and salt to taste in a small mixing bowl, whisking to blend well. Set aside.

3. Place a nonstick sauté pan over medium-high heat. Lightly coat with vegetable spray. Add just enough of the egg mixture to lightly coat the bottom of the pan, swirling the egg to cover the bottom completely. Cook for about 1 minute, or until completely set. Flip from the pan and continue spraying and cooking until you have used all of the egg mixture.

4. When all of the egg has been cooked, roll up each "pancake," cigar-fashion, and cut crosswise into thin strips. Open the strips and shake them loose. Set aside.

5. Place a wok over high heat. Add the remaining 4 teaspoons sesame oil and the peanut oil and, when the oil is hot but not smoking, add the jalapeño, shallot, and garlic and sauté for about 30 seconds, or just until fragrant. Stir in the yellow squash, zucchini, bean sprouts, leek, carrot, and bell pepper, tossing for about 1 minute, or just until the vegetables have begun to wilt. Add the curry sauce and the reserved noodles, tossing constantly to blend the vegetables with the noodles and sauce, and cook for about 4 minutes, or just until heated through. Season with salt and pepper to taste.

6. Remove from the heat and transfer to a large platter. Sprinkle the reserved egg strips over the top along with the scallion and cilantro and serve.

. . . .

2 tablespoons peanut oil

1 shallot, peeled and minced

1 tablespoon minced fresh ginger

1 tablespoon minced garlic

2 tablespoons Thai yellow curry paste (see Notes)

$^1/_4$ cup rice wine (see Notes)

1 cup chicken broth (see Notes)

2 cups unsweetened coconut milk

2 tablespoons low-sodium soy sauce

Salt and freshly ground pepper

1. Heat the oil in a heavy-bottomed saucepan over medium heat. Add the shallot, ginger, and garlic and sauté for 1 minute. Lower the heat and stir in the curry paste. Cook, stirring frequently, for about 4 minutes, or until the vegetables have sweat their liquid but have not taken on any color.

2. Raise the heat and add the rice wine. Bring to a boil, then lower the heat and simmer for about 1 minute. Immediately add the broth and again bring to a boil. Simmer for about 6 minutes, or until the liquid has reduced by half. Add the coconut milk and continue to simmer until the liquid has again reduced by half, about 5 minutes. Stir in the soy sauce and salt and pepper to taste. Remove from the heat and strain through a fine sieve into a clean bowl and set aside until ready to use. If not using immediately, cover and refrigerate for up to 3 days.

NOTES: *Rice noodles, sesame oil, Thai yellow curry paste, and rice wine are available at Asian markets, specialty food stores, and some supermarkets.*

You can add 1 tablespoon of sriracha *(smooth Thai chili paste) or other chili-pepper-based hot sauce to the curry sauce for additional heat.*

Substitute canned low-sodium, fat-free chicken broth, if desired.

Black Pepper Crab

Serves 6

This is one terrific dish for a crowd. It is the perfect equalizer, as everyone can get down and dirty slurping the meat from the crab shells. There must be hundreds of variations of this traditional recipe, but I'd like to think that this is the closest you will come to the real thing. Although this is always made with crab, if great crab is not available to you, try large shrimp or Alaskan king crab legs.

3 large (about 1³/₄ pounds) live Dungeness, blue, or mud crabs,
　　cut into pieces (see Note)
2 cups clam juice or chicken broth
3 tablespoons freshly ground pepper
4 tablespoons honey
4 tablespoons low-sodium soy sauce
2 teaspoons freshly grated ginger
About ¹/₄ cup peanut oil
3 cloves garlic, peeled and crushed
¹/₂ cup sherry
1 tablespoon cornstarch dissolved in 1 tablespoon cold water
¹/₄ cup chopped fresh cilantro
¹/₄ cup chopped scallion
6 cups cooked white rice (optional)

1.　Place the crab pieces in a large, shallow container (such as a glass baking dish).

2.　Combine the clam juice, pepper, honey, soy sauce, and ginger in a small mixing bowl. When well blended, pour over the crab, tossing to coat well. Cover with plastic wrap and refrigerate for 1 hour.

3. Remove the crab from the marinade, reserving each.

4. Heat the oil in a wok over medium-high heat. Add the crab and stir-fry for 3 minutes. Add the crushed garlic and stir-fry for 2 minutes more, or until the garlic is just turning golden brown. Immediately add the sherry to keep the garlic from burning. Cook for about 3 minutes, or until the sherry has almost evaporated.

5. Add the reserved marinade and bring to a simmer. Cover and simmer for about 5 minutes, or until the crab is bright red. Stir in the cornstarch slurry and bring to a simmer, stirring constantly, for about 3 minutes, or until slightly thickened. Remove from the heat and place equal portions of the crab in 6 shallow soup bowls. Ladle the broth over the crab and sprinkle the cilantro and scallion over the top. Serve with the rice, if desired.

NOTE: *You will want each person to have 3 to 4 good-sized pieces of crab, so buy accordingly. Have the fishmonger kill, clean, and cut each crab into 2 to 4 pieces, depending on the size.*

Traditional Wedding Pineapple Rings

This is a very typical sweet-yet-savory dish that would be served at a Malaysian wedding. If the pineapple is too ripe, it will fall apart during the cooking process, so be sure that you purchase one that is just beginning to ripen. Although this is served as a sweet, I have used it as a garnish for ham, pork, and roasted game.

Serves 6

. . . .

1 large, not–quite–ripe pineapple, peeled

8 cups cold water

3 whole cloves

3 cardamom seeds

One 3–inch cinnamon stick

$^1/_2$ cup sugar

1 teaspoon ground turmeric

2 tablespoons peanut oil

2 red bird chili peppers (or other small red chili peppers), well washed, stems removed, seeded, and cut crosswise into thin slices

1 shallot, peeled and sliced

$^1/_2$ cup light corn syrup

2 tablespoons rice wine vinegar, or more to taste (see Note)

2 tablespoons chopped fresh mint

1. Cut the pineapple crosswise into $^1/_2$- to $^3/_4$-inch-thick rings. Neatly remove the core from each ring (a small cookie cutter or hors d'oeuvre cutter works well).

2. Place the water in a large pot over high heat. Add the cloves, cardamom seeds, cinnamon stick, sugar, and turmeric and stir to dissolve the sugar. Bring to a boil and then lower the heat to a simmer. Simmer for 10 minutes.

3. Add the pineapple rings and raise the heat. Bring the mixture to a boil. Lower the heat and simmer for 10 minutes. Remove from the heat and drain well, separately reserving the pineapple and 1 cup of the cooking liquid, strained through a fine sieve. Set aside.

4. Heat the oil in a large, deep sauté pan over low heat. Add the chili peppers and shallot and sauté for about 4 minutes, or just until very fragrant. Add the reserved cooking liquid, the corn syrup, and the vinegar. Raise the heat and bring to a boil. Lower the heat and simmer for 5 minutes, or until the liquid has thickened slightly. Add the reserved pineapple rings and return to a simmer. Simmer for 3 minutes, or until the mixture is very syrupy. Remove from the heat and allow the pineapple to cool in the syrup.

5. Serve the pineapple rings at room temperature with some of the syrup drizzled over the top and sprinkled with the mint. May be served at room temperature or chilled. Store, covered and refrigerated, for up to 1 week.

NOTE: *Rice wine vinegar is available at Japanese or other Asian markets and some specialty food stores.*

Golden Coconut-Banana Croquettes

When I first tasted these croquettes in Singapore, all I could think of were the *zeppole* (Neapolitan) and *sfinci* (Sicilian) (see page 283) of my childhood. These Italian fried pastry fritters are still traditionally served on Saint Joseph's Day in every southern Italian household. This is such a clear example of how so many similar dishes have evolved in widely dissimilar cuisines.

Serves 6

. . . .

2 large eggs, at room temperature

$^1/_2$ cup sugar

$^1/_4$ teaspoon salt

1 cup all-purpose flour

1 cup unsweetened coconut milk

5 very ripe bananas, peeled and chopped

$^1/_2$ cup unsweetened coconut flakes, toasted

About 6 cups vegetable oil

About $^1/_2$ cup confectioners' sugar

1. Beat the eggs and sugar together in the bowl of an electric mixer. Add the salt and continue beating until the mixture is very thick. With the mixer running, slowly add the flour. When all of the flour has been incorporated, add the coconut milk and then the bananas, mixing just until the batter is smooth. Fold in the coconut flakes. Cover and refrigerate for about 1 hour, or until well chilled.

2. When ready to cook, heat the oil in a deep fryer over high heat until it reaches 350°F on an instant-read thermometer.

3. Drop the chilled batter by the tablespoonful into the hot oil. Fry, turning frequently with a slotted spoon, for about 3 minutes, or until golden brown and cooked through. Using a slotted spoon, remove the croquettes from the oil and place on a double layer of paper towels to drain. Continue frying until all the batter has been used.

4. While the croquettes are still warm, place the confectioners' sugar in a fine sieve and, hitting against the edge of the sieve, dust with the sugar. Serve warm.

Lychee Sorbet with Asian Fruit Salad

Even if you have never traveled to Southeast Asia, the flavors of this dessert will take you there. If you can't find the lychees required to make the ice, substitute any one of the delicious, commercially available tropical fruit purees. This is one of the most refreshing summertime cookout desserts that I know.

Serves 6

. . . .

1/2 cup sugar

1/2 cup water

3 cups lychee puree (see Note)

1/2 cup fresh lime juice

1/2 cup sake

One 16-ounce can coconut milk

Freshly grated zest of 1 lime

Asian Fruit Salad (recipe follows)

1 cup fresh pomegranate seeds (optional)

1. Combine the sugar and the water in a large, heavy-bottomed saucepan over high heat. Bring to a boil. Add the lychee puree, lime juice, sake, coconut milk, and lime zest and return to a boil. Remove from the heat and allow to cool.

2. Pour the cooled mixture into a large, shallow glass baking dish. Place in the freezer and freeze for at least 4 hours or up to 3 days.

3. A couple of hours before you're ready to serve, place 6 shallow soup bowls in the refrigerator to chill.

4.   When ready to serve, scrape the ice to make crystals. Using an ice-cream scoop, scoop a ball of the lychee ice into the center of each of the chilled soup bowls. Spoon some of the fruit salad around the edge of each bowl. Sprinkle with the pomegranate seeds, if desired, and serve.

NOTE: *Fresh or canned lychees may be used to make the puree if lychee puree is not available.*

ASIAN FRUIT SALAD

2 tablespoons fresh lime juice

2 tablespoons fresh lemon juice

2 tablespoons honey

1 tablespoon plum wine

1 tablespoon plum sauce

6 fresh lychees, peeled, seeded, and cut in half lengthwise

3 guavas, peeled, seeded, and cut into chunks

2 mandarin oranges, peeled and sectioned

1 cup fresh papaya chunks

1 cup fresh mango chunks

1 cup fresh pineapple chunks

2 bananas

1 tablespoon julienned fresh mint

1. Combine the lime juice, lemon juice, honey, plum wine, and plum sauce in a small mixing bowl. Set aside.

2. Combine the lychees, guavas, mandarin oranges, papaya, mango, and pineapple. Cover and refrigerate for up to 3 hours.

3. When ready to serve, peel and cut the bananas crosswise into thin rounds, then add them to the mixed fruit along with the mint. (Do not allow the bananas to sit too long, as they will soften and turn unappetizingly brown.) Add the reserved lime juice mixture to the fruit and toss to combine. Serve immediately.

The Americas

Part of the job of being a chef in a well-known restaurant is to serve as the restaurant's goodwill ambassador. Until recently, it was the job of the restaurant owner, but with the recognition now given new American cuisine and the advent of Food Network, chefs have become the face of the industry. This responsibility is not as glamorous as it might seem.

When traveling to charitable events, the chef is usually responsible for bringing meals representative of his or her menu. This means having ready all of the components of the menu in place, packing them in transportable containers with dry ice, and shipping them overnight to the final destination, where the dish has to be prepared and served just as it would be in your restaurant.

It takes a tremendous amount of planning and coordination, and you have to make sure that your own kitchen can function while you're away!

In a two-year period alone, I cooked at thirty different events in thirty different cities as well as traveling to eight countries, many of which were in Latin or South America. Although these culinary excursions can be exhausting, I love doing them because I always make new friends and return with new ingredients for my staff and me to play with—which, of course, spawns great new menu ideas.

On one of my South American trips to Chile, I was to be a guest chef (along with Jean-Louis Palladin, Douglas Rodriguez, and Christopher Gross) for a charitable banquet to be attended by 250 people. I wanted to combine American ingredients with a local product to highlight a spirit of friendship in the kitchen, so as soon as I arrived, I made a trip to the local outdoor market to see if I could find something typically Chilean to feature on my menu. I discovered what is now on menus all across America, Chilean sea bass. I had never seen or heard of it before then.

The fish was perfect for my menu. It had a very high oil content and would stay moist for a longer cooking period than most fish—something I had to take into consideration when cooking larger quantities for a crowd. I was delighted to feature this indigenous product in my American meal. I also discovered some great Chilean red wines, so I was able to go the distance and garnish the rich fish with a sauce made from wines of the region. The Chileans had not yet experienced red wine with fish, so my dish caused much comment and appreciation.

For a non-work-related trip, I headed for Venezuela. One of my cooks, Elena Omana, was Venezuelan, and her aunt had a travel agency in Caracas. Elena knew that I loved to explore new places and that I was looking for some inspiration, so she booked a trip through her aunt that had me in the jungle one day, the rain forest the next, on to an island, then back into the city. It was to be a quick but total immersion in Venezuelan culture and cuisine.

The first day, I arrived in Canaima, a vast national park that is home to Angel Falls, the highest waterfall in the world. Wanting to make sure that I saw it all, I also booked a tour guide, who happened to be a Peruvian Indian. He had already been booked by a couple from Miami, who, he said, wouldn't mind my joining their trek. He first took us hiking up a very steep cliff to show us his home, a cave tucked under a ledge overlooking the cliffs. He then prepared a great campfire lunch while we all got acquainted.

As it turned out, Ricardo de Montoya, a Colombian American in the coffee business, and his American wife, Sidney White, were die-hard food enthusiasts. This helped create new bonds of friendship as our guide introduced us to foods and flavors that we had never before experienced. Rick and Sid assured me that they would soon see me in New York, and after a few days, I went on to discover other parts of the country.

Two days after we had separated and 1,500 miles away from where we had parted, I heard my name called while I was walking on a secluded beach in Los Roques, an archipelago off the eastern coast. I looked out across the water and saw Rick and Sid sunbathing on a boat. I swam out for a reunion, and our friendship was forever sealed by this serendipitous meeting.

About a year later, I was at the Tribeca Grill late one night packing up for a dinner in Miami, where thirty chefs from all over the country were scheduled to prepare a dinner for 3,000 people to raise money for the Hurricane Andrew Relief Fund. On my

way home from the restaurant in the early-morning hours, I was the victim of an attempted carjacking. I was shot at several times as I ran from the scene, and then watched in awe as the gunman aimed toward my truck and shot out my two front tires. After hours of filling out police reports on my brush with death, I was able to make my seven-thirty A.M. flight. I arrived in Miami still rattled by the experience.

That night, my adrenaline flowed with the excitement of being with my colleagues from all over the country and the enthusiasm of the diners supporting a worthy cause. The overwhelming generosity of spirit that I felt was the perfect antidote for my frightening experience earlier in the day. When I finally collapsed in my room, I noticed the message light on my telephone blinking. I checked and there was Rick's voice asking me to join him and Sid on their boat for a little Sunday spear fishing. I was delighted to accept, as I thought a little relaxation would do me good.

Early the next morning, I joined the de Montoyas on their boat and we headed out into Biscayne Bay. Rick had promised that we would spear some fish and catch lobsters and then he would cook his famous paella for a crowd that evening. It sounded like the best tonic I could find. We found more than our share, but I decided to take one more look and got caught in a fast current flowing through a finger channel. Because I was so tired and unfamiliar with how to negotiate the furious water, I started to drown. Fortunately, Rick swam out to save me.

Once home, Rick made me a revitalizing drink and told me to rest while he got dinner started. I sat there thinking that I had escaped death twice in one weekend, that I had witnessed the suffering of people whose lives had been torn apart by an act of nature, and that through it all, there were enormous numbers of people who were trying to set things right in the world. It gave me a whole new outlook on life, and on my life, in particular. I can tell you, sharing Rick's paella in the de Montoya home that night, surrounded by thirty or so new friends, was the most satisfying meal of my life.

Rick's Paella

This is a spectacular paella that comes from my friend Ricardo de Montoya. It takes a fair amount of work to complete, but I will guarantee that the taste is worth the effort. There is almost no dish more suited to feeding a crowd of hungry people than a brimming pan of paella, rich and elegant with shellfish, fish, sausage, and poultry. Before making the dish, read through the entire recipe, as some elements from the paella (such as the chicken bones, shrimp shells, and parsley stems) are used in the broth. Rick suggests that you invest in a paella pan, which makes a great centerpiece for the table and gives diners the opportunity to pick and choose their meal.

Serves 6

Paella Broth (recipe follows)

3 live 1¼-pound lobsters

18 mussels, well scrubbed and beards removed (see Notes, page 169)

18 small littleneck clams, well scrubbed (see Notes, page 169)

1 teaspoon saffron threads

6 tablespoons plus 1 teaspoon olive oil

8 ounces Spanish chorizo, cut crosswise into ¼-inch-thick
    slices (see Notes, page 169)

8 ounces serrano ham or other fine-quality ham, diced

2 pounds chicken, boned, skinned, and cut into 1-inch cubes

1 pound monkfish or other firm white fish, cut into 1-inch cubes

8 ounces squid, cleaned, tentacles cut in half, and bodies cut into rings

18 large shrimp, peeled and deveined

12 medium sea scallops

Sea salt

6 cloves garlic, peeled and minced

1 onion, peeled and finely diced

1 red bell pepper, well washed, cored, seeded, and finely diced

1 yellow bell pepper, well washed, cored, seeded, and finely diced

2 cups Uncle Ben's Original Converted white rice

1 large beefsteak tomato, well washed, cored, seeded, and diced

1 cup julienned roasted red peppers

$^1/_2$ cup chopped fresh flat-leaf parsley

1 tablespoon fresh thyme leaves

2 teaspoons Spanish smoked paprika

Freshly ground pepper

$^1/_2$ cup cooked English peas (optional)

1.   Place the broth in a stockpot over high heat. Bring to a boil and add the lobsters. Again, bring to a boil and boil for about 3 minutes, or just until the lobsters are bright red. Using tongs, lift the lobsters from the broth and set aside. Lower the heat to keep the broth at a bare simmer.

2.   Separate the head, tail, and claws from each lobster. Cut the tails in half lengthwise and lightly crack the claws. Set aside. Remove any dark material from the heads and return the heads to the broth.

3.   Raise the heat under the broth and bring to a rapid simmer. Add the mussels and clams and cook for about 4 minutes, or just until the shells open. Using a slotted spoon, remove the shellfish from the broth and set aside. Lower the heat, add $^1/_2$ teaspoon of the saffron, and keep the broth at a bare simmer.

4.   Heat 2 tablespoons of the oil in a large sauté pan over medium heat. Add the chorizo and ham and sauté for about 2 minutes, or until the chorizo has rendered some of its red oil. Using a slotted spoon, lift the meat from the pan, keeping the pan over the flame, and set on a double layer of paper towels to drain.

5.   Add the chicken to the pan and sauté for about 4 minutes, or just until the meat is lightly browned. Using a slotted spoon, lift the chicken from the pan, keeping the pan over the flame, and set on a double layer of paper towels to drain.

6.   Add 2 tablespoons of the remaining oil to the pan. When very hot, add the monkfish, squid, shrimp, and scallops. Season with sea salt to taste and sauté for about 2 minutes, or just until the seafood is beginning to color. Using a slotted spoon, lift the seafood from the pan and place on a plate.

7. Heat 2 tablespoons of the remaining oil in a paella pan or other large, heavy-bottomed pan over medium heat. Add half the garlic along with the onion and red and yellow bell peppers. Sauté for about 2 minutes, or just until very fragrant. Stir in the rice and sauté for about 3 minutes, or until the rice is beginning to color. Add 5 cups of the simmering strained broth and bring to a gentle simmer. Lower the heat and simmer, stirring occasionally, for 20 minutes, or until the rice is al dente.

8. Ten minutes before the rice is ready, add the reserved chorizo, ham, and chicken to the rice, tossing to combine.

9. While the rice is cooking, heat the remaining 1 teaspoon oil in a medium sauté pan. Add the remaining 3 cloves garlic and sauté for 1 minute. Stir in the tomato, roasted peppers, and parsley along with the remaining $1/2$ teaspoon saffron and cook for about 1 minute, or just until warmed slightly. Remove from the heat and set aside.

10. When the rice is about 3 minutes from being ready, toss in the reserved lobster tails and claws, monkfish, squid, shrimp, and scallops. If the rice seems dry, add a bit of wine or clam juice. Cover and steam for the remaining time period.

11. Uncover the rice and season with the thyme leaves, the smoked paprika, and sea salt and pepper to taste. Add the roasted pepper mixture and toss to mix. Bury the reserved mussels and clams in the rice. Turn off the heat, cover, and steam for 2 minutes more. Uncover and, if desired, stir in the peas. Serve immediately.

. . . .

¹/₄ cup peanut oil

Shells from 18 large shrimp

1¹/₄ cups dry white wine, plus more as needed

Bones from 2 pounds chicken

2 cloves garlic, peeled and chopped

2 ribs celery, well washed, trimmed, and chopped

2 leeks (white part only), well washed and chopped

1 large carrot, peeled, trimmed, and chopped

1 onion, peeled and chopped

3 ripe tomatoes, well washed, cored, seeded, and chopped

2 bay leaves

1 bunch fresh flat-leaf parsley stems

1 sprig fresh thyme

1 tablespoon fresh tarragon leaves

1 teaspoon saffron threads

1 teaspoon black peppercorns

Pinch of cayenne pepper

¹/₂ cup brandy

¹/₂ cup Madeira wine

3 cups clam juice, plus more as needed

Juice of 1 lemon

8 cups water

Coarse salt and freshly ground pepper

1. Heat the oil in a stockpot over medium-high heat until almost smoking. Add the shrimp shells and sauté for a minute or two, or until the shrimp shells turn bright red. Remove from the heat and place in a blender with ¹/₄ cup of the white wine and process to a smooth paste. Set aside.

2. Return the pot to medium heat. Add the chicken bones, garlic, celery, leeks, carrot, and onion and sauté for about 7 minutes, or until the bones are taking on some color and the vegetables have wilted.

3. Stir in the reserved shrimp paste. When well blended, add the tomatoes, bay leaves, parsley stems, thyme, tarragon, saffron, peppercorns, and cayenne. Raise the heat and bring to a boil. Add the remaining 1 cup white wine along with the brandy and Madeira, and, using a long wooden match, ignite the alcohol. Let the flame burn out and then add the clam and lemon juices, stirring to blend. Add the water and salt and pepper to taste and again bring to a boil. Lower the heat and simmer, skimming any impurities that rise to the top, for about 1 hour, or until the broth is very fragrant and well seasoned.

4. Remove from the heat and strain through a fine sieve into a clean container, pushing on the solids to extract all of the flavor. Discard the solids. If not using immediately, allow the broth to cool and store, covered and refrigerated, for up to 3 days, or freeze for up to 3 months.

NOTES: *Rick removes the beards from the mussels and scrubs the mussels and clams with a stiff brush, then he places them in a deep bowl in cold salt water. He adds 1 tablespoon of all-purpose flour and stirs to combine. He places the bowl in the refrigerator for at least 3 hours or up to 8 hours. All of the sand carried in the shellfish falls to the bottom of the bowl and the shellfish are grit free.*

Spanish chorizo is a highly seasoned sausage made from smoked pork and has a deeper, smokier flavor than Mexican chorizo, which is made from fresh pork.

Tres Leches Cake

Almost every Latin culture has a version of this unbelievably sweet cake. It really does need a cup of good, strong coffee to balance its richness. Since it is best served after it has chilled for a day, it is an ideal make-ahead dessert when company is expected. It is also a great conversation piece, as everyone will try to guess how the dense cake is made.

Serves 12
. . . .

9 large eggs, separated

2 cups sugar

1 teaspoon pure vanilla extract

1 tablespoon baking powder

$^1/_2$ cup milk

2 cups cake flour

Tres Leches Cake Filling, chilled (recipe follows)

Sweet Frosting (recipe follows)

1 cup unsweetened coconut flakes, toasted

1. Preheat the oven to 350°F.

2. Lightly grease a 13 × 9 × 2-inch glass baking dish. Set aside.

3. Combine the egg yolks with the sugar and beat in the bowl of an electric mixer for about 5 minutes, or until pale and thick. Beat in the vanilla extract.

4. Dissolve the baking powder in the milk. Beat half the milk mixture into the egg yolk mixture, then add 1 cup of the flour, beating to incorporate. Repeat the process, beating until a smooth batter is formed.

5.   Beat the egg whites until stiff peaks form. Fold half the beaten egg whites into the batter, just until the batter has lightened slightly. Fold in the remaining egg whites until the mixture is well blended. Do not overmix, or the cake will be tough. Pour the batter into the prepared dish, smoothing the top with a spatula. Place in the preheated oven and bake for 30 minutes, or until a cake tester or toothpick inserted into the center comes out clean.

6.   Remove from the oven and place on a wire rack to cool.

7.   When cool, invert the cake onto a serving platter. Using the end of a wooden spoon, poke holes in neat rows down the cake. Slowly pour the chilled filling over the cake, allowing the filling to soak into the holes as you pour so that the cake can absorb all of the filling.

8.   Using a spatula, swirl the frosting over the top and sides of the cake to completely cover. Sprinkle the coconut over the top of the cake, pressing down lightly so that it adheres to the frosting. Cover lightly with plastic wrap and refrigerate for at least 3 hours or up to 24 hours. Serve well chilled, cut into squares.

TRES LECHES CAKE FILLING

· · · · · · · · · · · · · · · · · · ·

1 1/2 cups heavy cream

3 large egg yolks

2 ripe bananas, peeled and chopped

1 cup unsweetened coconut milk

1 cup sweetened condensed milk

One 5-ounce can evaporated milk

2 tablespoons dark rum

1 teaspoon pure vanilla extract

1. Place the heavy cream in a small saucepan over medium heat. Bring to a boil, then immediately lower the heat and simmer, watching carefully that it doesn't boil over, for 8 minutes, or until reduced to 1 cup. Remove from the heat.

2. Using an electric mixer, beat the egg yolks until light and fluffy. Slowly add the reduced cream, beating until cool and foamy. Add the bananas and beat just to blend. Add the coconut milk and then the sweetened condensed milk and evaporated milk, beating well. Beat in the rum and vanilla extract. Lightly cover with plastic wrap and refrigerate for at least 2 hours, or until well chilled. (The filling may be made up to 1 day in advance of use.)

SWEET FROSTING

1 1/2 cups sugar

1 cup light corn syrup

1/2 cup water

3 large egg whites

1. Combine the sugar, corn syrup, and water in a heavy-bottomed saucepan over medium heat. Bring to a boil, stirring frequently. Lower the heat and simmer for about 15 minutes, or until a clear syrup forms and the liquid reaches 234°F on a candy thermometer. Take care that the syrup does not begin to caramelize and turn golden brown. Remove from the heat and set aside.

2. Using an electric mixer, beat the egg whites until stiff peaks form. Beating constantly, add the hot syrup in a slow, steady stream. Beat for about 10 minutes, or until the frosting is shiny, fluffy, almost cool, and stiff peaks can be held. Use within 1 hour.

The Middle East

Although I have been to Israel several times and have had the thrill of traveling through the Sinai desert in Egypt, I have not yet had the opportunity to visit all of the other countries in the area that hold great fascination to me. A brief glimpse into the Bedouin camps on the banks of the Red Sea across from Jordan was enough to tell me that there was much to experience in this intriguing part of the world.

My visits to Israel have centered on cooking for charitable events. I have made many friends in Israel and have seen the significance of family and friends in this impassioned land. I have felt a deep kinship with both the Arab and Israeli communities in their reverence for the community of food.

There is one story that, more than any other travel tale, speaks to the idea of this book. In 1992, Chef Shalom Kadosh of the Sheraton Group–Jerusalem and Michael Ginor, owner of Hudson Valley Foie Gras, coordinated dinners in Jerusalem and Tel Aviv to benefit Hadassah. Shalom hosted four chefs from the United States: Todd English (Olives, Boston), Roberto Donna (Galileo, Washington, D.C.), Jean-Louis Palladin (who had restaurants in Las Vegas and New York), and me. It was during the period of the peace accords and we got off our plane in Tel Aviv welcomed by a throng of well-wishers holding banners. I thought that they had confused us for diplomats arriving for the peace talks, but a huge banner reading "Welcome, Chefs for Peace" told us otherwise. An overzealous publicist, perhaps? No matter; we were surprised and most appreciative of the honor.

I came away with many funny tales about the two kosher-style dinners that we created, mostly having to do with the Frenchman (Jean-Louis) and the Italian (Roberto) trying to discern and follow Jewish dietary laws. Having grown up in New York in an area where you were either Italian or Jewish, I was, fortunately, in familiar territory.

Jean-Louis was, as always, assigned the foie gras course. Before he could even begin the preparations, the *mashgiach* (supervising rabbi) had to kosher the livers. In order for him to do so, he had to put the lobes on a grill to char them until no blood

remained. The absentminded rabbi strolled the kitchen as flames leaped five feet into the air, charring the foie gras beyond recognition. He then chucked the blackened livers into a bucket of ice water. While this procedure created a kosher duck liver, it also created an unusable one for a French chef. We looked at Jean-Louis just as the pin was being pulled from the grenade—"What are you doing, you *@#~!!!? I'm from Gascony, you are killing zee foie gras, you *@#~!!!! Stop right now—don't touch my livers!"

Jean-Louis brazenly concocted a plan to outfox the rabbi by slow-roasting the foie gras in a back kitchen, where he hoped that no one would notice him. But he got caught and we got thrown out of the kitchen, which could have led to the cancellation of the event and the complete closure of the hotel. Some quick behind-closed-doors negotiations with the general manager of the hotel gained us reentry. We agreed to sacrifice all eighty pieces of foie gras, and the show went on.

Shalom Kadosh, knowing that we would have our fill of dining out, graciously arranged a marvelous meal for us at the home of an extraordinary cook, Miriam Cohen. Miriam is a Sephardic Jew from Morocco who spoke French fluently but little English, so Miriam and Jean-Louis immediately became fast friends. She created a meze-style meal for us featuring flavors and ingredients combined in new and irresistible ways. Sitting around Miriam's table was an extraordinary experience, as she had brought together American, French, Italian, Israeli, and Arab chefs. As I glanced around the table, I couldn't help but notice that all conversation and attention were on Miriam's food. There was no discussion of religion or politics; there were no barriers of language or social class. It was simply about the food.

The recipes that follow all come from Miriam Cohen. They are just a few of the many that she cooked for us at that notable meal. When I contacted her years later about including them in this book, she was as accommodating and generous as I remembered. It was only as an afterthought that she told me she was now the private chef for Israel's prime minister, Ariel Sharon.

This trip was made even more memorable because it sealed my friendship with Jean-Louis, who, sadly, passed away a couple of years ago after a very full but too-short life. He was an extraordinary man and probably the most gifted chef I've ever known. He was creative, a master of classic French techniques and styles, and extremely charismatic. When Jean-Louis was in a room, all eyes were on him. Although I never worked for or with him in his restaurants, we often traveled together to many of the charitable events that we did with other chefs. He gave every chef, even the journeymen, the utmost respect, and as a consequence, we all acknowledged him as a master. He embraced America with a vengeance. He was one of the first chefs to search out artisanal producers and he put a great many small farmers on the culinary map. He was a champion of American products and hands-on producers. He brought chefs together in new ways, always in a celebration of life.

Eggplant Cured in Lemon

This is a very traditional dish that is popularly served at festive occasions, particularly weddings. You can add chili peppers and replace the parsley with cilantro for a more intense flavor. Frying the eggplant makes this quite a rich dish that is a great accompaniment to roast

Serves 6 to 8

. . . .

chicken. If you use Japanese or Chinese eggplant, salting is unnecessary, as it is not as bitter as the larger globe eggplant.

3 eggplants, peeled, trimmed, and quartered

Coarse salt

About 6 cups vegetable oil

3 cloves garlic, peeled and minced

$^1/_4$ cup fresh lemon juice

$^1/_4$ cup red wine vinegar

$^1/_2$ teaspoon ground cumin, toasted, plus more to taste

Freshly ground pepper

$^1/_2$ cup chopped fresh flat-leaf parsley

$^1/_2$ cup finely diced red bell pepper

1. Cut each eggplant quarter in half and place on a clean, dry work surface. Generously sprinkle with coarse salt. Let stand for 15 minutes or until the bitter juices have been released. Using paper towels, pat the eggplant dry.

2. Heat the oil in a deep fryer to 350°F on an instant-read thermometer. Add the eggplant and fry for about 6 minutes, or until golden brown. Using a slotted spoon, transfer the eggplant to a double layer of paper towels to drain.

3. Cut the fried eggplant into 1-inch cubes. Place the cubes in a mixing bowl and add the garlic. Toss to combine, then add the lemon juice, vinegar, cumin, and pepper to taste and toss to coat well. Taste and, if necessary, adjust the seasoning with salt, pepper, and cumin.

4. Place the eggplant in a serving dish. Sprinkle with the parsley and bell pepper and serve at room temperature.

Khrime: Moroccan-Style White Fish

In Israel, this dish is made with gray mullet steaks that are not quite as tender as halibut and cod, which are more widely available in the States. This is one of the most frequently made Moroccan fish dishes and consequently there are many versions of it. Some cooks add lots of chili peppers, some lemon juice and vinegar, and others make a very mild dish suitable for children. If serving this as an entrée, you might want to use Israeli couscous or a fragrant short-grained rice as an accompaniment.

Serves 6

. . . .

6 cloves garlic, peeled and sliced

2 large beefsteak tomatoes, peeled, cored, seeded, and diced

1 jalapeño chili pepper, well washed, stem removed, seeded, and diced

1 red bell pepper, well washed, cored, seeded, and diced

$^1/_2$ cup chopped fresh cilantro

2 cups light fish stock or water

$^1/_2$ cup dry white wine

$^1/_2$ cup olive oil

1 teaspoon paprika

$^1/_2$ teaspoon ground turmeric

Six 1-inch-thick *buri* fish steaks (about 8 ounces each) (see Note)

Coarse salt and freshly ground pepper

1. Combine the garlic, tomatoes, jalapeño, bell pepper, and cilantro in a large, shallow, heavy-bottomed saucepan. Add the fish stock, wine, oil, paprika, and turmeric and stir to combine. Nestle the fish into the vegetables and add enough water to barely cover the

fish. Season with salt and pepper to taste and place over medium-high heat. Bring to a simmer. Lower the heat and cook at a bare simmer, basting frequently, for about 25 minutes, or until the fish flakes easily when a knife is inserted.

2. Remove from the heat and, using a slotted spoon, lift the fish steaks to a serving platter. Again using a slotted spoon, scoop most of the vegetables from the pan and spoon them over the fish.

3. Place the pan with the cooking liquid over medium-high heat and bring to a boil. Boil for about 10 minutes, or until the liquid has thickened slightly and is reduced to somewhat less than 2 cups. Pour the hot sauce over the fish and serve immediately.

NOTE: *In America, use mullet or grouper.*

Oven-Baked Lamb Chops

This dish is, to me, a bit like a ratatouille with lamb. These are flavors found throughout the Mediterranean. Like many Israeli dishes, you will find many versions of this one. Some are highly seasoned with cumin and sweet spices, some have a fair amount of chili peppers, and others have lots more vegetables—it really depends upon the origination of the cook. Israeli cuisine is another offshoot of "fusion" cooking.

Serves 6

. . . .

½ cup plus 3 tablespoons olive oil

2 teaspoons paprika

1 teaspoon coarse salt

Six 8-ounce shoulder lamb chops, trimmed of excess fat

½ cup Wondra flour

Freshly cracked black peppercorns

1 cup dry red wine

2 cups beef broth

10 cloves garlic, peeled

3 onions, peeled and quartered

3 large beefsteak tomatoes, well washed, cored, seeded, and quartered

1. Preheat the oven to 400°F.
2. Combine the ½ cup oil, paprika, and salt in a small bowl.
3. Using a pastry brush, lightly coat each lamb chop with the seasoning mixture, reserving any that remains. Then, lightly dust both sides of each chop with the Wondra flour and cracked black peppercorns.

4. Heat the 3 tablespoons oil in a large frying pan over medium-high heat. When very hot but not smoking, add the seasoned chops, in batches, if necessary, and sear, turning once, until both sides are lightly browned.

5. Place the seared chops in a shallow baking dish large enough to hold them in a single layer. Set aside.

6. Keeping the frying pan on medium-high heat, add the wine and bring to a boil, scraping the bottom of the pan with a wooden spoon to release all of the browned bits. Add the broth and again bring to a boil. Remove from the heat and pour the liquid over the lamb chops. Add any of the remaining seasoning mixture to the pan. Nestle the garlic, onions, and tomatoes around the chops.

7. Tightly wrap the entire dish with aluminum foil and place in the preheated oven. Bake for 20 minutes, then lower the temperature to 300°F and continue to bake for 2 hours more, or until the meat is very tender and falling off of the bone and the liquid has reduced to a sauce. Remove from the oven, unwrap, and transfer to a serving platter. Serve hot.

Artichoke Bottoms Stuffed with Veal

When I first tasted this dish, I was reminded of my mom's stuffed artichokes. Although the Italian version is much simpler, with the whole artichoke used and no meat in the stuffing, I could see the evolution of the dish. These are most often found on an appetizer tray or used as a first course in a more elaborate dinner.

Serves 6

. . . .

6 large artichokes, well washed and prepared for stuffing
  (see Note, page 185)
Veal Stuffing (recipe follows)
1 cup seasoned bread crumbs, or as needed
1 large egg, beaten
$1/4$ cup plus 2 tablespoons peanut oil
1 onion, peeled and chopped
2 ribs celery, well washed, trimmed, and diced
3 cups chicken broth
$1/2$ teaspoon ground turmeric
$1/2$ teaspoon freshly ground pepper

1. Generously pack each artichoke bottom with the stuffing. Use your fingers to push the stuffing down into the artichoke, making a neat, symmetrical filling.
2. Place the bread crumbs in one shallow bowl and the egg in another.
3. Carefully holding the stuffed artichokes upside down, dip the stuffing end first into the bread crumbs and then into the egg. Set aside.

4. Heat the ¼ cup oil in a large sauté pan over medium-high heat. Add the stuffed artichokes, meat side down, and fry for about 2 minutes, or until golden brown. Using a slotted spoon, carefully lift the artichokes from the pan and place on a double layer of paper towels to drain.

5. Heat the 2 tablespoons oil in a large, shallow, heavy-bottomed saucepan (large enough to hold the artichoke bottoms snugly) over medium heat. Add the onion and sauté for about 2 minutes, or just until soft. Stir in the celery. Add the chicken broth, turmeric, and pepper and stir to combine.

6. Carefully place the stuffed artichokes, meat side up, in the saucepan. Bring to a simmer, then lower the heat and cook at a bare simmer for about 45 minutes, or until most of the liquid has evaporated and the bottoms are tender. Remove from the saucepan and serve hot or at room temperature.

. . . .

12 ounces lean ground veal

1 onion, peeled and coarsely grated

3 tablespoons chopped fresh flat-leaf parsley

$^1/_2$ teaspoon paprika

$^1/_2$ teaspoon ground cumin

$^1/_2$ teaspoon freshly ground pepper

1 large egg, beaten

2 tablespoons olive oil

1$^1/_2$ tablespoons fresh white bread crumbs

Coarse salt

Combine the veal with the onion, parsley, paprika, cumin, and pepper in a mixing bowl. Add the egg and stir to blend. Add the oil and bread crumbs and season with salt to taste. If the mixture seems a bit dry, add water, a tablespoonful at a time, until the desired moistness is reached. Cover and refrigerate until ready to use.

NOTE: *Instructions for cleaning artichokes:*

On a cutting board, cut the thick stem off the bottom of each artichoke, then turn it around and cut off the top of the artichoke, about 2 inches from the tip, or about 1 inch from the heart, leaving just 1 layer of leaves intact above the heart.

Hold the artichokes in lemon water while peeling and cleaning. Peel off all of the outer leaves and reserve for steaming. Using a grapefruit spoon or a fork, dig out the center of the heart, discarding the fibrous middle, and create a pocket to stuff. Rinse and drain.

Using a paring knife, carefully trim around the bottom of each artichoke heart to make uniform while trimming the tough outer layer.

Sephardic-Style Baklava

Usually thought of as Greek, this very sweet dessert is also typically found on the Sephardic table. I have made it many times for special events because it can be made so far in advance. You can use almost any type of nut, but almonds and pistachios are Middle Eastern favorites.

Makes about 45

- - - - - - - - - - - - - - - - - -

2 packages frozen phyllo dough

3 tablespoons solid vegetable shortening, softened

1 cup finely chopped walnuts

1 cup finely chopped unsalted pistachios

1 cup finely chopped almonds, toasted

3$^{1}/_{4}$ cups granulated sugar

$^{1}/_{4}$ cup packed light brown sugar

1 tablespoon ground cinnamon

1$^{1}/_{2}$ pounds (6 sticks) unsalted butter, melted

3 tablespoons honey

1 tablespoon fresh lemon juice

2 cups water

1. Remove the phyllo dough from the freezer and bring to room temperature. Do not remove the plastic that it is wrapped in.

2. When the phyllo is at room temperature, preheat the oven to 400°F.

3. Using the vegetable shortening, coat the bottom and sides of an $18 \times 11 \times 2$-inch baking pan. Set aside.

4. Combine the chopped walnuts, pistachios, and almonds with $\frac{1}{4}$ cup of the granulated sugar, the light brown sugar, and the cinnamon. Set aside.

5. Working with 1 sheet of phyllo at a time and keeping the remaining phyllo covered with the plastic or wrapped in a clean, slightly damp kitchen towel, place a piece of phyllo in the bottom of the prepared pan. Using a pastry brush, generously coat the phyllo with some of the melted butter. Continue layering and buttering until you have used 4 sheets of the phyllo.

6. Spread an even layer of the reserved nut mixture over the buttered phyllo. Place a sheet of phyllo over the layer of nuts and continue buttering and layering until you have used 2 more sheets. Continue layering the nuts and the buttered phyllo until you have used all of the nut mixture. Cover the last layer of nuts with 4 sheets of buttered phyllo. Gently pat the last sheet down to make a neat fit.

7. Using a very sharp knife, cut the layered phyllo into diamond shapes by cutting across on the diagonal every 2 inches in both directions to make about 45 pieces. (The baklava may be made up to this point, tightly wrapped in freezer wrap, and frozen for up to 3 months.)

8. Place in the preheated oven and bake for 10 minutes. Lower the heat to 350°F and bake for 15 minutes more. Then, lower the heat to 300°F and bake for an additional 15 minutes, or until the baklava is golden brown and crisp. Remove from the oven and place the pan on an angle with paper towels under the edge so that the excess butter can drain off while the baklava cools.

9. Combine the remaining 3 cups granulated sugar with the honey, lemon juice, and water in a heavy-bottomed saucepan over high heat. Bring to a boil, then lower the heat and simmer for 10 minutes, or until the liquid is slightly thick and bubbly. Remove from the heat and allow to cool for 10 minutes.

10. Pour the syrup over the entire surface of the cooled baklava, using a spatula to evenly spread it out. Let stand for 40 minutes, or until the syrup has been absorbed. Cover lightly with plastic wrap and let stand for about 3 hours before serving to allow the syrup to penetrate completely.

11. The baklava can be served or covered and stored in a cool, dry place for up to 2 weeks.

Ma'amoul

These cookies are quite familiar to many cooks in southern Europe, where dried fruits are the sweet of choice. I have made these with great success using dried apricots in place of the dates. These are good keepers, which makes them perfect to have on hand for unexpected guests.

Makes about 40

. . . .

> 2 1/2 cups all-purpose flour
>
> 1/2 cup semolina flour (see Note)
>
> 1/2 pound (2 sticks) cold unsalted butter, cubed
>
> 2 teaspoons blended oil (half olive oil and half vegetable oil)
>
> 1/4 to 1/2 cup water
>
> 1 cup chopped walnuts, toasted
>
> 1/2 cup chopped pitted dates
>
> 1/4 cup granulated sugar
>
> 1/4 cup packed light brown sugar
>
> 1 teaspoon ground cinnamon
>
> About 1 cup confectioners' sugar

1. Place the all-purpose and semolina flours in the large bowl of a heavy-duty electric mixer fitted with a dough hook. Add the butter and oil and mix on low speed until a crumbly dough forms. Begin adding the water, a bit at a time, mixing until a smooth dough forms. You may need more or less water than called for. Do not overprocess, or the mixture will turn pasty.

2. Transfer the dough to a clean, dry work surface and knead it into a ball. Tightly wrap in plastic and refrigerate for 20 minutes.

3. Combine the walnuts, dates, granulated and brown sugars, and cinnamon in a small mixing bowl. Mush together with your fingers until almost pastelike. Set aside.

4. Preheat the oven to 350°F.

5. Remove the dough from the refrigerator and unwrap.

6. If you have a *ma'amoul* mold, form the dough into walnut-sized pieces and, working with 1 piece at a time, press the dough into the mold. Insert 1 tablespoon of the nut filling into the center and then, using your fingertips, close the dough around the filling. Invert the mold and tap the cookie out. (If you don't have a *ma'amoul* mold, follow the same process but hold the walnut-sized piece of dough in the palm of your hand, hollow out the center to receive the filling, and close the dough over the filling with your fingertips.) As each cookie is formed, place it on an ungreased cookie sheet, leaving about $^1/_2$ inch between cookies.

7. When all of the cookies are formed, gently press on the top of each one with the tines of a dinner fork to make a line design.

8. Place in the preheated oven and bake for about 30 minutes. (Do not allow the cookies to color—they should be almost white.)

9. Remove the cookies from the oven and, while still hot, roll each one in the confectioners' sugar to coat heavily. Set aside to cool before serving.

NOTE: *Semolina flour (coarsely ground durum wheat flour) is available at Middle Eastern markets, specialty food stores, and some supermarkets.*

Although many cooks become chefs by working their way up through all of the kitchen jobs, I felt that learning the classics was the best way for me to train as a restaurant chef. To me, it was like building a strong house that would withstand the elements. The classic French repertoire that I learned at the Culinary Institute of America has been my bedrock.

When I began training to be a chef, it was a prerequisite to study abroad, but that, too, has changed. America is now producing many of the world's most creative chefs, and as a consequence, most young cooks stay right at home and learn from their American masters. Although travel remains important to broaden the palate and hone kitchen techniques, Paris is not necessarily the first and only stop.

What I didn't know when I began my training was how hard a chef's life can be. When I was a student, I had the freedom to travel, to experiment, to take my time learning new skills and techniques, and to embrace new cultures. Although I had worked extremely hard in the various restaurant jobs that I had held, I had never had the full responsibility of running a restaurant, even a small one. But that's how it has always been for chefs—you go from wading in calm, shallow waters to swimming in the turbulent ocean.

When making the leap from cook or sous-chef to chef, abilities other than cooking have to be developed: You must learn business and management skills; you must be creative in both the kitchen and the dining room; you must have people skills, both to manage personnel and to interact with guests in the dining room. You have to be prepared to wear many more hats than just a chef's toque—that of a businessman (or - woman), host, mentor, psychiatrist, artist. You also have to be prepared to spend more of your life in the restaurant kitchen than at home.

I have usually had a multiethnic staff whom I have always encouraged to bounce concepts back and forth. This helped in the development of new menus at the Tribeca Grill and it was especially helpful when we needed to be inventive for special events. Nothing creates a better work environment than to make your coworkers feel as though they are part of a team, with their input equal to yours. Through this trust, I have learned much to augment my foundation in the French classics.

In the twenty or so years since I began cooking, the public perception and status of chefs have changed enormously. It used to be a craftman's job, one that was not looked upon with much regard. Now it is a job to be coveted with pride in accomplishment. Television, beginning with Julia Child and right up to Emeril Lagasse, has had the greatest impact in this change. Chefs have gone from being domestic labor, with their category next to maids and butlers on government listings, to being international celebrities.

The Tribeca Grill

I spent almost twelve years in the kitchen of the Tribeca Grill and I loved the intensity of it, especially the early years, when reservations were at a premium. Movie stars, politicians, socialites, people on the party circuit—you name it, they were clamoring to get in. On some nights, the kitchen would prepare over 700 meals and each one of them had to shine. I quickly went from the frying pan into the fire.

The Tribeca Grill is set in one of New York's trendiest neighborhoods and it creates a very special backdrop for dining and entertaining. There is the main restaurant itself, along with the Skylight Room (a small, intimate dining room) and the huge second-floor

loft space (with its own kitchen), which can be kept open and spacious or set with elegant tables for a formal sit-down dinner (and which has been the scene of many, many celebrity and charitable events).

Throughout my years at Tribeca, I gathered a huge repertoire of food, drink, and decor ideas. Since the restaurant is on the first floor of the building that houses the Tribeca Film Center (home to Miramax Films and Tribeca Productions), many of the events were celebrity packed and, consequently, demanded chic and trendsetting stylishness. Here are some of my favorite recipes, chosen to service all types of banquets and special events held at the restaurant.

Trio of Tartares

Sauté of Foie Gras with Parsnips and Sour Cherries

Pepper-Crusted Rack of Venison, Glazed Root Vegetables,
and Lingonberry Sauce

Poached Quince with Fourme d'Ambert, Watercress,
and Candied Walnuts

Fresh Plum Tart with Lemon Verbena Ice Cream

When putting together a formal restaurant menu, it is important to titillate all of the senses. For sight, you want to focus on presentation with the colors and textures displayed in each course. For touch, a balance of texture must be apparent. Pleasant aromas must activate the sense of smell. The tastes must blend well on the palate. And the ears must be perked with a balance of crunchy and soft sounds. These same goals should be met with a formal menu at home.

Be aware of sweet, sour, salty, bitter, and spicy elements in the dishes. Spicy dishes should never be served first, as you don't want to inhibit the palate from tasting what follows.

Each course should have its own identity and character while still reflecting your personal style.

The menu should follow a logical sequence of protein, with the heaviest coming last—fish, shellfish, fowl, red meat, game.

Seasonal ingredients are a must and should be considered for all dishes and garnishes.

Sauces must not be repeated throughout the menu. Work with vinaigrettes, broths, cream-based sauces, fruit- or vegetable-based sauces, and natural juices. If at all possible, avoid using sauces of the same color in varying courses.

If a cold course is part of the menu, place it first.

If the dinner is to be accompanied by wines or if wine is an important component of a dish, refrain from using ingredients that are not wine-friendly, such as artichokes and asparagus.

Be mindful of ingredients that are particularly acidic. They often conflict with the subtle qualities of the wine.

When preparing a menu, it is important to customize it for its intent and for the specific diners. Holidays and special occasions will warrant one type of menu, family gatherings quite another. Romantic occasions rate a menu featuring amorous ingredients like caviar, oysters, and chocolate. A women's lunch will require dishes quite different from those you might plan for a sales meeting.

The following menu will, I hope, bring all of these elements together.

197

WORKING AS A CHEF

Trio of Tartares

In recent years, with the wide acceptance of sushi and sashimi, some variation of a raw fish tartare has been found on many restaurant menus. Tuna tartare is a particular favorite. In this recipe, I have brought together three beautifully colored

Serves 6

and textured fish tartares and highlighted their freshness with the saltiness of caviar.

48 paper–thin slices English cucumber

Scallop Tartare (recipe follows)

Salmon Tartare (recipe follows)

Tuna Tartare (recipe follows)

1 cup crème fraîche, whipped

1 heaping tablespoon osetra caviar

Twelve 2–inch-long fresh chive points

1. Working with 1 plate at a time and using a 2-inch-round-by-2-inch-deep ring mold, overlap 8 slices of the cucumber to make a solid bottom in the mold. Add about 2 tablespoons of the scallop tartare and carefully smooth it over the cucumber. Place about 2 tablespoons of the salmon tartare on top of the scallop tartare and carefully smooth the top. Place about 2 tablespoons of the tuna tartare on top of the salmon tartare and carefully smooth the top. Place a dollop of whipped crème fraîche on top of the tuna tartare. Garnish the dollop with about $1/2$ teaspoon of the caviar. Remove the ring mold and continue making tartare towers until you have made 6.

2. Place 2 chive points in the dollop on each tower. Lean a phyllo cap on the dollop and serve immediately.

SCALLOP TARTARE

8 ounces sea scallops

4 cups water

1 cup dry white wine

1 bay leaf

1 sprig fresh flat-leaf parsley

6 tablespoons extra-virgin olive oil

2 tablespoons low-sodium soy sauce

1 tablespoon fresh lemon juice

$1^1/_2$ teaspoons rice wine vinegar (see Note, page 201)

$1^1/_2$ teaspoons white wine vinegar

$1^1/_2$ teaspoons freshly grated lemon zest

$1^1/_2$ teaspoons minced drained vinegar-packed capers

1 teaspoon *sambal olek* or other chili paste (see Note, page 201)

Coarse salt and freshly ground pepper

1. Pick the muscle, if any, off the side of each scallop.

2. Combine the water, wine, bay leaf, and parsley in a saucepan over high heat. Bring to a boil. Add the scallops and poach for 1 minute, or until just opaque and almost rare. Drain the scallops well and refresh under cold running water. Pat dry.

3. Cut the scallops into a very fine, even dice. Place in a mixing bowl, cover with plastic wrap, and refrigerate.

4. Whisk the oil, soy sauce, lemon juice, rice wine vinegar, white wine vinegar, lemon zest, capers, and *sambal olek* together. Taste and adjust the seasoning with salt and pepper. Set aside.

5. When ready to serve, add just enough of the dressing, about 3 tablespoons, to the scallops to lightly moisten. Reserve the remaining dressing for another use. Use the tartare as directed in the master recipe or serve alone with crisp toasts.

2 tablespoons Dijon mustard

1 tablespoon mayonnaise

1 tablespoon fresh lemon juice

1 teaspoon *sriracha* or other chili-pepper-based hot sauce

(see Note, page 201)

Dash of Worcestershire sauce

Coarse salt and freshly ground pepper

8 ounces boneless, skinless salmon, finely diced and well chilled

1.   Combine the mustard, mayonnaise, lemon juice, *sriracha,* and Worcestershire sauce in a small nonreactive container. Season with salt and pepper to taste. Cover and refrigerate.

2.   When ready to serve, place the salmon in a small mixing bowl. Add just enough of the dressing, about 3 tablespoons, to lightly moisten. Reserve the remaining dressing for another use. Use the tartare as directed in the master recipe or serve alone with crisp toasts.

TUNA TARTARE

1/4 cup low-sodium soy sauce

2 tablespoons cold water

1 tablespoon mirin (see Note)

1 tablespoon sake

1/2 teaspoon sugar

1/2 teaspoon minced fresh ginger

1/4 teaspoon wasabi paste (see Note)

1/4 teaspoon minced garlic

8 ounces sushi-grade tuna, finely diced and well chilled

1. Combine the soy sauce, water, mirin, sake, sugar, ginger, wasabi paste, and garlic in a small nonreactive container. Cover and refrigerate.

2. When ready to serve, place the tuna in a small mixing bowl. Add just enough of the dressing, about 3 tablespoons, to lightly moisten. Reserve the remaining dressing for another use. Use the tartare as directed in the master recipe or serve with crisp toasts.

NOTE: *Rice wine vinegar,* sambal olek, sriracha, *mirin, and wasabi paste are available at Asian markets, specialty food stores, and some supermarkets.*

Sauté of Foie Gras with Parsnips and Sour Cherries

Foie gras always adds a note of luxury to a formal menu. The availability of excellent American foie gras is, for the most part, due to my great friend Michael Ginor, of Hudson Valley Foie Gras, who has

Serves 6

perfected the art of producing duck livers as good as, if not better than, those of the French.

$^1/_3$ cup sugar

$^1/_3$ cup sherry vinegar

2 cups pitted Bing cherries (see Notes)

$1^1/_2$ pounds parsnips, peeled and trimmed

$1^1/_2$ cups water

2 tablespoons unsalted butter

2 tablespoons heavy cream, at room temperature

Coarse salt and freshly ground pepper

About 6 cups vegetable oil

1 pound grade A foie gras, cut into six equal portions (see Notes)

1. Combine the sugar and sherry vinegar in a heavy-bottomed saucepan over medium heat. Cook, stirring frequently, for about 3 minutes, or until the mixture is bubbling vigorously. Stir in the cherries and continue to cook, stirring frequently, for 5 minutes more, or until the mixture has thickened slightly. Remove from the heat and set aside (see Notes).

2. Using a mandoline or Japanese vegetable slicer, shave the parsnips to get 12 long slivers about $^1/_{16}$ inch thick (see Notes). Set the slivers aside and chop the remaining parsnips.

3. Combine the water and butter in a saucepan over medium heat. Add the chopped parsnips and bring to a boil. Lower the heat and cook at a bare simmer for about 15 minutes, or until the parsnips are very tender and the liquid has been absorbed. Remove from the heat and place in the bowl of a food processor fitted with the metal blade. Add the cream and process to make a smooth puree. Scrape the puree from the bowl of the food processor into the top half of a double boiler. Taste and adjust the seasoning with salt and pepper. Cover lightly and place over simmering water to keep warm.

4. Heat the oil in a deep fryer over high heat to 365°F on an instant-read thermometer. Add the reserved parsnip slivers and fry for about 10 seconds, or just until the slivers are golden. Using a slotted spoon, lift the slivers from the oil and place on paper towels to drain.

5. Place a nonstick sauté pan over high heat until very hot but not smoking. Add the foie gras and cook, turning every 30 seconds, for about 2 minutes, or until the foie gras is exuding fat and turning crispy and brown. Turn and sear the other side for about 2 minutes, or until nicely browned. Using a slotted spatula, remove the foie gras to a warm plate.

6. Place an equal portion of the parsnip puree in the center of each of 6 plates. Place a piece of foie gras in the center of the puree and spoon the reserved cherry sauce over the top. Garnish each plate with 2 parsnip slivers and serve.

NOTES: *If fresh cherries are not available, do not hesitate to use frozen.*

Foie gras is available from fine butchers, at some specialty food stores, and by mail order from D'Artagnan (see Sources, page 335).

The cherry sauce may be made up to 3 days in advance of use. Store tightly covered and refrigerated. Reheat before serving.

You can make the parsnip slivers and the puree a day in advance of use. If the weather is very dry, you can store the slivers at room temperature wrapped in plastic. If not, store them in an airtight container. Store the puree tightly covered and refrigerated. Reheat in a double boiler before serving.

Pepper-Crusted Rack of Venison, Glazed Root Vegetables, and Lingonberry Sauce

Serves 6

It has only been in recent years that venison has been commercially farmed. Some of the best comes from a New Zealand company, Cervena, which has done much to promote its virtues. Where wild game has to be marinated and, usually, braised to tenderize it, lean, low-calorie farmed venison can be prepared any way a cook desires. Although the flavor of farmed game is much more delicate than that of the meat of wild animals, it remains intense enough to stand up to a rich sauce or spicy accent such as the pepper crust in this recipe.

¹/₄ cup chestnut (or other richly flavored) honey

2 tablespoons Dijon mustard

¹/₄ cup vegetable oil

Three 16-ounce racks of baby venison, Frenched (see Notes, page 208)

Pepper Crust for Venison (recipe follows)

Glazed Root Vegetables (recipe follows)

Lingonberry Sauce (recipe follows)

6 small branches fresh rosemary

1. Preheat the oven to 450°F.

2. Combine the honey and mustard in a small mixing bowl and set aside.

3. Heat the oil in a large sauté pan over medium-high heat. Add the venison racks, outer side down, and sear, turning occasionally, for about 6 minutes, or until nicely colored. Remove from the heat and, using a pastry brush, lightly coat the racks with the honey-

mustard mixture. Using your hands, press an equal portion of the pepper crust onto each coated rack.

4. Place the racks in a roasting pan in the preheated oven and bake for about 12 minutes, or until an instant-read thermometer inserted into the thickest part reads 145°F, for medium-rare. (The venison will continue to cook after it is removed from the oven.)

5. Remove the venison from the oven and let rest for a couple of minutes. Cut the racks into chops and then place an equal portion of chops (usually 3) in the center of each of 6 plates. Spoon the glazed root vegetables around the chops and drizzle the lingonberry sauce over the chops and around the edge of the plate. Garnish with a sprig of rosemary and serve.

¹/₄ cup Szechuan peppercorns (see Notes, page 208)

2 tablespoons black peppercorns

2 tablespoons green peppercorns

2 tablespoons white peppercorns

³/₄ cup Italian Seasoned Bread Crumbs (page 30)

1 tablespoon coarse salt

2 tablespoons chopped fresh flat-leaf parsley

2 tablespoons chopped fresh cilantro

1. Grind all of the peppercorns in a spice grinder until processed to a medium grind. Transfer to a small mixing bowl. Stir in the bread crumbs and salt.

2. Just before ready to use, stir in the parsley and cilantro.

GLAZED ROOT VEGETABLES

. . . .

4 tablespoons (¹/₂ stick) unsalted butter

2 tablespoons olive oil

12 baby white turnips, peeled, cut in half lengthwise, and blanched

12 cipollini onions, peeled and blanched

2 celeriac (celery root), peeled, cut into ³/₄-inch cubes, and blanched

1 large rutabaga, peeled, cut into ³/₄-inch cubes, and blanched

Coarse salt and freshly ground pepper

1 cup chicken broth

¹/₄ cup chopped mixed fresh herbs (such as parsley, chives,
        thyme, and rosemary)

1. Heat the butter and oil in a large sauté pan over medium-high heat. Add the turnips, onions, celeriac, and rutabaga and cook, tossing occasionally, for about 5 minutes, or just until the vegetables begin to take on some color. Season with salt and pepper to taste.

2. Add the chicken broth and bring to a boil. Lower the heat and simmer, tossing occasionally, for about 5 minutes, or until the liquid has almost evaporated and the vegetables are beautifully glazed.

3. Remove from the heat, taste, and, if necessary, adjust the seasoning with salt and pepper. Just before serving, toss in the herbs.

. . . .

2 cups port wine

2 shallots, peeled and chopped

1 teaspoon white peppercorns

2 cups veal demi-glace (see Notes)

1 tablespoon unsalted butter, softened

2 tablespoons lingonberry jam (see Notes)

Coarse salt and freshly ground pepper

1.   Combine the port wine, shallots, and peppercorns in a saucepan over medium-high heat. Bring to a boil, then lower the heat and simmer for about 20 minutes, or until the liquid has reduced to $1/2$ cup.

2.   Stir in the demi-glace and return to a simmer. Simmer for about 10 minutes, or until the liquid has reduced by one-quarter. Remove from the heat and strain through a fine sieve into a small saucepan.

3.   Place the saucepan over medium heat and return the sauce to a simmer. Whisk in the butter and, when well emulsified, the jam. Season with salt and pepper to taste.

4.   Place in the top half of a double boiler over hot water until ready to serve or place in a nonreactive container, cover, and refrigerate for up to 3 days. Reheat just before serving.

NOTES: *Venison is available from quality butchers and by mail order from D'Artagnan (see Sources, page 335). The butcher will French the racks for you. If you want to do it yourself, simply scrape the meat from the bones with a small sharp knife until the bones are cleaned and make handles for the chops.*

Szechuan peppercorns are available at Asian markets, specialty food stores, and some supermarkets.

Veal demi-glace is available from quality butchers and at specialty food stores.

Lingonberry jam is available at Scandinavian markets and some specialty food stores.

Poached Quince with Fourme d'Ambert, Watercress, and Candied Walnuts

Serves 6

. . . .

3 large quinces

2 cups Merlot or red Zinfandel wine

1 cup sugar

One 2-inch cinnamon stick

1 whole clove

2 large bunches watercress, well washed, dried, and trimmed
     of thick stems

Walnut Vinaigrette (recipe follows)

Coarse salt and freshly ground pepper

Eighteen 1 1/2-ounce triangles fourme d'Ambert cheese

Candied Walnuts (recipe follows)

1/4 cup chopped fresh chives

6 slices raisin-walnut or cinnamon-raisin toast, cut into triangles
     (optional)

1.   Peel the quinces and cut them in half lengthwise. Carefully core and then cut each half lengthwise into 4 wedges.

2.   Place the quinces in a heavy-bottomed saucepan. Add the wine, sugar, cinnamon stick, and clove and place over medium heat. Bring to a simmer, then lower the heat and cook at a bare simmer for about 1 hour, or until the quinces are tender and have taken on a reddish color. Do not allow the quinces to cook too fast, or they will be tender before they have reddened. Remove from the heat and pour through a fine sieve, separately reserving the quinces and the cooking liquid. Pick the cinnamon stick and clove from the quinces and return the spices to the cooking liquid. Set the quinces and liquid aside to cool.

3. When the quinces and the liquid have cooled, combine them in a nonreactive container. Cover and place in the refrigerator to marinate for at least 24 hours or up to 1 week.

4. When ready to serve, using a slotted spoon, lift the quinces from the liquid and pat dry. (You can reserve the liquid, covered and refrigerated, for use as a poaching medium for other fruits such as apples, pears, or peaches.)

5. Place 4 pieces of quince around the edge of each of 6 plates.

6. Place the watercress in a mixing bowl with just enough of the walnut vinaigrette to moisten. Toss to lightly coat. Season with salt and pepper to taste and mound an equal portion in the center of each of the plates. Add 3 triangles of cheese and 3 candied walnuts to each plate. Sprinkle the chopped chives over the top and serve with raisin-walnut or cinnamon-raisin toast points, if desired.

WALNUT VINAIGRETTE

. . . .

$^1/_4$ cup red wine vinegar

2 teaspoons Dijon mustard

$^1/_2$ cup walnut oil

$^1/_4$ cup light olive oil

Coarse salt and freshly ground pepper

Place the vinegar and mustard in the bowl of a small food processor fitted with the metal blade. Process to blend. With the motor running on low, slowly drizzle in the walnut oil and then the olive oil, processing until well emulsified. Season with salt and pepper to taste and set aside until ready to use.

CANDIED WALNUTS

4 ounces walnut halves

1 tablespoon molasses

2 tablespoons light corn syrup

1 teaspoon paprika

1 teaspoon cayenne pepper

$^1/_4$ teaspoon freshly ground pepper

$^1/_4$ teaspoon ground cumin

1. Preheat the oven to 200°F.

2. Bring a small saucepan of water to a boil over high heat. Add the walnuts and return to a boil. Boil for 1 minute, then remove from the heat and drain well. Using paper towels, pat the nuts dry.

3. Place the dry nuts in a single layer on a small baking pan. Place in the preheated oven and dry for 30 minutes. Remove from the oven and set aside. Do not turn off the oven.

4. Combine the molasses, corn syrup, paprika, cayenne, pepper, and cumin in a small mixing bowl, whisking to blend. Add the walnut halves and toss to coat well.

5. Place a wire rack on the baking pan and lay the coated walnuts out on the rack in a single layer. This will allow the molasses coating to drip off and will keep the nuts from burning in the sweet syrup.

6. Place the nuts in the preheated oven and roast for 1 hour, or until the nuts are no longer sticky. Remove from the oven and allow to come to room temperature in a cool, dry place. The nuts will become smooth and shiny as they cool. Store in an airtight container for up to 3 weeks.

Fresh Plum Tart with
Lemon Verbena Ice Cream

This is typical of a guaranteed best seller—a simple tart that almost everyone likes, garnished with an exotically flavored ice cream that intrigues. These tarts can be made with any firm fruit and served with a fine-quality ice cream or gelato. You could also, as I might do for restaurant service, make a plum sauce to drizzle around the edge of the plate to make a fancier dessert.

Serves 6

. . . .

1 cup honey

2 vanilla beans

2 sheets frozen puff pastry, thawed according to package directions
    (see Note)

12 large firm, ripe plums, well washed

Plum Compote (recipe follows)

2 tablespoons sugar

Lemon Verbena Ice Cream (recipe follows)

6 sprigs fresh lemon verbena (optional)

1. Preheat the oven to 400°F.

2. Place the honey in a small saucepan. Split the vanilla beans lengthwise and scrape the seeds into the honey. (Place the scraped beans in granulated or confectioners' sugar to make vanilla sugar, or store them, well wrapped and refrigerated, to flavor sauces.) Place over medium heat and bring to a boil. Remove from the heat and set aside.

3. Cut the puff pastry sheets into six 5-inch circles. Place the pastry rounds on a nonstick baking sheet and set aside.

4. Cut the plums in half lengthwise and remove and discard the pits. Using a small, sharp knife, cut each half into thin slices. Set aside.

5. Using a spatula, lightly coat each pastry round with the plum compote.

6. Working in concentric circles to a decorative pattern, cover each pastry round with the reserved plum slices. Sprinkle an equal portion of sugar over each tart. Place in the preheated oven and bake for about 6 minutes, or just until the pastry is golden and crisp. Remove from the oven and allow to cool.

7. When ready to serve, reheat the honey glaze just to warm. Using a pastry brush, lightly coat each plum tart with the honey glaze. Place a small scoop of the ice cream in the center and garnish with a sprig of lemon verbena, if desired.

NOTE: *You will need enough puff pastry to make six 5-inch circles. Check the size of the sheets when you purchase them to make sure you have enough.*

PLUM COMPOTE

8 large firm, ripe plums, peeled, pitted, and quartered

$^1/_4$ cup water

$^1/_4$ cup sugar, plus more to taste

$^1/_4$ teaspoon fresh lemon juice, plus more to taste

$^1/_2$ vanilla bean

2 tablespoons mirabelle eau-de-vie (French plum brandy)

1.   Combine the plums, water, sugar, and lemon juice in a heavy-bottomed saucepan over medium heat. Split the vanilla bean lengthwise and scrape the seeds into the plums, reserving the bean to flavor sugar or sauces (see page 213). Bring to a boil, then lower the heat and cook at a bare simmer, stirring frequently, for about 15 minutes, or until very thick. After the mixture has cooked for about 5 minutes, taste, and, if necessary, adjust the flavor with additional sugar or lemon juice. Stir in the mirabelle and remove from the heat. Allow to cool.

2.   When cool, strain the mixture through a fine sieve, discarding the liquid. (Alternately, you can place the liquid in a small saucepan over medium-high heat and simmer until very thick and saucy. The sauce can be drizzled on the plate when serving.) Place the plums in a small nonreactive container with a lid and reserve until ready to use.

LEMON VERBENA ICE CREAM

2 cups half-and-half

1 cup heavy cream

2 tablespoons powdered milk

$^3/_4$ cup sugar

1 tablespoon finely chopped fresh lemon verbena

6 large egg yolks, at room temperature

1. Combine the half-and-half, cream, powdered milk, $^1/_2$ cup of the sugar, and lemon verbena in a heavy-bottomed saucepan over medium heat. Bring to a simmer and remove from the heat.

2. While the cream mixture is heating, whisk the egg yolks together with the remaining $^1/_4$ cup sugar.

3. Whisk a bit of the hot cream into the eggs to temper them. Slowly whisk the tempered eggs into the hot cream. Return to low heat and cook, stirring constantly, for about 5 minutes, or until thickened.

4. Remove from the heat and strain through a fine sieve into a clean bowl. Place in a larger bowl of ice and, stirring frequently, allow the mixture to cool.

5. Pour into the container of an ice-cream machine and process according to manufacturer's directions.

HORS D'OEUVRES

So many special events at Tribeca were cocktail parties where only hors d'oeuvres were served that we developed quite a repertoire of tiny bites. Some of our hors d'oeuvres were extremely elegant and quite difficult to put together, while others were as simple and straightforward as you could get. Whatever we served had to be easy to eat, beautiful on the platter, and a tempting accompaniment to drinks.

Hors d'oeuvres should feature contrasts in texture, flavor, and color. When giving a large cocktail party, you should try to put together at least six to eight different hors d'oeuvres, allowing six to eight pieces total for each guest. Just like we professionals do, always have a fair number that can be made ahead of time so that last-minute preparations are kept to a minimum and unexpected guests can be served by a relaxed host.

Present the hors d'oeuvre selection on interesting plates, platters, and trays decorated with colorful garnishes or flowers. Line the platter or tray with coarse salt, multicolored peppercorns, dried spices, or a dry version of a component in the hors d'oeuvres.

Hors d'oeuvres are not meant to be a full meal but are meant to stimulate the palate. You should offer a mix of flavors and always have something for non–meat eaters. Interesting bits of food or deluxe offerings like caviar are always great conversation starters, so they help get a party buzz going.

The following recipes are just a few of my favorites. They offer a bit of the luxe, a bit of the do-ahead, and quite a few flavors from around the world.

Chicken Skewers "Cordon Bleu"

. . . .

Six 8-ounce boneless, skinless chicken breast halves, trimmed of all fat

6 thin slices fine-quality baked ham

About 48 fresh spinach leaves, well washed and stems removed

6 thin slices Emmentaler cheese

1 cup Wondra flour

3 large eggs, beaten

One 12-ounce package panko bread crumbs (see Note)

Coarse salt and freshly ground pepper

About 6 cups vegetable oil

Herb Cream Sauce (recipe follows)

1. Lay the chicken breast halves out on a cutting board and, using a sharp chef's knife, butterfly each breast half by cutting through one side into the middle almost through to the opposite side. Lift up the top flap of chicken and open up the entire breast half into a butterfly shape.

2. Working with one at a time, place a butterflied breast on a piece of plastic wrap. Cover it with a piece of plastic wrap of the same size. Using a cleaver or other heavy object (such as a small cast-iron frying pan), pound the breast until it is about ⅛ inch thick. Continue pounding until all of the chicken has been flattened. Remove and discard the plastic wrap.

3. Lay 6 pieces of plastic wrap, each large enough to enclose a rolled chicken breast, out on a clean, dry work surface. Place a butterflied chicken breast on each piece of plastic. Lay a piece of ham on top of the chicken, then cover the ham with an even layer of spinach leaves (about 8). Place a piece of cheese on top of the spinach.

4. Starting from the end closest to you, roll the layered chicken breast into a compact cylinder. Pull the plastic wrap over the cylinder to enclose it. Twist the ends closed to firm the roll and seal it tightly. Tape the roll closed with Scotch tape. Place the roulades in the freezer until frozen through, at least 2 hours. (The roulades may be made up to this point and stored, frozen, for up to 3 months.)

5. When ready to fry, remove the roulades from the freezer. Place the flour, eggs, and bread crumbs in descending order in large, shallow bowls. Season each with salt and pepper to taste. Working with 1 frozen roulade at a time, dip it first into the flour and then into the eggs, shaking off the excess; finally, roll the roulade in the bread crumbs. Set aside.

6. Preheat the oven to 350°F.

7. Heat the oil in a deep fryer over high heat to 350°F on an instant-read thermometer. Place the coated roulades in the hot oil and fry, turning occasionally, for about 4 minutes, or until crisp and golden brown. Using a slotted spoon, transfer the roulades to a double layer of paper towels to drain.

8. When all of the roulades are drained, using a serrated knife, cut each roulade crosswise into ½-inch-thick pieces. Place a small skewer (or large toothpick) through the bottom of each slice. Place on a nonstick baking pan in the preheated oven and bake for about 7 minutes, or just until cooked in the center.

9. Place a small bowl of the cream sauce in the center of a serving platter. Remove the skewers from the oven, decoratively arrange them around the sauce, and serve.

NOTE: *Panko bread crumbs are coarse Japanese bread crumbs that when fried make a very crisp, crunchy crust. They are available at Asian markets and some specialty food stores.*

HERB CREAM SAUCE

1 cup fresh flat-leaf parsley leaves, blanched

1 cup chopped scallions, blanched

$^{1}/_{2}$ cup chopped fresh chives, blanched

1 tablespoon unsalted butter

2 small shallots, peeled and minced

$^{1}/_{4}$ cup dry white wine

2 cups heavy cream

1 cup chicken broth

Coarse salt and freshly ground pepper

1. Place the blanched parsley, scallions, and chives in a blender and process to a smooth puree, adding water as needed. Set aside.

2. Heat the butter in a saucepan over medium heat. Add the shallots and sauté for about 3 minutes, or just until softened. Add the wine and bring to a boil. Boil for about 10 seconds. Add the cream and broth and again bring to a boil. Lower the heat and simmer for about 20 minutes, or until the liquid has reduced by half. Season with salt and pepper to taste and remove from the heat.

3. Strain the reduced liquid through a fine sieve into a mixing bowl and allow to cool.

4. Whisk the reserved herb puree into the reduced liquid. Cover and refrigerate (or freeze for up to 3 months) until ready to use.

5. When ready to use, place the amount needed in a small saucepan over medium heat and heat just enough to take the chill off. Do not cook, or the color will flatten. Serve barely warm.

Sesame Beef with Ginger Plum Sauce

Makes 28

. . . .

Two 1-pound strip loin or rib-eye steaks, trimmed of all fat

Coarse salt and freshly ground pepper

$^1/_2$ cup sesame seeds

2 tablespoons vegetable oil

Ginger Plum Sauce (recipe follows)

1. Place 28 8-inch bamboo skewers in cold water to cover and let soak for at least 1 hour.

2. Using a sharp knife, trim a thin edge off all sides of the steaks to make neat rectangles (about 7 inches long by 4 inches wide by 1 inch thick). Cut each steak lengthwise into 7 pieces about 4 inches long and 1 inch wide.

3. Place the 14 pieces alongside one another with the length facing away from you. Pierce 2 bamboo skewers up through each piece of meat so that when the meat is cut in half lengthwise, after cooking, you will have 2 skewers of beef of equal size. (The skewers may be assembled up to this point, covered, and refrigerated for up to 24 hours or frozen for up to 3 months.)

4. When ready to cook, season the skewers with salt and pepper to taste and roll in the sesame seeds to completely coat.

5. Heat the oil in a nonstick griddle over medium-high heat. Place the skewers in the hot oil and sear, turning occasionally, for about 2 minutes, or until nicely browned but still rare in the center.

6. Transfer to a cutting board and cut each skewer in half lengthwise to make 2 skewers of equal size. Lay the skewers out on a serving platter, cut side up to show the beautiful rare meat. Serve immediately with the ginger plum sauce on the side.

GINGER PLUM SAUCE

One 15-ounce jar golden plum sauce (see Note)
1 cup chicken broth
1 tablespoon minced fresh ginger

Place the plum sauce, chicken broth, and ginger in a small saucepan over medium-high heat. Bring to a boil, then lower the heat and simmer for about 15 minutes, or until the mixture is thick enough to coat the back of a spoon. Remove from the heat and strain through a fine sieve into a serving bowl. Serve immediately or cover and refrigerate for up to 2 weeks. Reheat when ready to use.

NOTE: *Golden plum sauce is available at Asian markets and some specialty food stores.*

Foie-Gras-Stuffed Figs with White Truffle Honey

Makes 40

. . . .

10 ounces foie gras mousse (see Notes)

40 firm fresh Black Mission figs, well washed and dried

6 tablespoons white truffle honey (see Notes)

$^1/_4$ cup fresh mint chiffonade

1. Bring the mousse to room temperature.

2. Using a paring knife, cut about $^1/_2$ inch off the stem end of each fig. Using a small melon baller, carefully scoop the flesh from the figs, leaving a shell about $^1/_8$ inch thick; reserve the flesh.

3. Line a baking sheet with parchment paper. Place the hollowed-out figs on the baking sheet and set aside.

4. Divide the fig flesh in half. Set one half aside and mix the honey into the other.

5. Preheat the oven to 350°F.

6. Place the foie gras mousse in a small mixing bowl. Add the reserved plain fig flesh and stir to combine. Set aside.

7. Fill each fig "shell" with the foie gras mixture. (The figs may be prepared up to this point and stored, covered and refrigerated, for up to 2 days.)

8. When ready to serve, place the filled figs in the preheated oven and bake for 4 minutes, or just until barely warmed through.

9. Remove from the oven and place a dollop of the reserved fig-honey mixture on top of each fig. Garnish with a few pieces of the mint chiffonade and serve warm.

NOTES: *Foie gras mousse is available from D'Artagnan (see Sources, page 335), from some fine butchers, and at specialty food stores.*

White truffle honey is available at specialty food stores.

Warm Poppy Crisps with Red Wine–Shallot Marmalade

Makes 30

. . . .

1 large egg

1 tablespoon water

$^1/_4$ cup poppy seeds

$^1/_4$ cup yellow cornmeal

2 sheets frozen puff pastry, thawed according to package directions

Red Wine–Shallot Marmalade (recipe follows)

1. Place the egg in a small mixing bowl. Whisk in the water until well blended.

2. Combine the poppy seeds and the cornmeal in a small mixing bowl. Set aside.

3. Lay each piece of puff pastry out on a clean, dry work surface. Using a pastry brush, lightly coat the pastry with the egg wash. Sprinkle the poppy seed–cornmeal mixture over the pastry and, using the palms of your hands, press the mixture into the pastry.

4. Carefully flip each piece of coated pastry. Spread the marmalade over each piece in an even layer.

5. Using a sharp knife, cut each piece of pastry in half lengthwise, making two rectangles of equal size. Working with 1 piece at a time, roll each long side about one-quarter of the way in toward the center, then roll in again until the two sides meet each other in the center. Flip over one last time, so that the top side is flat, and the bottom of the roll has two sections. Wrap each roll in plastic and place in the freezer for at least 2 hours or up to 3 months.

6. When ready to bake, preheat the oven to 375°F. Line 2 baking sheets with parchment paper or use nonstick baking sheets.

7. Unwrap the frozen pastry rolls and cut each one crosswise into $1/4$-inch-thick slices. Place the pastry slices on the baking sheets, leaving at least $1/2$ inch between each piece.

8. Place in the preheated oven and bake for about 15 minutes, or until golden brown and crisp. Remove from the oven and serve warm.

RED WINE—SHALLOT MARMALADE

2 tablespoons blended oil (half olive oil and half vegetable oil)

2 pounds shallots, peeled and finely diced

1 cup dry red wine

1 cup port wine

2 tablespoons red wine vinegar

2 tablespoons balsamic vinegar

$^1/_2$ cup sugar

1. Heat the oil in a heavy-bottomed saucepan over medium heat. Add the shallots and sauté for about 5 minutes, or just until soft. Add the red and port wines along with the red wine and balsamic vinegars. Stir in the sugar and bring to a boil. Lower the heat and simmer for about 20 minutes, or until the mixture is thick and syrupy, taking care that the sugar does not scorch. Remove from the heat and set aside to cool.

2. When cool, use as directed in the master recipe, serve as a condiment with meat or game, or cover and refrigerate for up to 1 month.

Roasted Fingerling Potatoes with Wild Mushrooms

Makes 45

. . . .

15 large fingerling potatoes, peeled and cooked

1 tablespoon olive oil

4 ounces oyster, chanterelle, shiitake, or cremini mushrooms, or a mix,
      cleaned and chopped

2 tablespoons minced shallots

$^1/_4$ teaspoon minced garlic

$^1/_4$ cup crème fraîche (see Note)

2 tablespoons minced fresh chives

1 tablespoon heavy cream

1 tablespoon truffle oil, plus more for serving (see Note)

Coarse salt and freshly ground pepper

Forty-five 3-inch-long fresh chive points

1. Cut the ends off each of the fingerling potatoes to make neat almost-rectangles. Cut each potato crosswise into 3 equal pieces about 1 inch long. Using a demitasse spoon or a tiny melon baller, scoop out the center of each potato piece almost to the bottom to make 45 neat little potato cups. Reserve the scooped-out flesh.

2. Line 2 baking sheets with parchment paper or use nonstick baking sheets. Place the potato cups on the prepared sheets. Set aside.

3. Preheat the oven to 350°F.

4. Heat the olive oil in a large sauté pan over medium heat. Add the mushrooms, shallots, and garlic and sauté for about 3 minutes, or until the mushrooms and shallots have softened completely. Remove from the heat and set aside to cool.

5. Combine the cooled mushroom mixture, the reserved potato flesh, the crème fraîche, minced chives, heavy cream, and truffle oil in the bowl of a food processor fitted with the metal blade. Process, using quick on-and-off turns, just until blended. Season with salt and pepper to taste. Place in a pastry bag fitted with a scalloped tip.

6. Pipe an equal portion of the potato mixture into each of the potato cups, coming up about $1/4$ inch over the top. (The potatoes may be prepared up to this point and stored lightly covered and refrigerated.)

7. Place the filled potato cups in the preheated oven and bake for 6 minutes, or until slightly colored and hot in the center. Remove from the oven and, if desired, drizzle with truffle oil. Garnish each cup with a chive point and serve hot.

NOTE: *Crème fraîche and truffle oil are available at specialty food stores.*

Although *antipasto* simply means "before the meal" and can, in fact, be used to describe hors d'oeuvres or appetizers—both hot and cold—it has come to mean a large platter of assorted vegetables, meats, cheeses, salads, and pickled, marinated, or cured vegetables or fruits that are served with crusty bread or breadsticks. An antipasto platter is usually much more substantial than passed hors d'oeuvres and less formal than a plated appetizer.

Despite the fact that most antipasto platters, particularly those served in restaurants, feature Italian specialties, this does not have to be so. And even if it is, the foods can be Italian-inspired but far beyond the olives, roasted peppers, and sausages of my childhood. Most of the recipes that follow have some Italian ancestry, but they are a far reach from the old familiars.

In fact, when I make an antipasto, I like to pull together Italian-flavored dishes, then mix them with some French charcuterie, Asian pickles, and American standards. It's fun to include some sushi and sashimi along with cured and/or smoked meats. The truth is, an antipasto platter is the perfect place to bring many cultures together in harmony.

Balsamic-Glazed Cipollini Onions

Serves 6

2 pounds cipollini onions, peeled

$^1/_3$ cup extra-virgin olive oil

Coarse salt and freshly ground pepper

$^1/_2$ cup balsamic vinegar

1 tablespoon sugar

$^1/_4$ cup port wine

1 tablespoon chopped fresh rosemary

1. Preheat the oven to 450°F.

2. Combine the onions with the oil and salt and pepper to taste. Place the seasoned onions in a baking dish large enough to hold them in a single layer. Place in the preheated oven and roast for 15 minutes, or until well caramelized and tender. Remove from the oven and set aside to cool.

3. When the onions are cool enough to handle, peel off the outer layer. Place the onions in a serving bowl and set aside.

4. Heat the balsamic vinegar, sugar, and port wine in a small saucepan over medium heat. Cook for about 3 minutes, or until bubbly. Stir in the onions and continue to toss, covering the onions completely with the syrupy vinegar, until the liquid evaporates and the onions are glazed. Add the rosemary and season with salt and pepper to taste. (The onions may be prepared to this point up to a week in advance. Store covered and refrigerated. Bring to room temperature before serving.) Lay the onions out on a platter in a single layer to dry at room temperature for 30 minutes. Serve at room temperature.

Cauliflower Cresspeda
with Lemon-Pepper Aïoli

Serves 6

. . . .

1 head cauliflower, well washed and trimmed of all leaves

3 cups all-purpose flour

2 tablespoons baking powder

Coarse salt and freshly ground pepper

4 large eggs

$^1/_4$ cup freshly grated Parmesan cheese

About 1$^1/_2$ cups water

About 6 cups vegetable oil

Lemon-Pepper Aïoli (recipe follows) (optional)

1. Break the cauliflower into 4 large portions. Place in a saucepan with lightly salted cold water to cover by 2 inches. Place over medium-high heat and bring to a boil. Lower the heat and simmer for about 5 minutes, or just until tender when pierced with the point of a small, sharp knife. Remove from the heat and drain well. Place in a colander under cold running water to stop the cooking. Pat dry.

2. Break the cauliflower into small florets. Set aside.

3. Combine the flour and baking powder in a mixing bowl. Season with salt and pepper to taste.

4. Combine the eggs and grated cheese in another mixing bowl. Slowly whisk the egg mixture into the flour, adding as much water as needed to reach a pancake-batter consistency. Season with salt and pepper to taste.

5. Heat the oil in a deep fryer over high heat to 350°F on an instant-read thermometer.

6. Working with a few pieces at a time, dip the cauliflower florets into the batter and then drop them into the hot oil. Fry, turning occasionally, for about 3 minutes, or until golden and crisp. Using a slotted spoon, transfer the cauliflower to a double layer of paper towels to drain.

7. Serve warm with the lemon-pepper aïoli as a dipping sauce, if desired.

LEMON-PEPPER AÏOLI

2 large egg yolks

2 tablespoons fresh lemon juice, warmed

1 tablespoon white wine vinegar, warmed

2 tablespoons chopped fresh flat-leaf parsley

1 tablespoon freshly grated lemon zest

1 teaspoon coarsely ground pepper

$^{1}/_{2}$ teaspoon minced garlic

$^{1}/_{4}$ teaspoon ground turmeric

Coarse salt

$^{1}/_{2}$ to $^{3}/_{4}$ cup olive oil

1. Place the egg yolks in a blender. With the motor running, add the warm lemon juice and vinegar.

2. With the motor at the lowest speed, add the parsley, lemon zest, pepper, garlic, turmeric, and salt to taste. When all of the ingredients are blended, begin adding the oil in a slow, steady stream. Process until the mixture begins to resemble mayonnaise. Stop the motor immediately or the aïoli will get too hot and break up.

3. Scrape the aïoli from the blender into a small serving bowl. Serve immediately or cover and refrigerate for up to 1 day.

Roasted Beets with Ricotta Salata

Serves 6

. . . .

2 red beets

2 yellow beets

$^1/_2$ cup water

3 tablespoons olive oil

Coarse salt and freshly ground pepper

2 cloves garlic, peeled and minced

1 small red onion, peeled and diced

$^1/_2$ cup hazelnut oil

$^1/_4$ cup extra-virgin olive oil

$^1/_3$ cup apple cider vinegar

6 ounces *ricotta salata,* crumbled

$^1/_2$ cup chopped hazelnuts, toasted

2 tablespoons chopped fresh chives

1. Preheat the oven to 375°F.

2. Trim the tops (discard, or wash well and sauté in a little olive oil, salt, and pepper for a delicious extra on the antipasto platter) from the beets and wash the beets well. Pat dry. Place the beets in a baking dish with the water. Add the olive oil and salt and pepper to taste and toss to coat evenly. Place in the preheated oven and roast for about 1 hour, or until the beets are tender when pierced with the point of a small, sharp knife. Remove from the oven and set aside to cool.

3. When cool enough to handle, push the skins from the beets, keeping the two colors separate until ready to put the salad together. Cut the beets into quarters.

4. When ready to serve, combine the garlic and onion in a mixing bowl. Add the hazelnut oil, extra-virgin olive oil, and apple cider vinegar and toss to combine. Toss in the red and yellow beets and transfer to a serving bowl. Sprinkle with the *ricotta salata,* hazelnuts, and chives and serve.

Marinated Chickpeas with Roasted Garlic and Lemon

Serves 6

. . . .

$^1/_2$ cup olive oil

4 cloves garlic, peeled and quartered

1 teaspoon red pepper flakes

2 pounds cooked chickpeas (garbanzo beans), drained

1 small red onion, peeled and diced

1 red bell pepper, well washed, cored, seeded, and diced

Zest of 1 lemon

Coarse salt and freshly ground pepper

2 tablespoons Chianti vinegar or red wine vinegar, plus more to taste

Juice of 1 lemon, plus more to taste

$^1/_4$ cup chopped fresh flat-leaf parsley

1. Combine the oil and garlic in a small sauté pan and bring to a simmer over low heat. Cook at a bare simmer, tossing the garlic occasionally, for about 5 minutes, or until the garlic is evenly golden on all sides. Remove from the heat and add the red pepper flakes to the hot oil. Set aside to cool.

2. Place the chickpeas in a mixing bowl and add the onion, bell pepper, lemon zest, and salt and pepper to taste.

3. Pour in the cooled olive oil mixture. Add the vinegar and lemon juice and mix well to incorporate.

4. Stir in the chopped parsley, cover the mixture, and refrigerate for at least 1 hour or up to 1 day.

5. Taste and, if necessary, adjust the seasoning with lemon juice or vinegar and salt, before serving.

Serves 6

. . . .

2 1/2 cups fresh orange juice, strained

36 thin stalks asparagus, well washed and trimmed

1 cup fresh basil stems

1 1/4 cups olive oil

1/3 cup white balsamic vinegar

2 teaspoons Dijon mustard

Coarse salt and freshly ground pepper

1/2 cup basil chiffonade

1. Place the orange juice in a small saucepan over medium-high heat. Bring to a boil, then lower the heat and simmer for about 45 minutes, or until the juice has reduced to 1/2 cup. Remove from the heat, pour into a mixing bowl, and set aside to cool.

2. Bring a large pot of lightly salted cold water to a boil over high heat. Add the asparagus and blanch for 1 minute. Drain well and refresh under cold running water. Pat dry and set aside.

3. Combine the basil stems with 1 cup of the oil in a small saucepan over medium heat. Bring to a boil, then remove from the heat and set aside to steep for 10 minutes. Strain through a fine sieve, discarding the basil stems.

4. Add the vinegar and mustard to the cooled orange juice and whisk until well blended. Whisking constantly, beat in the flavored oil. Season with salt and pepper to taste and set aside.

5. Preheat and oil a grill.

6. Toss the asparagus with the remaining ¼ cup oil and season with salt and pepper to taste. Place on the hot grill and cook, turning frequently, for about 4 minutes, or just until al dente. (The grilling time will depend on the thickness of the asparagus.)

7. Transfer the asparagus to a serving platter. Whisk the vinaigrette and then pour it over the warm asparagus. Toss to coat. Sprinkle the basil chiffonade over the top and serve warm or at room temperature.

Chafing dishes are most often used on a buffet table for informal parties at home or for large parties where full table service is not possible. Chafing dishes, which are easily rented, make service an absolute snap: less staff is needed to serve, or guests can simply help themselves. When planning recipes for a chafing dish, you need to make sure that they can withstand sitting over a fairly constant low heat without drying out and that they have enough texture and color to stay fresh-looking throughout service.

When entertaining at home, a buffet offers the opportunity to use beautiful linens and a combination of plates and serving pieces, since the buffet table does not require the formality of a traditionally set table. If the buffet table is not large enough to hold both dining pieces and serving pieces, use a smaller side table for plates, silverware, and napkins. If you are serving dessert from the same buffet table, be certain to remove all other dishes and, if necessary, cover the table with clean linens. If space allows, present the dessert buffet in another setting, along with coffee and tea.

Here are some pointers for a successful buffet:

Make a list of all the items required—food, beverages, ice, serving pieces.

Plan for an excess of plates, glass, silverware, and napkins—two to three times the number of guests will ensure that no one has to look for a clean plate.

The buffet table should feature three to four entrées and four to five accompaniments such as salads, starches, and/or vegetables. This is the perfect time to introduce foods from other cultures along with their side dishes. Bread, butter, and condiments can be placed around the chafing dishes.

Prepare a printed menu that can sit on the buffet so that guests can easily identify their choices.

Prepare the decor for the table so that the entire buffet is a balance of color and texture.

Set the table up the day before the event. This will give you time to select varying levels for stacking plates and serving pieces and to use your space wisely.

Place food items in a sensible order—cold items and salads, then entrées and sides, and so on.

Refill the chafing dishes often to keep the dishes looking fresh and inviting. Make sure hot items remain hot and cold remain cold.

As the party goes on, condense the dishes or platters into smaller containers so that the buffet table remains attractive.

Seared Baby Chicken with Monterey Jack Spoon Bread

Serves 6 as an entrée; 12 on a buffet table

This is a terrific chafing-dish recipe that combines two favorite flavors—almost-fried chicken and corn. You can adjust the heat as you wish, cutting out or adding chili peppers to lower the thermostat or build a fire. Since the spoon bread can be made in advance, this is a snap to put together for easy entertaining.

Six 1^1/$_2$ pound *poussins* (baby chickens) or Cornish game hens,
    split in half and deboned, well washed and dried

5 shallots, peeled and sliced

4 cloves garlic, peeled and crushed

2 bay leaves

2 jalapeño chili peppers, well washed, stems removed,
    seeded (if desired), and chopped

1 ancho chili pepper, stem removed, crushed

^{1}/$_2$ cup roughly chopped fresh flat-leaf parsley

2 tablespoons roughly chopped fresh thyme

2 tablespoons roughly chopped fresh rosemary

1 tablespoon black peppercorns

1^1/$_2$ cups blended oil (half olive oil and half vegetable oil)

4 tablespoons (^{1}/$_2$ stick) unsalted butter

Coarse salt and freshly ground pepper

Monterey Jack Spoon Bread (recipe follows)

1. Place the chicken halves in a large bowl or plastic container with a lid. Add the shallots, garlic, bay leaves, jalapeños, ancho, parsley, thyme, rosemary, and peppercorns. Pour the oil over the top and toss vigorously to combine. Cover and refrigerate for 8 hours or up to 24 hours.

2. Preheat the oven to 400°F. Using the butter, generously coat two baking pans. Set aside.

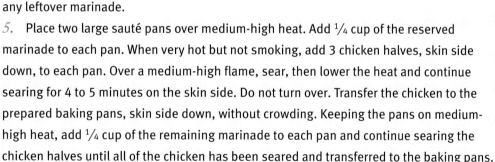

3. Remove the chicken halves from the refrigerator, uncover, and lift from the marinade. Using paper towels, pat the chicken dry. Season with salt and pepper to taste and set aside.

4. Strain the marinade through a fine sieve. Measure out and set aside 1 cup. Discard the solids along with any leftover marinade.

5. Place two large sauté pans over medium-high heat. Add ¼ cup of the reserved marinade to each pan. When very hot but not smoking, add 3 chicken halves, skin side down, to each pan. Over a medium-high flame, sear, then lower the heat and continue searing for 4 to 5 minutes on the skin side. Do not turn over. Transfer the chicken to the prepared baking pans, skin side down, without crowding. Keeping the pans on medium-high heat, add ¼ cup of the remaining marinade to each pan and continue searing the chicken halves until all of the chicken has been seared and transferred to the baking pans.

6. Place the chicken in the preheated oven and bake for 12 minutes, or until the skin is very crisp and the chicken is cooked through but still moist.

7. Place the chicken halves on top of the spoon bread and transfer to the chafing-dish container placed over the heat source. Garnish the dish and serve.

12 tablespoons (1 1/2 sticks) unsalted butter

3 shallots, peeled and chopped

2 jalapeño chili peppers, well washed, stems removed, seeded,
    and chopped

1 clove garlic, peeled and chopped

2 cups fresh corn kernels (or thawed frozen corn kernels)

5 cups milk

1 cup yellow cornmeal

1/4 cup bourbon

2 tablespoons light molasses

Coarse salt and freshly ground pepper

8 large eggs, separated

2 cups grated Monterey Jack cheese

1. Heat 2 tablespoons of the butter in a large saucepan over medium heat. Add the shallots, jalapeños, garlic, and corn kernels and sauté for about 3 minutes, or just until the vegetables have softened.

2. Add the milk and bring to a boil. Immediately whisk in the cornmeal and cook, stirring constantly, for about 2 minutes, or until the cornmeal begins to thicken. Stir in the bourbon and molasses along with 8 tablespoons of the remaining butter, beating until well incorporated. Season with salt and pepper to taste, remove from the heat, and allow to cool.

3. Preheat the oven to 350°F. Using the remaining 2 tablespoons butter, lightly grease a 12 × 9-inch baking dish. Set aside.

4. Using a wooden spoon, beat the egg yolks into the cooled cornmeal mixture. When well incorporated, beat in the cheese. Taste and, if necessary, adjust the seasoning with salt and pepper.

5.   Using an electric mixer, beat the egg whites until soft peaks form. Gently fold the beaten egg whites into the cornmeal mixture.

6.   Spoon the batter into the prepared dish, using a spatula to smooth the top slightly. (The spoon bread can be made up to this point and stored, covered and refrigerated, for up to 2 days.)

7.   Place in the preheated oven and bake for 25 minutes, or until the top is golden and the edge is bubbling. Remove from the heat and place in the chafing dish, if using. If not using a chafing dish, remove from the oven and allow to cool for about 10 minutes before cutting into squares. Serve hot.

Filet Mignon with Horseradish Whipped Potatoes and Mushrooms and Pearl Onions

W ho doesn't love a piece of roast beef and mashed potatoes? This is a very elegant chafing-dish recipe that is perfect for more formal occasions. You can easily double or triple the potato and mushroom recipes and it is simple to roast up another filet for a crowd.

Serves 6 as an entrée;
12 on a buffet table

. . . .

One 5-pound tenderloin of beef, silver skin and fat removed,
   tied for roasting
1 cup blended oil (half olive oil and half vegetable oil)
4 shallots, peeled and sliced
4 cloves garlic, peeled and crushed
4 sprigs fresh thyme
4 sprigs fresh rosemary
2 bay leaves
$^1/_4$ cup chopped fresh flat-leaf parsley
2 tablespoons black peppercorns
Coarse salt and freshly ground pepper
Mushrooms and Pearl Onions (recipe follows)
Horseradish Whipped Potatoes (recipe follows)
$^1/_4$ cup chopped fresh chives

1. Place the tenderloin in a shallow container with a lid.

2. Combine the oil, shallots, garlic, thyme, rosemary, bay leaves, parsley, and peppercorns. Pour the oil mixture over the tenderloin and turn the meat over so that all sides are coated. Cover and refrigerate for at least 12 hours or up to 2 days, turning occasionally.

3. When ready to cook, preheat the oven to 450°F.

4. Remove the meat from the marinade and, using a paper towel, pat off any excess oil. Season with salt and pepper to taste.

5. Place the meat on a rack in a roasting pan. Place in the preheated oven and bake for about 25 minutes, or until an instant-read thermometer inserted into the thickest part of the meat reads 135°F for rare. (The meat will continue to cook after it is removed from the oven.) Remove from the oven and allow to rest for 5 minutes.

6. Untie the meat and, using a sharp knife, cut crosswise into ½-inch-thick slices. Lay the slices out, slightly overlapping, down the center of the chafing dish, making two adjoining lines, if necessary. Spoon the mushrooms and pearl onions over the meat and either spoon or pipe (using a pastry bag fitted with a large decorative tip) the whipped potatoes down each side. Transfer to the chafing-dish container placed over the heat source. Garnish with chopped chives.

1 tablespoon vegetable oil

8 ounces slab bacon, cut into $^1/_4$–inch dice

5 small shallots, peeled and minced

2 cups sliced cremini mushrooms

2 cups sliced button mushrooms

Coarse salt and freshly ground pepper

2 cups red or white pearl onions, blanched

$^1/_4$ cup chopped fresh chives

1. Heat the oil in a large sauté pan over medium heat. Add the bacon and sauté for about 6 minutes, or until the fat has been rendered and the bacon is very crisp. Using a slotted spoon, lift the bacon from the pan and transfer to a double layer of paper towels to drain.

2. Add the shallots to the fat in the pan and sauté for 2 minutes. Add the cremini and button mushrooms, season with salt and pepper to taste, and sauté for 5 minutes, or until the mushrooms have wilted. Stir in the pearl onions and sauté for 4 minutes more, or until the mushrooms have taken on some color and the onions are hot.

3. Remove from the heat. Add the reserved bacon and the chives and toss to coat. Taste and, if necessary, adjust the seasoning with salt and pepper. Serve hot.

HORSERADISH WHIPPED POTATOES

....

6 large Idaho potatoes, peeled and quartered

1 cup heavy cream

4 tablespoons ($^1/_2$ stick) unsalted butter

$^1/_4$ cup drained prepared horseradish, plus more to taste

Coarse salt and freshly ground pepper

1. Place the potatoes in a pot with lightly salted cold water to cover and bring to a boil over medium-high heat. Lower the heat and simmer for about 15 minutes, or until the potatoes are tender when pierced with the point of a small, sharp knife. Remove from the heat and drain well.

2. While the potatoes are cooking, combine the cream, butter, and horseradish in a small saucepan over low heat, stirring until the butter has melted. Remove from the heat and keep warm.

3. Place the hot potatoes in a ricer or food mill. Push the potatoes through the ricer or mill into a mixing bowl. Beating constantly, slowly add the cream mixture, beating until the potatoes are smooth and creamy. (Depending upon the moisture in the potatoes, you may not use all of the cream.) Season with salt and pepper to taste and, if necessary, additional horseradish.

4. Serve immediately or transfer to the top half of a double boiler over very hot water, cover lightly, and keep warm until ready to serve.

Fennel–Dusted Halibut with Flageolet Beans and Rock Shrimp and Lemon Vinaigrette

The delicate, slight licorice flavor of the fennel pollen adds a bit of intrigue to an otherwise quite simple dish. Halibut, being a very firm fish, can stand up well in a chafing dish, and the vinaigrette will add the necessary moisture.

This dish is a rather complex combination, but the three main elements—the succulent halibut, the slightly sweet beans, and the slightly salty shrimp—blend beautifully. The combination also stands up well to the heat of the chafing dish, but if it does

12 on a buffet table

begin to dry, drizzle a bit of extra-virgin olive oil over the top.

If you haven't tried them, flageolets, which are simply French kidney beans, are extremely tasty, with a very gentle, almost-green flavor. They are now sometimes available fresh or frozen in specialty food stores. If you find them, by all means use them—obviously without the presoak and long cooking time.

^{1}/$_2$ cup olive oil

2 shallots, peeled and finely minced

Juice and grated zest of 2 lemons

2 tablespoons white wine vinegar

^{1}/$_4$ cup chopped fresh chervil

Coarse salt and freshly ground pepper

Six 7–ounce halibut fillets

6 tablespoons fennel pollen, or ^{1}/$_2$ cup ground fennel (see Note)

2 tablespoons unsalted butter

Flageolet Beans with Rock Shrimp (recipe follows)

1. Heat ¼ cup of the oil in a saucepan over low heat. When the oil is hot, add the shallots and sauté for 3 minutes, or just until softened. Remove from the heat and allow to cool.

2. When the oil is cool, whisk in the lemon juice and zest, the vinegar, and 2 tablespoons of the chervil just until combined but not emulsified. Season with salt and pepper to taste.

3. Sprinkle the top of each halibut fillet with 1 tablespoon of the fennel pollen, rubbing it into the fish until it adheres. Season with salt and pepper to taste.

4. Preheat the oven to 350°F.

5. Heat two large ovenproof sauté pans over medium heat. Add the remaining 2 tablespoons of the olive oil to each of the pans. When very hot, add 3 fillets to each pan, seasoned side down, and sear for about 4 minutes, or until nicely colored.

6. Using a fish spatula, flip each fillet. Add 1 tablespoon of butter to each pan and place in the preheated oven. Bake for about 7 minutes, or just until the fish is barely cooked on the edges and the center remains almost raw. (The fish will continue to cook in the chafing dish.)

7. Remove the halibut from the oven and place over the beans and shrimp in the chafing dish. Transfer the dish to the chafing-dish container placed over the heat source.

8. Add the remaining 2 tablespoons chervil to the lemon vinaigrette. Spoon the sauce over the halibut and serve.

NOTE: *Fennel pollen, a delicately flavored Mediterranean seasoning, is available from specialty food stores.*

FLAGEOLET BEANS AND ROCK SHRIMP

. . . .

1 pound dried flageolet beans, well washed

2 ribs celery, well washed, trimmed, and cut in half crosswise

2 cloves garlic, peeled and smashed

1 onion, peeled and quartered

1 large carrot, peeled, trimmed, and quartered

1 tablespoon roughly chopped fresh thyme

2 quarts water

Coarse salt and freshly ground pepper

$^1/_4$ cup olive oil

4 small shallots, peeled and minced

1 teaspoon minced garlic

2 pounds rock shrimp, peeled and deveined

$^1/_2$ cup dry white wine

1 cup clam juice

3 tablespoons fresh lemon juice

2 tablespoons unsalted butter, softened

2 tablespoons minced fresh herbs (such as chervil, parsley, or chives,
     or a mixture, as desired)

1 tablespoon freshly grated lemon zest

1. Place the beans in cold water to cover by 2 inches and set aside to soak for 8 hours.

2. Drain the beans, discarding the soaking water. Place the beans in a large, heavy-bottomed saucepan. Add the celery, smashed garlic, quartered onion, carrot, and thyme. Add the water and place over high heat. Bring to a boil. Cover, lower the heat, and simmer for 45 minutes. Uncover and simmer for 10 minutes more, or just until the beans are tender. Season with salt and pepper to taste.

3. Remove the beans from the heat. Drain well, reserving 1 cup of the cooking liquid. Pick out and reserve the celery, garlic, onion, and carrot. Set the beans aside.

4. Cut the reserved celery, garlic, onion, and carrot into a fine dice and set aside.

5. Heat the oil in a large sauté pan over medium heat. Add the shallots and the minced garlic and sauté for 3 minutes, or just until the aromatics have sweat their liquid. Raise the heat to medium, stir in the shrimp, and sauté for 1 minute, or just until the shrimp begin to turn white. Add the wine and bring to a boil.

6. Stir in the reserved beans and then the clam juice, lemon juice, and butter. Bring to a simmer and simmer for 2 minutes.

7. Remove from the heat, taste, and, if necessary, season with additional salt and pepper. Spoon the mixture into a chafing dish. Stir in the reserved diced vegetables and garnish the top with the fresh herbs and the lemon zest. Follow the directions for serving in the master recipe, or if using without the halibut, transfer to the chafing-dish container placed over the heat source and serve.

Artichoke and Cheese Ravioli with Preserved Artichokes

This is bit more upscale than traditional cheese ravioli with red sauce. The rich butter sauce keeps the ravioli moist as it sits in a chafing dish. Don't overcook the tomatoes when heating them, as you want them to hold their shape in the dish.

Serves 6 as an entrée; 12 on a buffet table

2 cups vegetable or chicken broth

$^1/_2$ cup dry white wine

5 tablespoons balsamic vinegar

2 tablespoons roasted garlic puree

2 tablespoons fresh lemon juice

5 tablespoons unsalted butter

Coarse salt and freshly ground pepper

1 large leek (white part only), well washed and diced

One 16-ounce package frozen artichoke hearts, thawed, drained well, and quartered

1 pint red teardrop tomatoes, well washed and dried

1 pint yellow teardrop tomatoes, well washed and dried

Artichoke and Cheese Ravioli (recipe follows)

Preserved Artichokes (recipe follows)

$^1/_4$ cup chopped fresh chives

1.   Place the broth, wine, balsamic vinegar, garlic puree, and lemon juice in a small saucepan over medium-high heat. Bring to a boil and boil until reduced by half.

2.   Transfer the mixture to a blender and add 4 tablespoons of the butter. Process until the butter is incorporated. Season with salt and pepper to taste and place in the top half of a double boiler over hot water to keep warm.

3.   Heat the remaining 1 tablespoon butter in a large nonstick sauté pan over medium heat. Add the leek and sauté for 2 minutes, or just until softened. Add the artichoke hearts and sauté for about 5 minutes, or until golden. Add the red and yellow tomatoes and toss briefly just to combine. Add 1 cup of the reserved reduced sauce and cook for just a couple of minutes to heat through.

4.   Remove from the heat and strain through a fine sieve, separately reserving the vegetables and the sauce. If any of the reserved sauce remains, add it to the strained sauce.

5.   Place the vegetables in the center of the chafing dish. Spoon 30 ravioli over the vegetables and pour the sauce over the ravioli. Spoon the preserved artichokes around the edge of the dish and sprinkle the top with the chopped chives. Transfer to the chafing-dish container placed over the heat source.

ARTICHOKE AND CHEESE RAVIOLI

. . . .

¹/₄ cup olive oil

3 small shallots, peeled and minced

2 cloves garlic, peeled and minced

One 16-ounce can artichoke hearts, drained and quartered

Coarse salt and freshly ground pepper

¹/₂ cup mascarpone cheese

¹/₂ cup goat cheese or ricotta cheese

2 tablespoons freshly grated Parmesan cheese

2 tablespoons chopped fresh basil or flat-leaf parsley

1 egg

1 tablespoon water

6 sheets prepared pasta dough

1.   Heat 2 tablespoons of the oil in a large sauté pan over medium heat. Add the shallots and garlic and sauté for 2 minutes. Add the artichoke hearts, season with salt and pepper to taste, and sauté for 4 minutes, or just until the vegetables are beginning to color. Remove from the heat and allow to cool.

2.   When the artichoke mixture is cool, transfer to the bowl of a food processor fitted with the metal blade. Add the mascarpone, the goat cheese, and the Parmesan and process until smooth. Add the basil and give a quick pulse to incorporate. Scrape the mixture from the food processor bowl into a pastry bag fitted with a large plain tip. Set aside.

3.   Beat the egg with the water and set aside.

4.   Cover a ravioli mold with 1 sheet of the pasta dough. Pipe about a teaspoonful of the cheese mixture into each ravioli square. Using a pastry brush, lightly brush the corners of each ravioli with the egg wash. Cover the filled pasta sheet with another sheet of pasta dough and either press down to enclose or gently roll a rolling pin over the top to seal. Using a sharp knife, cut the sheets into individual ravioli. Continue making ravioli until you have used all of the filling. (The ravioli can be made up to this point and stored, covered and refrigerated, for 1 day, or frozen for up to 3 months.)

5. Place the ravioli in a large pot of rapidly boiling, lightly salted water. Return to a boil and boil for about 4 minutes, or until the ravioli float to the top. Drain well through a colander. Transfer the ravioli to a bowl, drizzle with the remaining 2 tablespoons olive oil, and season with salt and pepper to taste. Keep warm until ready to serve.

PRESERVED ARTICHOKES

2 tablespoons fresh lemon juice

12 baby artichokes with stems

2 cloves garlic, peeled

2 sprigs fresh rosemary

2 sprigs fresh thyme

1 lemon, well washed and quartered lengthwise

1 bay leaf

$^3/_4$ cup dry white wine

About 4 cups extra-virgin olive oil

1. Add the lemon juice to a large bowl of cold water. Set aside.

2. Wash the artichokes well. Using a sharp knife, cut the top off each artichoke. Trim off the tough outer leaves and peel the tough outer skin from the stem. Trim around the bottom to make a small, tight artichoke. Place the trimmed artichokes in the acidulated water.

3. Preheat the oven to 375°F.

4. Drain the artichokes well and place in a shallow baking dish large enough to hold them in a single layer. Add the garlic, rosemary, thyme, lemon quarters, and bay leaf. Pour the wine over the top and toss to combine. Pour in enough oil to just cover the artichokes.

5. Place the artichokes in the preheated oven and bake for about 40 minutes, or until the artichokes are very tender when pierced with the point of a small, sharp knife.

6. Remove from the oven and place on a wire rack to cool. When cool, transfer to a nonreactive container and store with oil, covered and refrigerated, for up to 1 month.

7. When ready to serve, remove from the refrigerator and bring to room temperature. Serve the artichokes whole or cut into quarters lengthwise.

NOTE: *Preserved artichokes may be used as is in salads or sandwiches or quickly sautéed to brown slightly for use in pasta or rice dishes. The flavored oil may be used in vinaigrettes or to sauté poultry or fish.*

Brooklyn Block Party

I moved to the Carroll Gardens neighborhood of Brooklyn while working at the River Café in 1984 and have never left. I love its diversity, strong immigrant population, and ethnic grab bag. Each street has its own defining mix in ethnicity, language, food, and fun. Carroll Gardens, with its strong Italian roots, has been my home base throughout my travels—it is where I have chosen to raise my children, and it is the place that keeps me grounded in the traditions of my own heritage.

Carroll Gardens has a strong sense of community that is often very hard to find in urban areas. I live on a small block in a neighborhood full of classic brownstones. Our little street could easily be a side street in southern Italy. Many of our neighbors are related and live in houses that have been family-owned for over 100 years. Residents are mostly craftsmen—electricians, carpenters, plumbers, general contractors—and when I renovated our house, everyone lent a hand. I felt like an Amish man at a barn raising.

I started throwing simple block-related parties for family occasions because our houses were too small to welcome our extended families. We'd line tables down the length of the block, everyone would contribute food and drink, and we'd celebrate birthdays, anniversaries, christenings, and even weddings. Someone would deejay and dancing was enjoyed by both the young and the old.

What ultimately became the first annual block party was thrown for my friend and fellow chef Michael Mina's

thirtieth birthday. It happened to fall on the same weekend that the James Beard awards were being held in Manhattan, so everyone was in town. We invited all of our friends and fellow chefs to the festivities. The food was prepared at the Tribeca Grill, we provided the drink, and over 200 people showed up. Since the local Court Street Festival was going on a block away, we had two parties in one, and even more people showed up.

The party was such a success that we decided to throw it every year. It was a relaxed, fun alternative to the more formal activities surrounding the Beard awards, plus families were welcome. Since our neighborhood church, Saint Mary's Star of the Sea, was in dire need of repairs, we decided to turn the block party into a fund-raiser for the church. We had a real street festival in the works.

As word of the party got around, everyone wanted to come. Our block welcomed all of the local politicians as well as chefs from all over the world. It became the yearly get-together, catch-up-on-news hospitality event. It was fun to share part of my home and neigh-borhood with chefs whom I had worked with on

charity events in their towns and who had often opened their homes and hearts to me. The block party was a great way for me to reciprocate their acts of generosity as well as to introduce them to Brooklyn and to show off my home.

Eventually the party grew to more than we could handle. We had to enlist the help of purveyors and local restaurants, who, as expected, generously donated not only food and drink but their time, as well as selling raffles to benefit the church. The Brooklyn Brewery and Brooklyn Soda lent their names as well as cases of liquid refreshment. It was such fun to see the church ladies and neighborhood characters mingle with the chefs. Everyone had a terrific time and the church got a new roof. Now that's fusion!

Pizza with Toppings

On a trip to Naples, I bought a wood-burning pizza oven that has, ever since being installed in my tiny backyard, provided the reason for many, many parties, particularly for the neighborhood kids. I make the dough and the sauce and then usually put out just a bunch of toppings and let them make their own.

One year, at the block party, the French contingent (Daniel Boulud and Jean-Louis Palladin, among others) took over the oven, making very "haute" pizzas. From our second-story terrace, a peanut gallery of the little ones had convened to watch. As the chefs were finalizing their masterpieces, the kids started screaming in disgust, "Youse guys don't know whacha doin'. That ain't pizza. We gotta come down and show ya how to make real pizza." Here's real pizza!

Makes 1

1 package active dry yeast

1 cup warm (115° to 120°F) water

About 3 cups all–purpose flour

2 tablespoons olive oil

¹/₂ teaspoon coarse salt

Vegetable oil

Pizza Sauce (recipe follows)

Pizza toppings (see Notes, page 264)

1. Place the yeast in the warm water in a large mixing bowl, stirring to dissolve. Using a wooden spoon, beat in 1 cup of the flour along with the olive oil and salt. When blended, beat in 1 cup of the remaining flour. The dough should begin to pull away from the sides of the bowl, forming a soft, sticky mass.

2. Sprinkle $\frac{1}{2}$ cup of the remaining flour over a clean, dry work surface, using your hands to spread it out so that they are lightly covered with flour. Scoop the dough from the bowl and sprinkle with a little bit of the remaining $\frac{1}{2}$ cup flour. Knead with your hands, adding flour as needed to make a dough that no longer sticks to your hands. (Alternately, the dough can be made in a heavy-duty electric mixer fitted with a dough hook or in a food processor fitted with the metal blade.)

3. When the dough is no longer sticky, push the heel of your hand down into the center and hold it for 10 seconds. If your hand comes up clean, the dough is ready. If the dough sticks to your hand, add a bit more flour and continue to knead until the 10-second test yields a clean hand. Shape the dough into a ball.

4. Lightly coat a large mixing bowl with vegetable oil. Roll the dough ball around the bowl to lightly coat it with oil and then place the dough in the center of the bowl. Tightly cover the entire bowl with plastic wrap. Place the dough in a warm, dry spot to rise for 45 minutes, or until doubled in size.

5. Remove the dough from the bowl and, using your fist, punch the dough down to deflate it. Knead the dough for 1 minute. (At this point, the dough can be wrapped in plastic and stored, refrigerated, for a day or two, or frozen for up to 3 months.)

6. Preheat the oven to 500°F. If using pizza stones, place them in the oven to preheat also.

7. Begin stretching the dough, pulling from the center out, until you have a circle about $\frac{1}{8}$ inch thick. Fit the dough into a large pizza pan. (Alternately, you can make a free-form pizza crust and, using a pizza or bread peel, transfer the prepared pizza directly to pizza stones or a baking sheet in the hot oven.)

8. Spoon the pizza sauce onto the prepared dough, using a spatula or the back of a large spoon to evenly spread it over the dough. Add any toppings desired and place in the preheated oven to bake for about 12 minutes, or until the crust is crisp and beginning to char slightly and the topping is bubbling hot.

9. Remove from the oven, cut into slices, and serve.

One 28-ounce can San Marzano whole peeled tomatoes,
with juice

2 fresh basil leaves, well washed and torn into pieces

1 clove garlic, peeled and minced (see Notes)

2 tablespoons tomato paste

1 teaspoon dried oregano

$^1/_2$ teaspoon freshly ground pepper

Coarse salt

1. Place the tomatoes in a saucepan (see Notes). Using your hands, crush the tomatoes until no large pieces remain.

2. Place the pan over medium heat and stir in the basil, garlic, tomato paste, oregano, pepper, and salt to taste. Bring to a simmer, then lower the heat and cook at a bare simmer, stirring frequently, for 15 minutes.

3. Remove from the heat and set aside to cool before using. (The pizza sauce may be made in advance of use and stored, covered and refrigerated, for up to 5 days, or frozen for up to 3 months.)

NOTES: *Almost anything can be a pizza topping. Some tasty combinations are as follows: crumbled Italian sausage, mushrooms, and onions with mozzarella or Parmesan cheese; grilled eggplant, grilled zucchini, sun-dried tomatoes, and mozzarella; baby artichokes, mushrooms, and tomatoes with smoked mozzarella; spinach and prosciutto with goat cheese; caramelized onions, gorgonzola cheese, and rosemary. You can forget about the sauce entirely and make white pizzas, which might be something like fontina,* taleggio, *ricotta, and mozzarella cheeses with basil and parsley; ricotta, mozzarella, and Parmesan with broccoli rabe; or mixed cheeses with anchovies, spinach, olives, and cracked black peppercorns.*

Feel free to add lots of garlic, if desired. Also, roasted garlic adds a sweetness that balances the acidity of the tomatoes. For a more aromatic flavor, you can add a small onion that has been sautéed in olive oil.

Many pizza cooks do not cook their sauce, as they feel that it tastes fresher if it has its first cooking in the hot oven. I do both cooked and uncooked sauces as well as one using raw tomatoes when they are dead ripe and juicy.

Pierogi

Almost every cuisine has some type of filled dough that is either fried or boiled: Italians have ravioli, Chinese eat wontons, Jews savor kreplach, Latins have empanadas, and Poles treasure their pierogi. In Brooklyn, there are a good number of Eastern Europeans, so we always include pierogi on our block-party menu. I call them Polish ravioli, but my Polish friends insist that ravioli are Italian pierogi! You can put almost any filling in a pierogi—meat, cabbage, cheese, sauerkraut, even fruit for a handheld dessert or snack.

Makes about 30

. . . .

1 package active dry yeast

²/₃ cup warm (115° to 120°F) water

1 large egg, beaten

4 tablespoons (¹/₂ stick) unsalted butter, melted

1 teaspoon coarse salt

2¹/₄ to 2¹/₂ cups all-purpose flour

¹/₄ cup vegetable oil, plus more for coating bowl

Egg and Scallion Filling (recipe follows)

8 tablespoons (1 stick) unsalted butter, cubed

Freshly ground pepper

1 cup chopped scallions

2 cups sour cream (optional)

1. Place the yeast in the warm water in a mixing bowl, stirring to dissolve. Let rest for 5 minutes.

2. Whisk in the egg, melted butter, and salt and blend well.

3. Begin adding the flour, 1 cup at a time, beating with a wooden spoon to incorporate the flour into the liquid. When a soft dough has formed, scrape the dough from the bowl onto a lightly floured work surface and knead until it is smooth and elastic. (This may be done in a heavy-duty electric mixer fitted with a dough hook or in a food processor fitted with the metal blade.)

4. Lightly coat a large mixing bowl with vegetable oil. Place the dough inside, cover, and place in a warm, dry spot to rise for 1 hour, or until doubled in size.

5. Divide the dough in half. Working with one half at a time, roll the dough out on a lightly floured work surface to a circle about $1/8$ inch thick. Using a cookie cutter or a sharp knife, cut the dough into 3-inch circles or squares. You should have about 30 pieces.

6. Place 1 teaspoon of the egg and scallion filling in the center of each piece of dough. Fold the dough over the filling to create either a half-moon (with round pieces) or a triangle (with square pieces), pressing along the edge to seal the dough together.

7. Bring a large pot of lightly salted cold water to a boil over high heat. Add the pierogi, without crowding the pot, and boil for about 1 minute, or until they float to the top. Using a slotted spoon, lift the pierogi from the water and place in a colander. Immediately rinse under warm running water to prevent sticking. Pat dry.

8. Combine the butter and the $1/4$ cup vegetable oil in a large sauté pan over medium heat. Add the pierogi (in batches, if necessary) and fry, turning frequently, for about $1^1/2$ minutes, or until the pierogi are lightly browned. Season with salt and pepper to taste. Remove from the heat and place on a serving platter. Sprinkle the chopped scallions over the top and serve with the sour cream on the side, if desired.

EGG AND SCALLION FILLING

. . . .

8 hard-boiled eggs, peeled and chopped

1 1/2 cups chopped scallions

3 tablespoons sour cream, plus more as needed

Coarse salt and freshly ground pepper

1. Combine the eggs, scallions, sour cream, and salt and pepper to taste in a mixing bowl. If the mixture seems too dry, add additional sour cream, a teaspoonful at a time.

2. Cover and refrigerate until ready to use.

Dry-Rubbed Spareribs with Don's Barbecue Sauce

Serves 6

What is there to say about spareribs? Everybody loves them, and at the block party, we cook tons of them on our big grills. And someone always complains that we haven't cooked enough! I sometimes even cook up a batch in my pizza oven to get that real down-home smoky flavor.

I sometimes coat my ribs with the dry rub and let them marinate for a couple of days so that the spices really dig right down into the meat.

2 slabs baby back pork spareribs
Dry Rub (recipe follows)
Don's Barbecue Sauce (recipe follows)

1. Preheat the oven to 275°F.
2. Either leave the slabs whole or cut them into individual ribs. If you are cooking on a grill, it is usually easier if the slabs are left whole.
3. Generously rub each side of the ribs with the dry rub. Place the ribs on nonstick baking pans in the preheated oven and bake for about 2½ hours, or until very tender.
4. Remove from the oven and wrap tightly with aluminum foil until ready to grill.
5. Preheat and oil the grill.
6. Using a pastry brush, generously coat the ribs with the barbecue sauce. Place on the preheated grill and cook, turning and basting with sauce frequently, for about 10 minutes, or just until the ribs are beginning to char.
7. Remove from the grill and, if in slabs, cut into ribs, and serve.

DRY RUB

1 cup paprika

$^1/_2$ cup Old Bay seasoning

$^1/_4$ cup packed dark brown sugar

2 tablespoons coarse salt

1 tablespoon chili powder

1 tablespoon garlic powder

1 tablespoon onion powder

1 tablespoon cayenne pepper

Combine the paprika, Old Bay seasoning, brown sugar, salt, chili powder, garlic powder, onion powder, and cayenne in a small nonreactive container. Use immediately or store, tightly covered, in a cool, dark place for up to 1 month.

DON'S BARBECUE SAUCE

. . . .

10 small shallots, peeled and sliced

1 clove garlic, peeled

1 onion, peeled and sliced

1 jalapeño chili pepper, well washed, stem removed, seeded, and sliced

2 tablespoons peanut oil

2 cups veal broth or other rich meat broth (see Note)

1 cup packed dark brown sugar

4 cups ketchup

3 tablespoons red wine vinegar, plus more to taste

1 tablespoon dry mustard

Coarse salt

---

1. Combine the shallots, garlic, onion, and jalapeño in a blender (or food processor) and process to a smooth puree.

2. Heat the oil in a large saucepan over medium heat. Add the aromatic puree, lower the heat, and cook slowly, without stirring, for about 12 minutes, or until very fragrant but with no color.

3. Add the broth, raise the heat, and bring to a boil. Add the sugar and stir to dissolve. Lower the heat and simmer for 5 minutes. Stir in the ketchup, vinegar, and mustard and bring to a simmer. Simmer for 10 minutes. Taste and adjust the seasoning with salt and, if necessary, additional vinegar.

4. Remove from the heat and allow to cool before using. The sauce may be stored, covered and refrigerated, for up to 2 weeks.

NOTE: *Veal broth is available from quality butchers and at some specialty food stores.*

Anna Nurse's Ham

Anna Nurse, a wonderful Italian cook and teacher, contributed this ham to our first block party. She also makes this for an annual brunch at the James Beard House given to raise funds for culinary scholarships. My wife loves this ham so much that she frequently makes this beautifully glazed masterpiece for our family get-togethers. The syrup that remains in the pan can be saved and used as a glaze for sweet potatoes or yams, winter squash, or pork roasts.

Serves 15 to 20

. . . .

One 12- to 18-pound smoked ham

15 large whole cloves

3 cups pineapple juice

1 pound dark brown sugar

One 16-ounce bottle dark corn syrup

1. Preheat the oven to 325°F.

2. Place the ham in a large roasting pan, fat side up. Using a small, sharp knife, score the entire surface of the ham in a diamond pattern. Stick the whole cloves into the center of the scored sections. Pour the pineapple juice over the ham and bake the ham in the preheated oven for 1½ hours.

3. Remove the ham from the oven and carefully pat on the brown sugar to completely cover the top of the ham. Drizzle the corn syrup over the ham, taking care not to dislodge the sugar. Return the ham to the oven and continue to bake, basting with the pan juices every 15 minutes, for about 2$\frac{1}{2}$ hours (12 minutes per pound, or 4 hours total for a 20-pound ham).

4. Remove the ham from the oven and set aside for at least 30 minutes or until cooled, basting frequently. Serve hot, warm, or at room temperature.

Braised Escarole Casserole

Block parties are a great way to bring neighbors together, and everyone is welcome to bring a dish. Our small block is very close-knit, and sometimes neighbors, like Joy Boggio, become family. She made this dish for our first block party, and it has become a favorite "family" recipe.

Serves 6

. . . .

2 cups Italian Seasoned Bread Crumbs (page 30)

$^1/_2$ cup freshly grated Parmesan cheese

$^1/_2$ cup freshly grated Romano cheese

4 cloves garlic, peeled and minced

$^1/_4$ cup julienned fresh basil

1 teaspoon red pepper flakes

1 teaspoon dried oregano

Freshly ground pepper

About 1 cup extra-virgin olive oil

3 pounds escarole, well washed, dried, and cut into 2-inch pieces

Coarse salt

Juice of 1 lemon

1 cup water

1. Combine the bread crumbs with the Parmesan and Romano cheeses in a mixing bowl. Stir in the garlic, basil, red pepper flakes, oregano, and pepper to taste. Set aside.

2. Heat about $^1/_4$ cup of the oil in a large, heavy-bottomed saucepan over low heat. Add one-quarter of the escarole, pressing it down into the oil. Season with lemon juice and salt and pepper to taste. Sprinkle with one-quarter of the bread crumb mixture and drizzle with

¼ cup of the remaining olive oil. Continue layering until you have 4 complete layers. Pour the water over the top. Cover and cook, without stirring, over very low heat for about 1 hour, or until the escarole is very tender and the layers have melded together.

3. Turn off the heat and let the casserole rest for 15 minutes. Serve hot, warm, or at room temperature directly from the saucepan.

NOTE: *For best results, a pressure cooker can be used. Cooking time will be cut in half.*

Baked Cardoons

If you have never eaten cardoons, you are in for a treat. They taste like a perfect balance of artichoke, salsify, and celery. Quite common throughout the Mediterranean and recently available throughout the United States, cardoons can be found from midwinter through late spring. This dish always elicits lots of comments as diners try to guess what they are eating, so it is a great dinner-party conversation starter. This recipe does not require any salt, as both the cheeses and the anchovies are quite salty.

Serves 6

1 cup heavy cream

Juice of 1 lemon

2$^1/_2$ pounds cardoons

5 tablespoons unsalted butter, melted

6 anchovy fillets, minced

$^1/_2$ cup Italian Seasoned Bread Crumbs (page 30)

$^1/_2$ cup freshly grated Parmesan cheese

$^1/_4$ cup chopped fresh flat-leaf parsley

2 tablespoons chopped fresh mint

Freshly ground pepper

$^1/_2$ cup shredded mozzarella cheese

1. Place the heavy cream in a small saucepan over medium heat. Bring to a simmer and simmer for about 15 minutes, or until reduced by half, watching carefully so that the cream does not boil over. Remove from the heat and set aside.

2. Add the lemon juice to a large bowl of cold water. Set aside.

3. Cut the bottoms from the cardoons to release the individual stalks. Trim off and discard the tops and the thorny edges. Wash well. Using a vegetable peeler, peel down the outer side of each stalk to remove the stringy fibers. Cut each stalk crosswise into 2-inch-long pieces. Immediately place the pieces in the acidulated water to keep them from discoloring.

4. Bring a large pot of lightly salted cold water to a boil over high heat. Add the cardoons and return to a boil. Lower the heat and simmer for about 10 minutes, or just until barely tender. Do not overcook. Drain well and pat dry.

5. Preheat the oven to 350°F. Using 1 tablespoon of the melted butter, lightly coat the inside of a 13 × 9 × 2-inch baking dish. Set aside.

6. Combine the anchovies, bread crumbs, Parmesan cheese, parsley, and mint. Season with pepper to taste. Add the remaining 4 tablespoons melted butter and stir to moisten the mixture.

7. Arrange the cardoons on the bottom of the prepared baking dish. Sprinkle the bread crumb mixture over the cardoons, spreading it out in an even layer. Drizzle the reduced cream over the top. Sprinkle the mozzarella over all. Place in the preheated oven and bake for 25 minutes, or until the top is golden brown and bubbling. Remove from the oven and serve.

New Shoes' Seafood Salad

New Shoes is my nickname for Jimmy Canora, who has been my project manager for a number of years. Jimmy is quite a character and takes great pride in his wardrobe (therefore the nickname), but he also has a great sense of humor and can take teasing with a laugh. His family is from Naples and this is their recipe for the traditional *frutti di mare*. Jimmy has made it for the block party, for restaurant events, and for our own parties at home. I think it is the best seafood salad that I have ever tasted.

Serves 6 to 8

. . . .

2 cups dry white wine

Juice of 3 lemons, juiced separately, peel reserved, plus more to taste

2$^1\!/_2$ pounds squid, cleaned, tentacles cut in half and bodies cut into rings

1 pound medium shrimp, peeled and deveined

1 pound bay scallops

One 28-ounce can scungilli, drained and thinly sliced (see Note)

1 cup extra-virgin olive oil

2 teaspoons minced garlic

18 mussels, well scrubbed and beards removed (see Note, page 169)

18 littleneck clams, well scrubbed (see Note, page 169)

3 ribs celery, well washed, trimmed, and finely diced

3 cloves garlic, peeled and slivered

2 shallots, peeled and thinly sliced

2 cups finely diced, seeded, peeled tomatoes

2 tablespoons red wine vinegar, plus more to taste

Coarse salt and freshly ground pepper

$^1/_4$ cup chopped fresh flat–leaf parsley

$^1/_4$ cup fresh basil chiffonade

1 teaspoon red pepper flakes, or to taste

1. Bring 2 quarts of lightly salted cold water to a boil in a stockpot. Add 1 cup of the wine, the juice of 1 lemon, and some of the reserved lemon peel and again bring to a boil. Add the squid tentacles and rings and bring to a simmer. Simmer for 4 minutes. Do not let the water return to a boil or the squid will toughen. Using a slotted spoon, lift the squid from the water and place in a colander. Place under cold running water to stop the cooking. Pat dry and set aside.

2. Return the water to a boil. Add the shrimp and scallops and bring to a simmer. Simmer for 3 minutes, or just until the shrimp is brightly colored and the scallops are barely cooked. Using a slotted spoon, lift the shrimp and scallops from the water and place in a colander. Place under cold running water to stop the cooking. Pat dry and set aside. Return the water to a boil. Add the scungilli slices and boil for 1 minute, then remove from the water and stop the cooking as above. Set aside.

3. Reserve and set aside 1 cup of the poaching liquid.

4. Heat 2 tablespoons of the oil in a large sauté pan over medium heat. Add 1 teaspoon of the minced garlic and stir to blend. Add the mussels and sauté for 1 minute. Add $^1/_2$ cup of the remaining wine, cover, and simmer for about 5 minutes, or just until the mussels open. Transfer the mussels with the juice to a large serving bowl. Set aside.

5. Wipe the sauté pan clean with a paper towel and return it to medium heat. Add 2 tablespoons of the remaining oil, the remaining 1 teaspoon minced garlic, and the clams and sauté for 1 minute. Add the remaining $^1/_2$ cup wine, cover, and simmer for about 5 minutes, or just until the clams open. Transfer the clams with the juice to the same bowl that holds the mussels.

6. Wipe the sauté pan clean with a paper towel and return it to medium heat. Add $^1/_2$ cup of the remaining oil along with the celery, slivered garlic, and shallots and sauté for 3 minutes, or until the garlic has begun to color. Add the tomatoes, vinegar, and the juice of the remaining 2 lemons and stir to combine. Season with salt and pepper to taste. Remove from the heat and allow to cool slightly.

7.   Add the reserved squid, shrimp, scallops, and scungilli to the mussels and clams. Add the tomato mixture, the reserved 1 cup poaching liquid, the parsley, basil, red pepper flakes, and the remaining $\frac{1}{4}$ cup oil and toss to combine. Cover with plastic wrap and refrigerate for at least 1 hour or up to 3 hours.

8.   When ready to serve, taste and, if necessary, adjust the seasoning with additional salt, pepper, lemon juice, or vinegar. Serve chilled.

NOTE: Scungilli *is the Italian word for whelk and it is sometimes used to refer to conch. It is naturally very tough and, when fresh, must be tenderized before cooking. Canned scungilli has been tenderized and is just fine for this dish. I use the La Monica brand, which is excellent. It is available at Italian markets and some specialty food stores.*

Tuscan Bread Salad with Sautéed Stone Fruits

Traditionally, *panzanella* is an Italian salad that uses stale bread as the base for ripe tomatoes, basil, and great extra-virgin olive oil and vinegar. Sometimes the bread is soaked in water and sometimes it is fried in oil, but whichever way, the bread sops up the savory juices and is absolutely delicious. I've taken the same idea using a rustic bread as the base for warm fruits that are accented with pungent basil, salty capers, and briny olives. It makes a provocative salad that looks spectacular on a buffet table.

Serves 6

2 cups cubed Italian country bread (such as foccacia or Tuscan)

1 cup extra-virgin olive oil

Coarse salt and freshly ground pepper

2 tablespoons unsalted butter

2 tablespoons sugar

3 large nectarines, well washed, halved, pitted, and cut into
$1/2$-inch dice

2 large peaches, peeled, halved, pitted, and cut lengthwise into
$1/2$-inch dice

2 large plums, well washed, halved, pitted, and cut into
$1/2$-inch dice

$1/2$ cup sliced, pitted Italian black olives

1 tablespoon drained vinegar-packed capers

$1/3$ cup red wine vinegar

$1/4$ cup fresh basil chiffonade

Cracked black peppercorns

1. Preheat the oven to 375°F.

2. Toss the bread cubes with 3 tablespoons of the oil and salt and pepper to taste. Spread out on a baking pan in a single layer and place in the preheated oven. Bake for about 6 minutes, or until golden brown. Remove from the oven and set aside.

3. Heat the butter and 1 teaspoon of the remaining oil in a large sauté pan over medium heat. Stir in the sugar and then the nectarines and peaches and sauté for about 3 minutes, or until the fruit is softening and taking on some color. Remove from the heat and set aside.

4. Combine 2 cups of the toasted bread cubes with 1 tablespoon of the remaining oil in a large serving bowl. Add the reserved sautéed fruit, the plums, olives, and capers. Season with salt and pepper to taste.

5. Whisk together the remaining oil with the vinegar. Add 2 tablespoons of the basil chiffonade and drizzle just enough of the dressing over the salad to moisten it. (You probably will not need all of the dressing.) Taste and, if necessary, adjust the seasoning with salt and pepper. Toss to combine.

6. Sprinkle the remaining 2 tablespoons basil chiffonade over the top and garnish with some cracked black peppercorns. Serve at room temperature.

Sfinci di San Giuseppe

Remember those *zeppole* and *sfinci* I mentioned back on page 156? Well, here they are in a slightly less sweet version than the Singapore croquettes. At the block party, we crank up the deep fryer and keep these babies coming as long as our batter lasts. Since they are best served warm, if you want to make them in advance, don't coat them with confectioners' sugar. When ready to serve, reheat them in a preheated 350°F oven and then dust them with the sugar.

Makes about 30

. . . .

2 cups Presto self–rising cake flour

¹/₂ cup granulated sugar

1 teaspoon baking powder

Pinch of salt

4 large eggs, beaten

1 pound ricotta cheese

1 teaspoon pure vanilla extract

About 6 cups vegetable oil

About 1 cup confectioners' sugar

1.　Combine the flour, granulated sugar, baking powder, and salt, then sift the dry ingredients into a large mixing bowl.

2.　Using an electric mixer, beat the eggs, ricotta, and vanilla until smooth. Beat the egg mixture into the dry ingredients to make a smooth, thick batter. Cover with plastic wrap and set aside to rise for 30 minutes.

3.　Heat the oil in a deep fryer over high heat to 350°F on an instant-read thermometer.

4. Drop the batter by the heaping teaspoon into the hot oil. Do not crowd the pan. Fry, turning occasionally, for about 4 minutes, or until puffed and golden. Using a slotted spoon, lift the fritters from the hot oil and place on a double layer of paper towels to drain. Please note that if the oil gets too hot, the fritters will get too brown before the center is cooked.

5. Place the confectioners' sugar in a fine sieve.

6. When the fritters are well drained, shake the confectioners' sugar over them and serve warm.

Peaches in Red Wine

In Tuscany, ripe peaches are hollowed out, stuffed with an amaretti cookie filling, and baked. In France, peaches are poached in a red wine syrup. I've combined a bit of both of these recipes for a marvelous summer buffet dessert. You can serve the peaches at room temperature or make them a few days

Serves 6

. . . .

ahead and serve them chilled. They're even better when served with homemade wine, like those I tried on my first trip to Sicily to meet my family.

4 cups fruity red wine (such as Beaujolais or Merlot)

1 tablespoon fresh lemon juice

1 cup sugar

3 strips orange zest

3 pounds firm, ripe peaches, peeled, cut in half lengthwise, and pitted

1. Combine the wine and lemon juice in a small saucepan over medium heat. Add the sugar and stir to combine. Add the orange zest and bring to a simmer. Simmer for 5 minutes. Remove from the heat.

2. Place the peaches in a shallow bowl. Pour the hot liquid over the peaches and set aside to marinate at room temperature for at least 1 hour or up to 6 hours.

3. Place in the refrigerator to chill for at least 3 hours or up to 24 hours before serving.

4. When ready to serve, transfer the peaches to a serving bowl. Strain the marinating liquid over the peaches through a fine sieve, discarding the solids, and serve with amaretti cookies, if desired.

Coming Full Circle

The tragic events of September 11, 2001, sent me, like many other Americans, on a search for meaning and understanding. For me, this meant going home. Not home to Brooklyn or even to my parents' house on Long Island but to Sicily. I wanted my children to experience the community of family and the intimacy of the shared table in a way that their great-grandparents had. I also felt that the peacefulness of Sicily would offer a sense of security and generational roots that would assist us all in an emotional recovery from 9/11. So, after a very sad but gratifying year, I packed up my family and, along with a few friends, went home. It was all that I could have hoped for.

September 11, New York City

Like that of millions of other Americans, my September 11 began as a very ordinary day. I was enjoying a spectacular Indian summer morning. As on every weekday, I drove my kids to their school, P.S. 321, in the Park Slope section of Brooklyn and was returning home to start my day. Driving down Ninth Street, I was shocked and, frankly, annoyed when two fire trucks shot past me blazing toward the Brooklyn-Battery Tunnel to Manhattan. I'd never seen fire trucks act so erratically and wondered what could be so urgent that they needed to drive so recklessly.

As I turned into my street, I saw my neighbors all outside, looking up at the sky, a bit dazed. Immediately everyone asked, "Have you heard? A plane hit the World Trade Center." Looking across the East River from my roof, I saw smoke rising above the towers. The brilliant blue sky was now speckled with tiny bits of paper glistening through the sunlight. Many full sheets, slightly burned around the edges, were also raining down on us, blowing east from the tip of Manhattan. The world had turned upside down.

I rode my bicycle down to the Brooklyn piers, directly across from the Twin Towers. I watched in disbelief as the towers tumbled. Less than a minute later, most of downtown Manhattan was lost behind a plume of deep, dark dust. It was all beyond my comprehension: What could I do? What could anyone do? Would the city survive? Should I get my family out to the relative safety of our family homes on Long Island? Should I try to get to work (the Tribeca Grill was eleven blocks from the disaster area)? What could I do to help?

It quickly became very apparent that businesses downtown would not be reopening and that I might not be back in my kitchen for weeks, if not months. I knew that the pantries, refrigerators, and freezers were filled with food and that the Tribeca kitchen could churn out meals for whoever might need them.

By the next morning, management and a group of employees were able to make it to the restaurant—some lived nearby, while others arrived with the help of an escort (a friend of the restaurant who was a retired police captain). The Tribeca Grill was just where I had left it the night before, but everything outside was covered with inches of gray ash. The area was highly restricted, emergency vehicles filled the streets, sirens wailed, and confusion reigned. I knew that this was the closest thing to a war zone that I would ever experience.

We went right to work. We emptied out the fridges and freezers and laid everything out on tables and then sorted it all out for the cooks and volunteers to prepare. We organized an assembly-line production and in minutes the volunteers started producing hundreds of sandwiches. The cooks took a rest and then started making a variety of pasta dishes, using the contents of the storeroom for inspiration. We hunted up aluminum pans and disposables from the catering kitchen upstairs and then walked it all down to Stuyvesant High School, where a temporary feeding center with a makeshift triage facility across the hall had been set up. There was no gas or electric and tons of food was piled high on tables. It felt like a big buffet set up in the middle of an emergency room. But it worked. The relief workers needed to eat—many of them had already been at Ground Zero for over twenty-four hours, and exhaustion, emotional and physical, was taking its toll. However, it was immediately clear that there had to be a more efficient, more sanitary way to feed them.

When I asked the workers at the center what was needed, almost everyone said, "Hot food and hot coffee." A Red Cross worker from Iowa said that, ideally, they needed a facility that could serve as both a feeding and a respite center. It should be close to the site but removed enough to give the workers a break from Ground Zero. I also ran into a friend, Martine La Fond, who was bringing water from a barge nearby and quipped, "I wish they could have brought some food, too."

On the way back up to the restaurant to pick up more food, I ran through some of the conversations—"respite center," "feeding center," "close to the site," "a barge delivering water." The solution might be right in front of us. Manhattan is an island. All streets below Fourteenth Street were blocked to general entry. Why not move meals by boat? We needed big boats, though. If we could find one, it could dock at the North Cove Marina at the World Financial Center, directly across from the Statue of Liberty out in the harbor.

That night, I called a friend, Vince Graceffo, a freelance boat captain, and told him of my idea. I asked him if he knew of any vessels that could fill the bill. He said, "I'm looking at one right now. It's called *Spirit of New York* and it's docked at Chelsea Piers." If nothing else, the name was sure perfect. I asked Vince to set up a meeting for the morning.

We met with Captain Greg Hanchrow, director of marine operations for Spirit Cruises (a dinner-boat cruise line that operates from Pier 61 at Chelsea Piers on the Hudson River). Vince and I presented our idea, and before we could finish, Greg said, "As far as I'm concerned, you can have the whole fleet." Operation "Chefs with Spirit" was under way.

We began the project thirty hours later, feeding the relief workers at a rate of 600 meals an hour. The demand was enormous and, to our amazement, we served over 20,000 meals during the first twenty-four-hour period. The *Spirit of New York,* now stationed at North Cove, had a seating capacity of 700 on the two decks, with two buffets set up on each deck. On the third deck were pillows and blankets with enough room for about 100 people to sleep. There were therapists, masseurs, and chiropractors on board. The USO sent in entertainment, and the telephone company provided free phone service so that the workers could check in at home.

All of New York's restaurant community was committed to the effort. Chef Gray Kunz gave his all to help organize the project. Every chef—from my mentors and friends Daniel Boulud and Charlie Palmer to neighborhood cooks—came together to prepare and even help transport and serve meals. Waitstaff, kitchen personnel, and support staff were at our side. The hospitality industry opened their hearts and purses in a most remarkable gesture of generosity (Nick Valenti of Restaurant Associates, alone, helped provide over 100,000 meals; Steve Hanson of B. R. Guest had every one of his restaurants donating meals and staff; Citarella donated food for weeks). Spirit Cruises provided boat staff. Volunteers of all ages, races, and creeds flooded in from all walks of life. Food donations came from all across the country, from giant corporations and from small family-owned storefront operations.

For me, the real poster child for "Chefs with Spirit" was Jack McDavid, the chef-owner of Jack's Firehouse in Philadelphia. One day, in the midst of a frantic moment on the boat, I bumped into Jack, a colorful chef with a deep southern drawl. At that moment, clad in overalls, he seemed to rise up from another time and place. "What are you doing here?" I asked. "I'm here to work, sir, and I've brought my boys with me. Just tell us what to do." He had driven up from Philly, loaded down with food and the

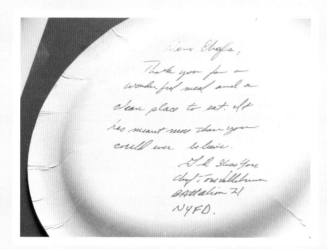

staff to see that it got to the workers, with absolutely no intentions except to help. It was at that moment that everything that I had ever learned about the restaurant community—its generosity, capabilities, and determination—came into play. No one said, "I can't"—everyone said, "Just tell me what to do."

One of my most vivid memories of this time occurred around midnight on the third or fourth day of operation. With the decks filled to overflowing and the USO singers entertaining, a fireman stood up in midsong and shouted, "I want to sing 'God Bless America.' " The singers stopped short and responded, "Great idea—let's all sing." Two by two, ten by ten, fifty by fifty, everyone stood. Everyone joined in harmony, loud and proud. When we finished, everyone turned to Ground Zero and saluted the victims of the savage attack on our ideals—the fathers, mothers, sisters, brothers, children, friends—and the grieving families that they had left.

My greatest treasure carried from the boat, beyond the love and humanity shown there, is a note written on a paper plate by a fireman, Chief Tom Vallebuona, Battalion 21, FDNY, that reads, "Dear Chefs, thank you for a wonderful meal and a clean place to eat. It has meant more than you could ever believe. God bless you."

The "spirit" generated by our Spirit Cruises to Ground Zero enveloped us all for weeks. Our goal was to keep it afloat at least long enough for the search-and-rescue phase of the recovery effort to be complete. This turned out to be three weeks and

600,000 meals later. Eventually, at the request of Mayor Rudy Giuliani, we turned over the operation to the American Red Cross, who kept it up and running for many more weeks. Once again, I had learned the power of food in bringing people together.

In the aftermath of this deeply emotional period, there was a huge shift away from haute cuisine, extravagant meals, and fancy dining to comfort food. The recipes that I share with you in this section are ones that we found ourselves cooking at home and even, occasionally, in the restaurant. They are satisfying, nourishing, hearty foods that are made even better when shared with friends and family.

Hearty Lentil and Tomato Soup

Almost every cuisine has some type of lentil dish and very often it is a soup or stew. Every Italian mom makes a special lentil dish, always serving it with a hunk of warm Italian bread to dunk. In our house, it has always been lentil soup that warms our winter days. I like to make a big pot so

Serves 6 to 8

. . . .

that we have leftovers that can be combined with cooked pasta and Parmesan cheese for another meal.

1 tablespoon olive oil

8 ounces pancetta, diced

1 small onion, peeled and finely diced

1 carrot, peeled, trimmed, and finely diced

1 rib celery, well washed, trimmed, and finely diced

1 leek (white part only), well washed and finely diced

2 cloves garlic, peeled and minced

4 ripe tomatoes, peeled, cored, seeded, and diced

1 pound lentils

12 cups chicken broth or water (see Note)

1 bay leaf

Coarse salt and freshly ground pepper

1 teaspoon red pepper flakes, or to taste (optional)

$^1/_4$ cup chopped fresh flat-leaf parsley (optional)

1 tablespoon chopped fresh thyme (optional)

1. Heat the oil in a large saucepan over medium heat. Add the pancetta and sauté for about 7 minutes, or until crisp. Add the onion, carrot, celery, and leek and sauté for another 3 minutes, or just until the vegetables begin to soften. Stir in the garlic and sauté for a minute or two more. Stir in the tomatoes and sauté for about 2 minutes, or just until wilted. Stir in the lentils, then add the chicken broth and bay leaf. Season with salt and pepper to taste and bring to a boil. Lower the heat and simmer for about 30 minutes, or until the lentils are soft. Add the red pepper flakes, if desired, and remove from the heat.

2. Stir in the parsley and thyme, if desired, just before serving.

NOTE: *If using water, cook for about 15 minutes more to allow the flavors to intensify.*

Bluepoint Oyster and Corn Chowder

This is a fancy version of a simple workingman's chowder. Bluepoints are the most commonly available Atlantic oysters and can be replaced with almost any other local type or not used at all. The soup base can be prepared the day before, with the vegetable garnish and finishing done on the day of service. The vegetables and oysters can also be mixed into the soup

Serves 6

. . . .

base just before serving. This soup is so rich and nourishing that a healthy portion could easily be counted as a meal. Served as a first course, you might want to ladle out only a cupful.

8 tablespoons (1 stick) unsalted butter

8 ounces lean bacon, finely diced

2 cups fresh corn kernels

$^1/_4$ cup finely diced leek (white part only)

$^1/_4$ cup finely diced celery

$^1/_2$ cup finely diced cooked potatoes

10 white peppercorns

2 sprigs fresh thyme

2 sprigs fresh flat-leaf parsley

1 bay leaf

4 shallots, peeled and sliced

2 ribs celery, well washed, trimmed, and cut into chunks

1 small white onion, peeled and diced

1 small fennel bulb, well washed, trimmed, and diced

1 clove garlic, peeled and minced

3 cups clam juice

1 cup dry white wine

$^1/_2$ cup dry vermouth

1 pint (about 20) bluepoint oysters, with juice

2 cups heavy cream

2 cups milk

Coarse salt and freshly ground white pepper

Tabasco sauce

2 tablespoons chopped fresh chives

1. Heat 2 tablespoons of the butter in a large sauté pan over medium heat. Add the bacon and sauté for about 4 minutes, or until the bacon has rendered most of its fat. Add the corn, leek, and finely diced celery and sauté for about 3 minutes, or just until the celery has softened. Stir in the potatoes and sauté for about 2 minutes, or just until heated through. Tent lightly with aluminum foil and keep warm.

2. Place the peppercorns, thyme, parsley, and bay leaf in a small piece of cheesecloth. Pull the edges up, and using kitchen twine, tie the cheesecloth into a little bag, making a bouquet garni. Set aside.

3. Heat 4 tablespoons of the butter in a heavy-bottomed saucepan over low heat. Add the shallots, celery chunks, onion, fennel, and garlic and sauté for about 8 minutes, or until the vegetables have sweat their liquid but not taken on any color. Add the clam juice, white wine, vermouth, and the reserved bouquet garni.

4. Drain the juice from the oysters and add it to the saucepan along with 5 of the oysters. Refrigerate the remaining oysters until ready to use. Raise the heat and bring the soup base to a simmer. Lower the heat and simmer for 20 minutes.

5. Combine the cream and milk in a saucepan over medium heat. Bring to a simmer, then lower the heat and cook at a bare simmer for about 20 minutes, or until reduced by half. Remove from the heat.

6. Strain the soup base through a fine sieve into a large, clean saucepan. Remove the 5 oysters from the sieve and discard the remaining solids. Chop the 5 oysters and add them to the strained soup base along with the reduced cream-milk mixture.

7. Place the enriched soup base over medium heat. Season with salt, white pepper, and Tabasco sauce to taste and bring to a simmer. Simmer for 10 minutes.

8.   While the soup is simmering, heat the remaining 2 tablespoons butter in a small sauté pan over medium heat. Add the reserved oysters and heat for about 2 minutes, or just until the edges begin to curl. Remove from the heat and, if very large, coarsely chop and set aside in the warm pan juices.

9.   Ladle equal portions of the hot soup into each of 6 shallow soup bowls. Spoon a mound of the reserved vegetable mixture in the center of each bowl. Place a generous serving of the warm oysters on top of the vegetables. Sprinkle with the chives and serve.

Turkey Meat Loaf with Cranberry Glaze

Meat loaf and mashed potatoes served together is a favorite combination at our house. It was the number one non-Italian dinner in my childhood and now it is a meal of choice for my own children. An old friend, Rose Klein, gave me this recipe. The turkey helps cut down on the fat, while the chicken broth and the cranberry glaze sort of work as fat replacements, as they keep the meat loaf really moist and flavorful. We usually make two meat loaves so we have sandwich makings left over. If company is coming, fancy up your meat loaf by adding some fresh herbs to the mixture and serving it with zesty cranberry chutney on the side.

Serves 6

. . . .

2 pounds lean ground turkey (see Note)

$3/4$ cup fresh bread crumbs

$1/4$ cup finely diced onion

3 large eggs, lightly beaten

$3/4$ cup milk

About $1/2$ cup chicken broth

Coarse salt and freshly ground pepper

$1/2$ cup pureed canned cranberry sauce

$1/4$ cup packed light brown sugar

1. Preheat the oven to 350°F. Lightly coat a nonstick 9-inch loaf pan with vegetable spray. Set aside.

2. Combine the turkey, bread crumbs, and onion in a mixing bowl. Add the eggs and milk and stir to combine. Stir in just enough chicken broth to make a very moist mixture. Season with salt and pepper to taste.

3. Combine the cranberry puree and brown sugar in a small mixing bowl. Using a spatula, spread the mixture over the bottom of the prepared loaf pan. Form the turkey mixture into a loaf shape and fit it into the pan. Place in the preheated oven and bake for 1 hour.

4. Remove the meat loaf from the oven and invert the pan onto a serving platter. Gently tap on the bottom to release the meat loaf. Cut crosswise into $1/4$-inch-thick slices and serve with your favorite potatoes and veggies.

NOTE: *If you use ground turkey-breast meat, the meat loaf will have much less fat and fewer calories, but it will also be quite a bit drier. Keep this in mind when adding the chicken broth.*

Oven-Roasted Citrus-Herb Chicken

Simple to put together, easy to cook, and great to eat! This dish has all the familiar qualities of a roasted chicken with just a bit more flavor. You can easily double or triple the recipe to feed a crowd and any leftovers will make great sandwiches or salads.

Serves 6

Three 2¹/₂-pound broiling chickens, cut into serving pieces,
    well washed and dried

³/₄ cup fresh lemon juice

³/₄ cup fresh orange juice

¹/₂ cup olive oil

1 large onion, peeled and sliced

1 teaspoon paprika

¹/₄ cup chopped mixed fresh herbs (such as rosemary,
    thyme, sage, and chives)

1 tablespoon minced garlic

Coarse salt and freshly ground pepper

2 lemons, well washed and quartered

1 orange, well washed and quartered

3 tablespoons bread crumbs, or as needed

1. Preheat the oven to 400°F.

2. Place the chicken pieces in a large bowl. Add the lemon juice, orange juice, oil, onion, paprika, herbs, and garlic. Season with salt and pepper to taste and toss to coat.

3. Place the chicken, skin side up, in a baking dish or roasting pan large enough to hold the pieces in a single layer. Pour the juice mixture over the chicken. Nestle the lemon and orange quarters into the pan. Sprinkle the top with bread crumbs.

4. Place the chicken in the preheated oven and bake, turning occasionally, for about 45 minutes, or until the skin is golden and slightly crisp. Using tongs, transfer the chicken to a serving platter. Pour the pan juices over the top and serve with lots of warm crusty bread to soak up the juices.

Four-Cheese Mac and Cheez

This is a jazzed-up version of mac and cheez that I devised using bits and pieces of leftover cheese. We liked it so much that I have continued to make it for the adults. Of course, the kids still prefer the old-fashioned kind, but I've found that most adults line up for seconds of my intensely flavored four-cheese variation.

Serves 6 to 8

- - - - - - - - - - - - - - - - - -

8 tablespoons (1 stick) unsalted butter

1 onion, peeled and minced

$^1/_4$ cup all-purpose flour

2 cups hot milk

1 cup shredded fontina cheese

1 cup shredded taleggio cheese

$^1/_2$ cup shredded Robiola cheese

1 pound farfalle, baby shells, orecchiette, or mezzi rigatoni, cooked and drained

Coarse salt and freshly ground pepper

$^1/_2$ cup shredded Gorgonzola cheese

$^1/_3$ cup Italian Seasoned Bread Crumbs (page 30)

1. Preheat the oven to 350°F.
2. Using 2 tablespoons of the butter, generously coat a 4-quart ovenproof baking dish. Set aside.

3. Melt 4 tablespoons of the butter in a large saucepan over medium heat. Add the onion and sauté for about 3 minutes, or just until softened. Stir in the flour, lower the heat, and cook, stirring constantly, for about 3 minutes, or until a smooth roux has formed.

4. Whisk in the hot milk, raise the heat, and bring to a boil, stirring constantly. Lower the heat and simmer, stirring constantly, for about 5 minutes, or until thickened. Remove from the heat and, using a wooden spoon, beat in the fontina, taleggio, and Robiola cheeses until smooth.

5. Add the cooked pasta to the cheese sauce and stir to combine. Season with salt and pepper to taste. Pour into the prepared baking dish, smoothing the top with a spatula.

6. Sprinkle the top with the Gorgonzola and then the bread crumbs. Dot the top with the remaining 2 tablespoons butter. Place in the preheated oven and bake for about 25 minutes, or until the top is golden and the edges are bubbling. Remove from the oven and serve.

The Very Best Brownies

I think that these are the best brownies
ever! I happen to love them with nuts and
peanut butter chips, but they are so rich
and chocolaty, they are almost as delicious
plain. You can fancy them up when
company comes by serving them warm
with a scoop of ice cream, a drizzle of
chocolate sauce, and a sprinkle of nuts.

Makes about 24

. . . .

Brownies are, to me, the great dessert
equalizer—kids love 'em, teenagers love
'em, and so do adults.

10 tablespoons unsalted butter, softened

¹/₄ cup Wondra flour

2 cups sugar

4 large eggs, at room temperature

1 teaspoon pure vanilla extract

1 cup sifted all-purpose flour

¹/₂ cup cocoa powder

¹/₂ teaspoon salt

1 cup walnut or pecan pieces, toasted (optional)

1 cup chocolate or peanut butter chips (optional)

1. Using 2 tablespoons of the butter, lightly coat an 11 × 7 × 2-inch baking pan. Add the
Wondra flour to the pan and shake to lightly coat. Shake out the excess flour and set aside.

2. Preheat the oven to 350°F.

3. Cream the remaining 8 tablespoons butter in the bowl of an electric mixer for 1 minute
just to soften. Add the sugar and beat until light and fluffy. Add the eggs, one at a time,
and beat to incorporate. Beat in the vanilla extract.

4. Combine the all-purpose flour, cocoa, and salt and sift the dry ingredients into the creamed mixture. Beat just to blend. Fold in the nuts and/or chips, if desired. Scrape the mixture into the prepared pan.

5. Place in the preheated oven and bake for about 25 minutes, or until a toothpick inserted into the center comes out almost clean. Remove from the oven and place on a wire rack to cool for 15 minutes. Cut into squares while still warm, but leave in the pan until cool.

6. Remove from the pan and serve, or store, covered, for up to 3 days.

All-American Cobbler

You can make this cobbler out of any juicy fruit. The most traditional cobblers are made from peaches, sweet cherries, or blueberries. One of my favorites is a peach-blueberry combination. Since the fruit is baked, frozen fruit works very well, so you can make cobblers all year round. If

Serves 6 to 8

. . . .

you want to use apples or pears, add some matching juice or nectar to create a nice, bubbly sauce.

2 cups all-purpose flour

4 teaspoons baking powder

1 cup plus 3 tablespoons sugar

$^1/_2$ cup plus 2 tablespoons cold unsalted butter

$^3/_4$ cup milk

4 to 5 cups berries, sliced stone fruits, or a mixture of both

1 large egg, beaten

2 tablespoons cornstarch

2 teaspoons fresh lemon juice

1 teaspoon ground cinnamon, nutmeg, allspice, or other
    spice of choice, or a mixture of spices (optional)

About 3 tablespoons cinnamon sugar

1. Place the flour, baking powder, and 3 tablespoons of the sugar in the bowl of a food processor fitted with the metal blade. Using quick on-and-off turns, add the $^1/_2$ cup butter, a bit at a time. When crumbly, add the milk and quickly process to a smooth dough. Set aside.

2. Preheat the oven to 375°F. Generously coat a 2-quart casserole or 9-inch square glass baking dish with the 2 tablespoons butter. Set aside.

3. Combine the fruit with the remaining 1 cup sugar in a mixing bowl. Stir until the sugar begins to dissolve. Add the egg, cornstarch, lemon juice, and, if desired, spice or spices. Pour into the prepared dish.

4. Drop the dough by the tablespoonful on top of the fruit. When the top is generously covered, sprinkle with the cinnamon sugar.

5. Place in the preheated oven and bake for about 35 minutes, or until the top is lightly browned, the dough is cooked through, and the fruit is bubbly.

6. Remove from the oven and let stand for 20 minutes. Serve warm with ice cream, heavy cream, whipped cream, or any light dessert sauce.

Return to Sicily

Over twenty years ago, on my first trip to Sicily (see page 53), I had made two promises. My great-uncle Vincenzo made me promise to someday bring my parents to Sicily—I was the link between the old and the new and he wanted me to be the one to bring the families together. And I made a promise to myself that when I was blessed with a family of my own, I would take them to Sicily so that they might understand their heritage.

I soon fulfilled my promise to Zio Vincenzo by taking my parents and my brother, Rob, back to St. Angelo di Brolo five years after my first trip. After September 11, thinking of all those who had dreams left unfulfilled, it felt imperative that I return with my wife and children. I particularly didn't want to put it off, as the future seemed so uncertain.

I wanted to slow the pace of our lives, and for the children to experience the peacefulness of the island and meet all of the relatives, and for my relatives to meet them. My kids were quite young, Alex six, Daniela five, and Nicky just eighteen months old, and I was not sure that my strategy to introduce them to the culture, food, music, and traditions of our family at such young ages would have any immediate effect, but providing them with a connection to their heritage seemed so important that I felt that it was worth the try.

Before traveling to Messina and St. Angelo, where most of our relatives resided, I wanted to explore the island and show my family all of the places that I had visited. We made our base in Mondello, a resort town just outside of Palermo, where the children could swim and play on the beach. We visited Erice, a breathtakingly beautiful hill town, for *dolci ericini,* the marvelous marzipan and pastries from Pasticceria Maria. Maria Grammatico learned to make traditional sweets such as *sospiri* ("sighs") and *belli e brutti* ("beauties and beasts") while a novice in a nunnery. (Sicilians do have a way with words—"virgin's breasts" and "chancellor's buttocks" give just a hint of some of the more salacious bakery items.) Her bakery is known as Sicily's finest, but it is her greatest fear that there is no interest among the young in carrying on with the rituals of handmade desserts, which would be a loss to the entire region.

In Trapani, we spent an afternoon in the fish and vegetable market on Piazza del

Mercato del Pesce. Trapani is an important port where traditional industries such as tuna fishing and coral and salt harvesting are still carried out. The market bustled with activity. Shoppers argued with merchants. Fishermen called out in lyrical songs praising their catches. Crates and barrels were filled to the brim with the freshest of fruits, vegetables, and fish. Huge tuna and swordfish were hanging from the rafters with hunks of meat cut out as it was purchased. Smoked and cured fish and meats, olive oils, olives, pickled vegetables, and breads filled stalls around the edge. It was as though we were in the center of a movie set.

In Palermo, we discovered the Vucciria ("the voices"), one of the world's oldest and most spectacular street markets. The stalls amble through a very old section of Palermo; olives, capers, nuts, spices, pasta, fresh vegetables and fish, sweets, breads, and storefronts where traditional dishes are ladled out of massive old pots tempted us at every turn. Here we purchased smoked swordfish, cured tuna, olives of every color and shape, pungent green olive oil, and everything else we needed for a hotel-room or beach antipasto.

Although the kids had certainly experienced good Italian food at home, like all other American children, fast food and junk food held great appeal to them. My greatest hope was to retrain their ideas about snacking and eating on the road. To some extent, the public markets did make an impression; however, it was the gelato shops on the rialto in Mondello that really caught their fancy. Of particular interest was *gelato con brioche,* a gigantic brioche roll that was split open and stuffed with a massive amount of the gelato flavor (or two) of their choice.

On our way to Messina, where my family had planned a big reunion, we stopped at the Regaleali Estate, a world-famous producer of fine Sicilian wines. Here Anna Tasca Lanza has developed her internationally known cooking school featuring the classic dishes of Sicily. The estate, in a magnificent setting in the heart of the island, is completely self-sustaining. Everything needed to feed the family and staff is grown and raised on land that stretches as far as the eye can see. Anna and her staff prepared a memorable lunch and then we walked the vineyards, visited the farm animals, tasted cheese in the cheese house, and saw all of the elements that came together to make an unbelievable life. We were all fascinated by the old-fashioned gas pumps located in front of the wine-storage barn, which customers used to pump their own wine. I had to chuckle as I remembered Alex questioning me as we drove through the mountains earlier that day, "Do they have a backyard?"

Then we were off to Messina. You can, perhaps, imagine what it was like at our family reunion to walk into a room full of non-English-speaking relatives, all of whom wanted to be the first to say hello. Hugs, embraces, kisses, pats, tears, all mingled with a babble of voices. The children were taken aback and the baby howled. Christine tried to keep order, and since I already knew almost everyone there, I tried to make my way quickly from person to person with a welcoming hug.

My cousins opened their beautiful home to us. Sitting on an outcrop overlooking the Strait of Messina, the expansive lawn faced out toward Calabria. Even with a light rain, it was a perfect spot for a party. Buffet tables were placed out on the lawn with the grill lit and ready to go. Jugs of red and white table wine were everywhere. There were over fifty relatives gathered (my grandfather had eight brothers and sisters) and all of the women had contributed a dish for the buffet. There was bruschetta, Involtini di Melanzane (page 323), stockfish and pasta, Aunt Vincenzina's Veal Spiedini (see page 325), fennel frittata, *involtini di pepperoni,* caponata, baked mussels, *tòrta di melanzane,* stuffed tomatoes, and on and on the dishes came. From St. Angelo, we had salami and cheeses made there. For dessert, we had *sfinci, gelatina di limone,* cookies of all kinds, and the famous Sicilian *cassata,* a layered cake filled with sweet ricotta and candied fruits.

The day was filled with so much emotion that even the gray skies and drizzle couldn't dampen the warmth. The children were hugged and caressed and treasured by people who had known their great-grandfather. Zìo Vincenzo had passed on, but his spirit was with us. Uncle Frank, my grandfather's only surviving brother, could not be with us, as he was too ill to travel, but in the middle of the afternoon, a cell phone was placed on my ear and I heard his feeble voice welcoming me back home. Shortly after that moment, we looked over toward Calabria and a double rainbow had formed, arching over the waters to Messina.

It seemed fitting to me to end this journal with a return to Sicily. All of the warmth of the table that led me into a career in the kitchen emanated from my Sicilian family: their love of conversation and good food and wine, their understanding of the importance of family, their generosity to friends and strangers alike. Sharing what they had was not something they had learned to do, it was what they had always done. And, in fact, it was in Sicily that I first came to understand how important this heritage was to me and will be for my children.

Bruschetta of Preserved Tuna, Anchovies, and Capers

Tuna is extremely popular throughout Sicily, often served, simply, as $1/2$-inch-thick grilled steaks. This is an easy-to-put-together version of the traditional Sicilian *involtini di tonno,* in which thin slices of tuna are pounded, wrapped around a stuffing of bread crumbs, capers, cheese, and lemon, and grilled or broiled. Either version makes a terrific hors d'oeuvre. In Sicily, bruschetta would be part of an antipasto.

1 pound bluefin tuna, preferably belly-cut, cut into 4 thick pieces (see Note)

Coarse salt and freshly ground pepper

$1^1/_2$ cups extra-virgin olive oil

1 tablespoon black peppercorns

4 sprigs fresh oregano

Twelve $1/_2$-inch-thick slices Italian country bread (such as
foccacia or Tuscan)

4 cloves garlic, peeled

2 tablespoons olive oil

6 anchovy fillets, chopped

2 tablespoons vinegar-packed, drained capers

$1/_2$ cup diced, peeled, and seeded tomatoes

$1/_4$ cup sliced black olives (optional)

2 tablespoons chopped fresh flat-leaf parsley

1.   Season the tuna with salt and pepper to taste. Place the seasoned tuna in a shallow saucepan along with the extra-virgin olive oil, peppercorns, and oregano. Place over low

heat and cook for about 8 minutes, or just until the oil is hot. Remove from the heat and allow the tuna to cool in the oil.

2. When cool, drain 1 cup of oil from the tuna. Using a pastry brush, lightly coat both sides of the bread with the tuna cooking oil.

3. Preheat and oil a grill.

4. Place the oiled bread on the hot grill and toast, turning frequently, for about 3 minutes, or until golden. Remove the toast from the grill and, while still warm, rub the top with 2 of

the whole garlic cloves, pressing down so that the garlic oil is absorbed into the bread. Set the toast aside. Slice the remaining 2 garlic cloves and set aside.

5. Drain the remaining oil from the tuna and reserve. Discard the peppercorns and oregano sprigs and flake the tuna into pieces. Set the tuna aside.

6. Heat the olive oil in a large sauté pan over medium heat. Add the anchovies, the reserved sliced garlic, and the capers and sauté for about 2 minutes, or just until the garlic starts to take on some color. Stir in the tomatoes, season with salt and pepper to taste, and toss to combine. Add the reserved flaked tuna and, if desired, the olives and sauté for about 2 minutes, or until heated through.

7. Remove from the heat and stir in the parsley. Spoon a generous portion on each piece of bread, drizzle with the reserved tuna cooking oil, and serve warm.

NOTE: *As a substitute, high-quality preserved tuna is available in jars at Italian specialty stores.*

Panelle

In Palermo, *panelle,* or chickpea pancakes, is a street food, usually seasoned with lemon juice and served between two slices of bread topped with some fresh ricotta cheese. To make the traditional version, you will need $3 \times 1^{1}/_{2}$-inch wooden panelle molds.

Makes 16

. . . .

However, for convenience, I have simply used baking pans and then cut out shapes from the firm batter.

1 tablespoon olive oil

2 teaspoons minced garlic

3 cups chicken broth

2 cups milk

1 cup chickpea flour (see Note)

1 teaspoon baking powder

Coarse salt and freshly ground pepper

$^{1}/_{4}$ cup chopped fresh flat–leaf parsley

About 6 cups vegetable oil

1 lemon, well washed and cut into wedges (optional)

1. Heat the olive oil in a small sauté pan over medium heat. Add the garlic and sauté for a few seconds, or just until the garlic begins to become golden. Immediately remove from the heat and scrape into a small bowl. Set aside.

2. Lightly coat a nonstick baking pan with vegetable spray.

3. Place the chicken broth and milk in a saucepan over medium heat. Add the reserved garlic-oil mixture. Combine the chickpea flour and baking powder and whisk it into the liquid. Season with salt and pepper to taste. Cook, stirring constantly with a wooden

spoon, for about 2 minutes, or until the mixture is very thick and pastelike. Stir in the parsley and remove from the heat.

4. Pour the batter into the prepared baking pan, pushing it out to an even layer about ⅛ inch thick. Cover lightly with plastic wrap and refrigerate for about 30 minutes, or until very cool. (If you have panelle molds, distribute the hot batter evenly in the molds and refrigerate as above. When cool, release the batter from the molds and proceed with the recipe.)

5. Using a small, sharp knife, cut the firm batter into 8 squares, then cut each square diagonally into 2 triangles (⅛-inch thick).

6. Place the vegetable oil in a deep fryer over high heat. Bring to 350°F on an instant-read thermometer. Add the batter triangles, a few at a time, and fry for about 3 minutes, or until golden and crisp. Using a slotted spoon, lift the panelle from the oil and place on a double layer of paper towels to drain. Continue frying until all of the batter triangles have been cooked. Season with salt and pepper to taste and serve as is, with a squeeze of lemon juice, or as a Palermo-style sandwich.

NOTE: *Chickpea flour is available at Italian markets and specialty food stores.*

Arancini

For lunch at Regaleali, we had our fill of Anna Tasca Lanza's famous *arancini* stuffed with rich meat *ragù*. They just kept coming, hot and aromatic, from the kitchen to the table. This is a more traditional recipe, using cheese in the center of the fried balls. In Sicily, *arancini*, which means "small orange," are used more as an appetizer. In the United States, many Sicilian Americans make large rice balls, spoon marinara sauce over them with melted mozzarella cheese on top, and serve them as a main course.

Makes 45

. . . .

6 cups chicken broth

3 tablespoons unsalted butter

1 small Spanish onion, peeled and finely diced

1 pound arborio rice

1 cup dry white wine

$^1/_4$ cup chopped fresh flat-leaf parsley

2 tablespoons freshly grated Parmesan cheese

Coarse salt and freshly ground pepper

$^1/_2$ pound mozzarella cheese

1 cup Nana's Fresh Marinara Sauce (page 8) or other marinara sauce, plus an additional 1$^1/_2$ cup for use as a dipping sauce (optional)

3 large eggs, beaten

1 tablespoon milk

1 cup Italian Seasoned Bread Crumbs (page 30)

About 4 cups vegetable oil

1. Place the chicken broth in a large saucepan over medium heat and bring to a simmer. Lower the heat and keep at just a bare simmer.

2. Heat 2 tablespoons of the butter in a large, shallow saucepan over very low heat. Add the onion and sauté for about 6 minutes, or until the onion has sweat its liquid and is soft but has not taken on any color.

3. Add the rice and sauté for about 3 minutes, or until the rice is glistening and beginning to toast. Raise the heat and add the wine. Cook, stirring constantly, for about 3 minutes, or until the wine has almost been totally absorbed by the rice. Adding 1 cup at a time, begin ladling the hot broth into the rice, stirring frequently. Cook for about 5 minutes, or until the liquid has been absorbed. Continue cooking and adding broth as above until all of the broth has been used or until the rice is almost creamy but still al dente. (You may not use all of the broth.) It is a good idea to vigorously shake the pan back and forth from time to time when not stirring to keep the rice moving without breaking the grains. This whole process should take about 30 minutes.

4. Stir in the remaining tablespoon butter along with the parsley and grated Parmesan cheese. Season with salt and pepper to taste.

5. Scrape the risotto into a large baking pan or dish, smoothing the top with a spatula. Cover lightly with plastic wrap and refrigerate to cool quickly.

6. Line 3 baking sheets with parchment paper. Set aside.

7. Cut the mozzarella into ³/₈-inch cubes. Set aside.

8. When the risotto has cooled, begin making the rice balls. Fill a small (about 1-ounce) scoop about three-quarters full with the cooled risotto. Place 2 cubes of mozzarella in the center, dot the cheese with marinara sauce, and then cover with enough risotto to fill the scoop. Pat down to firm the ball before releasing it from the scoop. Place on the prepared baking sheets and continue making balls until all of the risotto is used.

9. Combine the eggs and milk in a large, shallow bowl. Place the bread crumbs next to the eggs in a similar bowl.

10. Working with one at a time, turn the ball around in the palm of your hand to make a perfect round. Roll the ball in the egg mixture and then in the bread crumbs. Return the coated ball to the baking sheet. Continue breading until all of the balls have been coated. (At this point, the rice balls may be covered with plastic wrap and refrigerated up to 3 days or tightly wrapped in freezer paper and frozen for up to 3 months.)

11. Preheat the oven to 300°F.

12. Heat the oil in a deep fryer to 350°F on an instant-read thermometer. Drop the rice balls into the hot oil, a few at a time, and fry, turning occasionally, for about 3 minutes, or until golden brown. Using a slotted spoon, transfer the fried *arancini* to a double layer of paper towels to drain.

13. When drained, place on the baking sheets in the preheated oven to keep warm while you continue to fry the rice balls.

14. When all of the rice balls are fried, serve hot with warm marinara sauce as a dipping sauce, if desired.

Pasta con le Sarde

Anna Tasca Lanza prepared a most extraordinary platter of *pasta con le sarde* for us at Regaleali. This simple pasta is often referred to as the national dish of Sicily, as it combines many flavors of the cuisine in an intriguing way. It is traditionally made with wild fennel, fresh sardines, saffron, pine nuts, and raisins.

For Americans, the most elusive ingredient in this recipe is the wild fennel,

Serves 6

. . . .

which is abundant on the island. Wild fennel does grow here (particularly in California) but just doesn't often make it to the marketplace. If you can find it, by all means use it, but if not, use cultivated fennel.

2 pinches saffron threads

$^1/_2$ cup hot water

$^1/_4$ cup julienned sun-dried tomato

2 tablespoons dried currants

3 wild fennel bulbs with fronds

$^1/_2$ cup extra-virgin olive oil (preferably Sicilian), plus more as needed

1 large onion, peeled and cut into $^1/_4$-inch dice

$^1/_2$ cup dry white wine

1 pound sardines, cleaned, heads, tails, and bones removed

6 anchovy fillets, chopped

1 tablespoon tomato paste

1 pound dried pasta (such as bucatini or perciatelli)

$^1/_4$ cup fresh bread crumbs, toasted (see step 1, page 40)

1. Place the saffron threads in a small mixing bowl along with the hot water. Add the sun-dried tomato and the currants and set aside.

2. Wash the fennel under cold running water. Cut the tops from the bulbs, separately reserving them.

3. Clip the feathery fronds from the fennel stems and discard the stems.

4. Bring a large pot of very lightly salted cold water to a boil. Add the fennel fronds and cook for 1 minute just to blanch. Immediately refresh under cold running water and pat dry. Using a sharp knife, finely chop and set aside.

5. Return the water to a boil and add the fennel bulbs. Boil for about 8 minutes, or until tender when pierced with the point of a small, sharp knife. Using a slotted spoon, lift the bulbs from the water and set aside to cool slightly. Keep the water over low heat so that it remains at a bare simmer.

6. When cool, cut the fennel bulbs into $\frac{1}{4}$-inch dice. Set aside.

7. Heat the $\frac{1}{2}$ cup oil in a large sauté pan over medium heat. Add the onion along with the diced fennel and sauté for 3 minutes, or just until the onion has softened. Add the wine and bring to a simmer. Simmer for 1 minute. Add the sardines, anchovies, and tomato paste along with the reserved saffron mixture and 1 cup of the simmering water. Bring to a simmer and cook, stirring occasionally and pushing on the sardines to break them up, for about 10 minutes, or until the anchovies have dissolved and the sardines are almost mushy.

8. While the sauce is cooking, return the simmering fennel water to a boil and prepare the pasta according to package directions. Add the fennel fronds for the last 4 minutes of cooking time.

9. Drain the pasta, reserving 1 cup of the water. Add the pasta to the sauce, tossing to coat well. (If the sauté pan is too small, transfer the mixture to a warm mixing bowl and toss.) Add as much of the 1 cup water as needed to make a moist sauce.

10. Transfer to a serving platter. Drizzle with extra-virgin olive oil, sprinkle with the toasted bread crumbs, and serve.

Involtini di Melanzane

I had never had any pasta dish quite like this until the family reunion in Messina. Once I was back in New York, I kept experimenting until I got it right. These delicious rolls make a great addition to an antipasto platter or can be served as the pasta course in a traditional Italian meal.

Makes 45

. . . .

3 large eggplants, well washed and dried

Coarse salt

$^1/_2$ cup olive oil

Freshly ground pepper

2 pounds perciatelli pasta

3 large eggs, beaten

2 tablespoons milk

$^1/_2$ cup plus 2 tablespoons freshly grated Parmesan cheese

3 tablespoons Italian Seasoned Bread Crumbs (page 30)

1 pound fresh mozzarella cheese, cut into $^1/_4$-inch dice

About 4 cups Nana's Fresh Marinara Sauce (page 8) or
other marinara sauce

$^1/_2$ cup fresh flat-leaf parsley, chopped

1. Trim the ends from each eggplant. Using a slicing machine (or a very sharp knife), cut each eggplant lengthwise into 15 very thin slices. Lay the slices on a clean, dry work surface and generously sprinkle with salt. Let stand for about 20 minutes to allow the salt to draw out the bitter juices.

2. Preheat and oil a grill.

3. Using a paper towel, gently blot the moisture off the eggplant slices. Using a pastry brush, very lightly coat the eggplant with the oil. (If you use too much oil, it will flare up when you place the eggplant on the grill.) Place the eggplant on the grill and cook, turning as necessary, for about 1 minute, or just until the eggplant is slightly cooked and pliable. Remove from the grill and season with pepper to taste. Again, lay the eggplant out in a single layer on a clean, dry work surface.

4. Cook the pasta according to package directions. Drain well and place in a mixing bowl. Whisk together the eggs and milk and drizzle over the hot pasta, tossing to coat. Add the 2 tablespoons Parmesan cheese along with the bread crumbs, tossing to combine. Set aside to cool.

5. Preheat the oven to 350°F.

6. Lightly coat a lasagna or other large baking dish with olive oil. Set aside.

7. When cool, begin making the *involtini,* one at a time. Lift 8 strands of pasta and fold them in half to form a small bundle. Place the bundle in the center of 1 slice of eggplant. Lay 5 mozzarella dice on top of the pasta bundle and tightly roll the eggplant slice, cigar-fashion, up and over the filling. Place the eggplant in the prepared baking dish and continue making *involtini* until all of the eggplant is used and fitted into the dish.

8. Place a tablespoon of marinara sauce on top of each eggplant roll. Then sprinkle the tops with the parsley and then with the ½ cup Parmesan cheese. (The *involtini* may be made up to this point, tightly wrapped, and refrigerated for up to 2 days or frozen for up to 3 months.) Place in the preheated oven and bake for about 15 minutes, or just until hot in the center and the cheeses have begun to melt. Remove from the oven and serve hot.

Veal Spiedini

My great-aunt Vincenzina spent a whole day teaching me to make these her way. Everyone gathered around the kitchen table to heckle me as the very elegant Vincenzina went through the process step-by-step. She was a firm but loving instructor—I'll never forget the cooking lesson!

Serves 6

. . . .

$1/2$ cup extra-virgin olive oil (preferably Sicilian)

3 cloves garlic, peeled and minced

$1/4$ cup minced onion

$1/2$ cup fresh Italian bread crumbs

$1/2$ cup minced fresh flat-leaf parsley

$1/2$ cup freshly grated Pecorino Romano cheese

$1/3$ cup freshly grated caciocavallo cheese

Coarse salt and freshly ground pepper

12 veal cutlets (about $2 1/2$ pounds), pounded thin

About $1/3$ cup whipped unsalted butter

36 fresh bay leaves

2 large red onions (36 layered wedges)

1. Place 12 to 14 bamboo skewers in cold water to cover and let soak for at least 1 hour. (You will need 1 skewer for every 3 rolls.)
2. Preheat and oil a grill.

3. Heat $\frac{1}{4}$ cup of the oil in a small sauté pan over medium heat. Add the garlic and onion and sauté for about 2 minutes, or just until softened. Stir in the bread crumbs and parsley and sauté for 1 minute. Scrape into a mixing bowl and add the grated cheeses. Season with salt and pepper to taste.

4. Cut each piece of veal into thirds and lay the pieces out on a clean, dry work surface. Place about $\frac{1}{2}$ teaspoon of whipped butter in the center of each piece of veal, using your fingertips to spread it out slightly. Spoon a heaping tablespoonful of the bread crumb mixture on top of the butter. Roll the veal, cigar-fashion, up and over the filling, tucking in the ends, to make a neat, small packet. Trim the larger rolls down by cutting them in half to make an extra skewer or two.

5. Place 1 bay leaf and 1 piece of red onion on top of each veal roll. Place 3 rolls on each skewer, running the skewer through the roll to hold the bay leaf and onion in place.

6. Using a pastry brush, lightly coat the rolls with some of the remaining $\frac{1}{4}$ cup oil. Season with salt and pepper to taste and place on the preheated grill. Grill, turning occasionally and brushing with additional oil as needed, for about 6 minutes, or until lightly browned and cooked through. Remove from the grill and serve hot.

Crostata di Limone

This is a very light, almost chiffonlike, citrusy tart. In Sicily, lemons and limes are so abundant that they are used to flavor all types of foods. This is one of my most favorite Sicilian desserts. If you want to fancy it up, you can pipe rosettes of whipped cream over the top and garnish it with candied lemon peel.

Makes one 9-inch tart

. . . .

4 large eggs, separated

$^1/_2$ cup plus 2 tablespoons sugar

Juice and zest of 2 lemons

Juice and zest of 2 limes

Prebaked Pastry Shell (recipe follows)

1. Combine the egg yolks and sugar in the bowl of an electric mixer and beat until very light and thick. Add the lemon and lime juices and zest and beat to combine.

2. Transfer the mixture to the top half of a double boiler placed over simmering water. Cook, stirring constantly, for about 15 minutes, or until the mixture has thickened. Remove from the heat and set aside to cool.

3. Preheat the oven to 325°F.

4. Beat the egg whites until soft peaks form. Gently fold the beaten egg whites into the cooled egg yolk mixture, taking care not to deflate them too much. Spread the mixture into the pastry shell. Place in the preheated oven and bake for about 15 minutes, or until the center is set. Remove from the oven and place on a wire rack to cool slightly before cutting.

. . . .

1³/₄ cups all-purpose flour

¹/₂ cup ground almonds, toasted

¹/₂ cup sugar

Pinch of salt

8 tablespoons (1 stick) cold unsalted butter, cubed

1 large egg

1.   Combine the flour, almonds, sugar, and salt in the bowl of a food processor fitted with the metal blade. Process just to combine. Add the butter, a couple of cubes at a time, and process, using quick on-and-off turns, until the mixture is dry and crumbly. Add the egg and process just until the mixture comes together to make a soft dough.

2.   Scrape the dough from the processor bowl and form it into a disk. Cover with plastic wrap and refrigerate for 2 hours, or until well chilled.

3.   Lightly coat a 9-inch pie tin or tart shell with vegetable spray. Set aside.

4.   Preheat the oven to 325°F.

5.   Remove the dough from the refrigerator and place it on a lightly floured board. Using your fingertips, press the dough out slightly. Then, using a rolling pin, roll the dough out to a circle about 11 inches in diameter. Press the dough into the prepared tin or shell, either crimping the edges against the edge of the pie tin or trimming them to fit the edge of the tart shell. Prick the bottom with a fork, cover it with a piece of parchment paper, and weight it down with pie weights (or beans).

6.   Place in the preheated oven and bake for 10 minutes. Remove the paper and the weights and continue to bake for about 5 minutes more, or until the crust is golden brown. Remove from the oven and use as directed in the master recipe.

Ricotta Cookies

When we had these cookies in Sicily, I was filled with Christmas memories, as we always had this same treat back home at Christmas time. My mother-in-law, Maureen Fiorentino Buck, still makes them every year for my children. They are one of my favorite cookies, as their slightly crisp exterior is hidden by the confectioners'-

Makes about 120

. . . .

sugar icing so that when you bite into them, you get a hit of sugar, then a crunch, and finally a soft, sweet cheesy center.

4 cups all–purpose flour

2 tablespoons baking powder

1 teaspoon salt

$^1/_2$ pound (2 sticks) unsalted butter, softened

2 cups granulated sugar

2 large eggs

1 pound ricotta cheese

2 teaspoons freshly grated lemon zest

2 teaspoons freshly grated orange zest

2 teaspoons pure vanilla extract

1$^1/_2$ cups confectioners′ sugar

3 tablespoons milk

1. Preheat the oven to 350°F. Line at least 2 cookie sheets with parchment paper. Set aside.

2. Combine the flour, baking powder, and salt. Set aside.

3. Using an electric mixer, beat the butter and sugar on medium speed until well blended. Increase the speed to high and beat until light and fluffy.

4. Return the speed to medium and beat in the eggs, ricotta, lemon and orange zest, and vanilla extract.

5. Remove the bowl from the mixer and, using a wooden spoon, beat the dry ingredients into the creamed mixture until a firm dough forms.

6. Drop the dough by the teaspoonful onto the prepared cookie sheets, leaving about $1/2$ inch between cookies. Place in the preheated oven and bake for about 15 minutes, or until golden. Remove from the oven and place on wire racks.

7. Place the confectioners' sugar in a small bowl. Beat in the milk to make a barely thickened icing. Using a fork, drizzle the icing over the cookies while they are still warm.

8. Continue baking and finishing the cookies until all of the dough is used. Store, tightly covered, for up to 3 days.

Fig Cookies

Figs are everywhere in Sicily, fresh in season and dry all year round. Even the humblest of homes has a fig tree in the yard. Figs are very perishable, so when the trees are producing ripe fruit at a rapid rate, everyone dries what cannot be eaten. Although dried figs are eaten "as is" for dessert, with or without cheese, many Sicilian dishes also use them for

Makes 60

. . . .

enrichment. These cookies would be very extravagant treats, generally served only on holidays or special occasions—like my homecoming.

12 ounces dried Calimyrna figs

4 cups all-purpose flour

$^2/_3$ cup sugar

1 teaspoon baking powder

1 teaspoon salt

$^1/_2$ pound (2 sticks) unsalted butter, softened

5 large eggs

$^1/_2$ cup raisins

$^1/_3$ cup apricot (or orange) marmalade

$^1/_4$ cup finely diced candied orange peel

$^1/_4$ cup chopped almonds, pecans, or walnuts, toasted

$^1/_4$ cup mini chocolate chips

$^1/_2$ teaspoon ground cinnamon

$^1/_4$ teaspoon ground cloves

3 tablespoons Frangelico or amaretto liqueur

2 tablespoons milk

About $^1/_2$ cup multicolored nonpareils

1. Place the figs in boiling water to cover by 2 inches. Set aside to plump for about 20 minutes.

2. Combine the flour, sugar, baking powder, and salt in the bowl of a food processor fitted with the metal blade. Add the butter a bit at a time, using quick on-and-off turns, processing until the butter is incorporated and the mixture is powderlike. Add 4 of the eggs, pulsing until a thick dough forms.

3. Scrape the dough from the bowl onto a lightly floured work surface. Using your hands, pat the dough into a square about 1 inch thick. Wrap in plastic wrap and refrigerate while the filling is prepared.

4. Drain the figs. Trim off and discard the hard stem ends and chop. Place the chopped figs in a mixing bowl along with the raisins, marmalade, candied orange peel, almonds, chocolate chips, cinnamon, and cloves. Toss to combine, then add the Frangelico. Stir to combine. Set aside.

5. Beat the remaining egg with the milk in a shallow bowl. Set aside.

6. Preheat the oven to 350°. Lightly coat 3 nonstick cookie sheets with vegetable spray. Set aside.

7. Remove the dough from the refrigerator. Unwrap and place on a lightly floured work surface. Knead for a minute or two and then form the dough into an even log shape. Cut the log crosswise into 12 equal pieces.

8. Using your hands and working with 1 piece of dough at a time on a lightly floured work surface, flatten the dough out to a rectangle about 11 inches long by 3 inches wide. Continue until you have 12 rectangles.

9. Using a pastry brush, lightly coat the dough with the reserved egg wash. Spoon a line of fig filling down the center of the length of each rectangle. Roll the edges up and around the filling and, using your fingertips, seal the edges together. Gently roll the filled log back and forth to stretch it out to about 15 inches long. Continue until you have 12 filled logs.

10. Using a sharp knife, cut each log crosswise into five 3-inch-long pieces. Place the cookies on the prepared baking sheets. Using a small, sharp knife, make about 5 diagonal slices in the top of each cookie, without cutting into the filling. Using your fingertips,

carefully fold each cookie into a crescent shape and pull the ends closed. Leave about ¹⁄₂ inch between each cookie.

22. Using a pastry brush, lightly coat the tops with a bit of egg wash. While still wet, sprinkle with the nonpareils. Place in the preheated oven and bake for about 20 minutes, or until golden. Remove from the oven and place on wire racks to cool.

Sources

D'ARTAGNAN
280 Wilson Avenue
Newark, NJ 07105
(800) 327-8246
www.dartagnan.com
Wild game, meats, foie gras

D. COLUCCIO & SONS
1214–20 60th Street
Brooklyn, NY 11219
(718) 436-6700
Coluccioimport@aol.com
Oils, vinegars, San Marzano tomatoes,
cheeses, dried beans

CITARELLA
2135 Broadway
New York, NY 10024
(212) 874-0383
www.citarella.com
Meats, game, fish, specialty goods

DEAN & DELUCA
Mail Order Department
560 Broadway
New York, NY 10012
(212) 431-1691 / (800) 221-7714
Everything from soup to nuts (literally)

FOOD INNOVATIONS
1923 Trade Center Way, Suite 1
Naples, FL 34109
(888) 352-FOOD
www.foodinno.com
Fresh exotic seafood, cheeses,
farm direct produce

FRATELLI RAVIOLI
31 Browne Street
Brooklyn, NY 11231
(718) 222-3084
www.fratelliravioli.com
Specialty raviolis, pasta sauces

KATAGIRI
224 East 59th Street
New York, NY 10022
(212) 755-3566
www.katagiri.com
Japanese food products and housewares

PASTOSA RAVIOLI CORP.
7425 New Utrecht Avenue
Brooklyn, NY 11204
Fresh and stuffed pastas, fresh mozzarella,
Italian products

SAHADI'S
187 Atlantic Avenue
Brooklyn, NY 11201
(718) 624-4550
www.sahadis.com or Sahadis@aol.com
Middle Eastern specialty foods, spices,
nuts, grains

THE SAUSAGE MAKER
1500 Clinton Street
Buffalo, NY 14206
(716) 824-6510
Sausage-making equipment and
supplies

ZINGERMAN'S
620 Phoenix Drive
Ann Arbor, MI 48108
(888) 636-8162
www.zingermans.com
Specialty foods of all types

Special thanks to the following companies
for generously lending merchandise to be
used in the photographs in this book:

CRATE AND BARREL
650 Madison Avenue
New York, NY 10022
(212) 519-5735

FISHS EDDY
2176 Broadway at 77th Street
New York, NY 10024
(212) 873-8819

KORIN JAPANESE TRADING
56 Warren Street
New York, NY 10007
(212) 587-7021

MORE & MORE ANTIQUES
378 Amsterdam Avenue
New York, NY 10024
(212) 580-8404

SIMON PEARCE
500 Park Avenue on 59th Street
New York, NY 10022
(212) 421-8801

Index

ABOUT THE AUTHOR

DON PINTABONA *is one of the pioneers of contemporary American cuisine. During the past two decades, he has visited more than thirty countries and worked alongside some of the world's finest chefs, including Daniel Boulud, Charlie Palmer, and Georges Blanc. From 1990 to 2003, Pintabona was executive chef of the award-winning Tribeca Grill. His new restaurant, Trina, recently opened in the Atlantic hotel in Fort Lauderdale. He lives in Brooklyn with his wife and three children.*

ABOUT THE TYPE

This book is set in Fournier, a typeface named for Pierre Simon Fournier, the youngest son of a French printing family. He started out engraving woodblocks and large capitals, then moved on to fonts of type. In 1736 he began his own foundry and made several important contributions in the field of type design; he is said to have cut 147 alphabets of his own creation. Fournier is probably best remembered as the designer of St. Augustine Ordinaire, a face that served as the model for Monotype's Fournier, which was released in 1925.